The Boy from Altheimer

The Boy from Altheimer

FROM THE DEPRESSION
TO THE BOARDROOM

William H. Bowen

THE UNIVERSITY OF ARKANSAS PRESS / FAYETTEVILLE / 2006

Copyright © 2006 by The University of Arkansas Press

All rights reserved
Manufactured in the United States of America

10   09   08   07   06   5   4   3   2   1

Text design by Ellen Beeler

⊗   The paper used in this publication meets the minimum requirements of the American National Standard for Permanence of Paper for Printed Library Materials Z39.48-1984.

Library of Congress Cataloging-in-Publication Data

Bowen, William H., 1923–
The boy from Altheimer : from the Depression to the boardroom / William H. Bowen.
    p. cm.
  Includes bibliographical references and index.
    ISBN-13: 978-1-55728-818-9 (pbk. : alk. paper)
    ISBN-10: 1-55728-818-6 (pbk. : alk. paper)
    1. Bowen, William H., 1923–   . 2. Governors—Arkansas—Staff—Biography.
3. Clinton, Bill, 1946–   —Friends and associates. 4. Arkansas—Politics and government—
1951–   . 5. Fighter pilots—United States—Biography. 6. Lawyers—Arkansas—Biography.
7. Bankers—Arkansas—Biography. 8. Deans (Education)—Arkansas—Little Rock—
Biography. 9. University of Arkansas at Little Rock. William H. Bowen School of Law.
I. Title.
F415.3.B69A3 2006
976.7′053092—dc22
  [B]   2006001128

To my wife, Connie, and our children, Cynthia, Scott, and Patty

Here's The story of
a helluva guy —
for a helluva guy /

Bruno

19 Apr 07

Contents

Foreword

I've known Bill Bowen for over thirty years, and he's always been there when I needed him. Starting with my very first campaign, Bill provided invaluable contributions of advice, financial support, and friendship.

Eventually, Bill Bowen gave me something else, too: the chance to run for president. Although Bill had worked with me for years, he had never joined my administration until 1991, when I decided to run for president. Bill agreed to become my chief of staff, leaving Commercial National Bank and turning his life upside down so that I would always know the state government was in good hands in my absence. He took an hour to think it over before accepting. If you knew how decisive he usually is, you'd know that one hour is an unusually long time for Bill Bowen to make up his mind.

After Bill came on board, I knew he would make all the decisions he could, and when I needed to hear about a problem and make the call, Bill would make sure I did so. I knew that when decisions had to be made, Bill would make them, and when I needed to hear about a problem, Bill would tell me about it. I can honestly say that I could not have run for or become president if it weren't for Bill Bowen's selflessness and dedication to public service.

Bill has been helping people and serving his state and nation all his life. Besides his time as my chief of staff, Bill was a United States Navy fighter pilot during World War II, a tax attorney, president of a major bank, chief executive officer of a health maintenance corporation, dean of the law school that now bears his name, and a fine family man.

Bill has led a fascinating life, and I am pleased that he decided to share it with you. I have some experience with the process of writing an autobiography, and it is not a simple task. Bill, as usual, has done a great job.

I deeply admire Bill Bowen. After reading his book, I'm confident that you will too.

William Jefferson Clinton
January 2005

Introduction

Why did I write this book? The idea came into being in the office of U.S. Tax Court Judge Clarence V. Opper in the summer of 1951 in Washington, D.C. I was one of two law clerks employed by him; the other was Arnold Hoffman of New York City. Arnold was a first-generation American. His parents emigrated from Russia at the turn of the twentieth century.

We were discussing reports in the press of planning already underway to celebrate the one hundredth anniversary of the beginning of the Civil War. In passing, I had shared with Arnold that my grandfather, James Quinn Falls—my mother's father—was a Confederate soldier, but that he had died early and my mother, orphaned at age six, knew little about him or his experience. Arnold's interest in American history was such that he encouraged me to visit the National Archives on Pennsylvania Avenue during my lunch hour, since it was located only about two blocks from our office building.

I did so, returning less than pleased with my findings. Grandfather Falls was shown to have joined the Second Arkansas Mounted Rifles on May 15, 1861, at a site near Galla Rock in Pope County, where Galla Creek empties into the Arkansas River. The sources I consulted reflected that this unit was in the Battle of Pea Ridge near Bentonville, Arkansas, and that my grandfather had deserted in the summer of 1862. This did not agree with family legend and Arnold encouraged me to research it further. I undertook it fitfully.

As the one hundredth anniversary approached, Arnold and I had long parted ways. He was practicing in New York City and I in Little Rock when my interest in the Civil War came to the attention of a Shreveport, Louisiana, native whose grandfather had also served with the Second Arkansas Mounted Rifles. He invited me to join him in the research on this regiment, which resulted in a book published in Little Rock titled *Rebels Valiant*. The book reported that Grandfather Falls continued his service after a glitch in the summer of 1862—probably to help on the farm in Pottsville—in a consolidated regiment he joined in Tennessee that fought across Tennessee, Georgia, South Carolina, and North Carolina until the soldiers were discharged shortly after Appomattox in the spring of 1865.

A parallel interest was whetted on a visit to Alaska and Dutch Harbor, in the Aleutian Islands. I discovered some seven or eight books on the campaign in World War II, but no mention of the service of the 206th Coast Artillery Regiment of the Arkansas National Guard. My next older brother, John, died in service in the Aleutian Islands on October 19, 1942. To celebrate the fiftieth anniversary of the Japanese attack on Dutch Harbor (June 3–6, 1942), the 206th Coast Artillery Association returned for a reunion. They had employed the coauthors of the famous book, *Miracle at Midway,* a definitive account of that famous naval battle—which included a two-carrier task force attack on Dutch Harbor—to record their story. At the fiftieth anniversary ceremony in Dutch Harbor, the book *The Williwaw War: The Arkansas National Guard in the Aleutians in World War II* (Fayetteville: University of Arkansas Press, 1992), was distributed to participants.

Next, the Reverend William Ragsdale of Russellville, a Princeton graduate and retired Presbyterian minister, authored a book titled *They Sought a Land: A Settlement in the Arkansas River Valley, 1840–1870* (Fayetteville: University of Arkansas Press, 1997), a history of Pottsville, Pope County, Arkansas, its settlement and the creation of the Pottsville Associated Reformed Presbyterian Church. My mother's families—the Falls and Fergusons—were among the first sojourners to that part of Arkansas.

About the same time, Mrs. Bill Payne, a friend from Pine Bluff, provided me with a study of my family that totally surprised me—a story of a Hessian soldier named Johannes Reiden who landed in Brooklyn in 1776 with Hessian forces employed to help George III fight the Colonials. He fought in the battles of Brooklyn, Princeton, and Brandywine before he left the service in South Carolina at the end of the Revolutionary War. Then Johannes changed his name to John Reed, settled in Smith County, North Carolina, married a local girl of German descent, and had the good fortune to discover gold on his property. The mine, Reed Gold Mine, was so prolific that North Carolina was called the Golden State until 1848, after the western gold rush began. The riches equipped John's grandson to go to Pope County, Arkansas, before there was a Russellville, and in due course, he built a cotton gin in the Cardon Bottoms of the county, where my father learned to operate the gin when he was a teenager. The corrugated iron from the gin still stands.

My interest in my family history came to the attention of chancellor Charles Hathaway of the University of Arkansas at Little Rock, and he commissioned Laura Miller, then a recent graduate of UALR's public history program, to bring discipline to my studies and meanderings. She did so with the help of friends like Gray Clary Lyon, who reviewed the Altheimer chapter; Carol Griffey, who fashioned the account of First Commercial Bank, the bank's National Advisory Board, and my service as chief of staff to Gov. Bill Clinton; John Ryan, my colleague at Healthsource Arkansas, Inc., who guided the account of the partnership between Healthsource and St. Vincent Infirmary; professor Lynn Foster, who prepared the report of my service as dean of the UALR School of Law; and professor Scott Stafford, who reviewed my tax cases from my time as a lawyer.

Then Dr. Calvin Ledbetter, a long ago law associate and retired head of the Political Science Department at UALR, reviewed this collaborative work product with a recommendation of publication. So, the fellow law clerk Arnold Hoffman's suggestion fifty-three years ago has finally matured and it is with sincere gratitude and appreciation that I thank Chancellor Hathaway, Laura Miller, and the other contributors for their support and interest in bringing this study to fruition. I would also like to acknowledge Little Rock architect Tom Gray, who suggested the title for this book.

A word of warning to anyone disposed to write a book about his life. It is a significant and painful chore. You will encounter early and continuing misgivings about the appearance of bragging about yourself and your experiences. But if not undertaken, a chapter of family and community history will be lost. There is unlikely to be a telling of any part of the Altheimer story but for chapter 1 here. And life as it used to be in the Delta of Arkansas is already fading from view as those cultures disappear.

If a state like ours is to aspire to improve its citizenry and their life opportunities, it must know its roots and how we got where we are. These thoughts have steadied my hand in this undertaking.

William H. Bowen
2005

CHAPTER ONE

The Boy from Altheimer

I N HIS BOOK, *The Greatest Generation,* Tom Brokaw wrote of the men and women who came of age in the first decades of the twentieth century that they grew up in a time in which:

> economic despair hovered over the land like a plague. They had watched their parents lose their businesses, their farms, their jobs, their hopes. They had learned to accept a future that played out one day at a time. Then, just as there was a glimmer of economic recovery, war exploded across Europe and Asia . . . This generation was summoned to the parade ground and told to train for war . . . they quit school or went from cap and gown directly into uniform . . . They faced great odds and a late start, but they did not protest.[1]

Instead, he says, they answered their country's call and helped bring peace and prosperity for their fellow countrymen and the world.

I am a member of that generation, but I am uncomfortable in thinking of it as the "greatest"—particularly as compared to the generations that fought and lived through the Civil War and the "Great War," World War I. Born in the Arkansas Delta in the town of Altheimer on May 6, 1923, I have served as a U.S. Navy fighter pilot, attorney, bank president, chief of staff to Arkansas Gov. Bill Clinton, CEO of a health maintenance corporation, law school dean, and in numerous volunteer efforts before my "retirement" in 1997. I have lived during a remarkable period in our nation's history as the agricultural-driven society of my childhood gave way to the turmoil of the Depression and World War II, and the social upheaval in its aftermath. Although I grew up in a section of the country that was among the poorest in the nation, I nevertheless benefited from the stability of my family and community life. Growing up in a time and a place where individuals had little control over the capriciousness of nature and the land, I was lucky to guide my own destiny.

Life in the Arkansas Delta was difficult under the best of circumstances. As one historian noted, the physical environment itself "shaped a society, economy, and culture easily distinguishable from those in other sections of Arkansas."[2] After the Civil War, Delta towns grew rapidly due to several factors, including flood control efforts, improvements in transportation, and changes in cotton marketing and financing.[3] Like many others, my parents settled in the Arkansas Delta from the northwest part of the state, continuing a pattern of migration and settlement begun by their ancestors.

My maternal grandparents arrived in Pottsville (Pope County) by wagon train in 1852. My grandfather, James Quinn Falls, joined other families who were primarily from two Associate Reformed Presbyterian congregations in North and South Carolina. Because their eastern communities were becoming increasingly more populated and the soil less arable, they sought greater opportunities elsewhere for themselves and their families. The Pope County area of Arkansas became a destination for many because it lay on the main travel corridor to Fort Smith, which served as a jumping off point for wagon trains headed for California's gold fields.[4] After serving throughout the Civil War, first with the Second Arkansas Mounted Rifles—who fought at Wilson's Creek and Pea Ridge—and later as part of the Twenty-fifth Consolidated Rifles—whose members participated in battles across Tennessee, Georgia, and North and South Carolina—James Falls returned to Pope County, where he and his wife, Mary Ferguson Falls, had five children, including my mother, Ruth Falls.[5] They both died rather young, leaving my mother orphaned when she was six years old. Her brother, sisters, and an extended family of aunts, uncles and cousins looked after her as she was the baby of the family.

After my mother graduated from the local public schools, she entered South Carolina's Erskine College in 1906. It was then the only Associate Reformed Presbyterian College in the United States and was founded in 1836. My mother graduated in 1910—the year of Halley's Comet—schooled in the Bible, English, Scottish, and U.S. (principally southern) literature, plus Greek and Roman mythology, and the other studies then offered to "young ladies" in a liberal arts college. It turned her toward a lifetime of teaching—first her students, and then her own children and their friends. In 1910 and 1911, my mother taught in the Danville (Yell County) public schools, while she lived in the home of her uncle, a lawyer affectionately known as "Judge" Ferguson. She then taught until December 1913 in an Indian Mission of the Presbyterian Church in Durant, Oklahoma.[6]

As a veteran of World War II, I always took wry pleasure in my lack of German ancestry, until a little genealogy unearthed a paternal forefather named Johannas Reiden, a Hessian soldier who came to America in 1776 as part of a mercenary force hired by King George III of England to fight the colonials. He fought in several battles and finally left the service in Savannah, Georgia, and sought refuge in the backcountry of North Carolina. Enjoying life on the American frontier, he married and changed his name to John Reed. In 1799, his son, Bohannon, picked up a rock from a nearby creek to use as a doorstop. The rock turned out to be nearly pure gold. The resulting Reed gold mine brought riches the family never dreamed of and produced most of the gold for the Charlotte mint until the California Gold Rush of 1848.

John Reed's grandson later migrated to Pope County, Arkansas in 1857 and, after serving in the Confederate Army, became prominent enough to have Reed Mountain in Russelleville named after him. His daughter, Lena, married my grandfather, William Robert Bowen, newly arrived from Wartrace, Tennessee, and their first child, Robert James "Bob" Bowen, was my father. Lena Reed's brother, Albert, built a cotton gin at Cardon Bottoms in Pope County at the turn of the twentieth century and this gin became a training ground for my father. Because of his experiences working there, he began searching for richer cotton country in 1910. He first took a job with the Rose City Cotton Oil Mill in North Little Rock before moving to the cotton-rich Delta area of Altheimer. The Rose City Cotton Oil Mill was located on East Broadway in a rough part of town—my father was paid in cash on Saturdays and carried a shotgun on those days for protection.

My father had obtained what schooling was available in Pope County around the turn of the twentieth century. I believe he completed eight grades. As the oldest child in a large family, he began work early and was able to support himself by his middle teens. He trained to be a journeyman carpenter and he and his brothers, Albert and John, became skilled carpenters. In 1913, my father asked my mother to marry him and they wed on December 25 in Pottsville. They honeymooned at the Arlington Hotel in Hot Springs before settling down to their new life in Altheimer.

Located in Jefferson County, Arkansas, Altheimer developed in the aftermath of the Civil War and Reconstruction in one of the largest cotton-producing sections in the state. The key to its development was the creation of a railroad line from North Little Rock in 1886.[7] The town grew rapidly, displacing the small community of Cotton Center as the primary commercial center between Pine Bluff and Little Rock. In an article detailing Altheimer's growth, the *Arkansas Gazette* noted:

> less than two years ago it was a dense forest where roamed . . . wild beasts, is now the seat of civilization, where the hub of commerce is heard and opulent mercantile establishments rear in proud array their imposing fronts.[8]

By 1886, the town had about 250 residents and two cotton gins and farmers expected to ship five thousand bales of cotton that year.[9] With rising cotton prices and rich land, the future seemed bright for this small town.

The Altheimer of my youth looked like many other Delta towns. If one drove east on U.S. 79 from Pine Bluff in the 1930s, after about eighteen miles you were greeted by a small highway sign that read "Altheimer, Pop. 498." The business side of town was mainly on the north side of the highway. In town it was called Front Street. It was Altheimer's main street, and the only paved road in town.

From west to east in town you first encountered the ESSO wholesale plant operated by Mr. West. Next came the First Methodist Church, with residences on either side. Then came the Walt Gas and Oil Company, the town's water department and water tank, the First National Bank, and the post office. Front Street also housed about a two-block row of stores, including Doc Talioferro's (pronounced Toliver's) drug store, the Sing Company (a Chinese grocery), the Clemmons Dry Good Store, and then a one-block wide, one block-long street that connected Front Street with the Flat Bayou Bridge. Next came the Irving Sachs store, Benson's (Chinese), J. S. McDonnell Company, the ABC Store (Altheimer, Bowen, and Clary), the S&E Sachs Store, Bryson Liquor, the Kroger Store, and Wilson Company. Here the sidewalk ended. Next was a sandwich shop, then the Hoover Service Station. Flat Bayou ran east and west on the north side of town with U.S. 79 to the south framing about a two-block wide group of ten or so houses, including the Bowen house. The Cotton Belt Railroad paralleled U.S. 79 through town and was served by the Altheimer Depot between Front Street and the railroad track, almost exactly in midtown.

En route from Front Street to the Bayou Bridge, on the west side of the street, was Cassy Meek's butcher shop. On Saturdays and holidays, this street was filled with teams of horses and mules, wagons, and vintage cars. Across Front Street from the Bryson Liquor Store was a railroad crossing to State Highway 88. Destinations on 88 included the communities of Lake Dick, Cornerstone, and Reydel.

At the southeast corner of the railroad track and Highway 88 was Till Price's General Store. He and Meeks were the town's only two African American merchants. Making it an international community, next to the Till Price Store was Abraham Jabra Mercantile, a Lebanese-owned store.

On the south side of the railroad track were five cotton gins in a row, and a half block south of the middle gin—the Altheimer Gin—was the black-smith shop. On either side of U.S. 79 east of town and just beyond the white community were three blocks or so where African American families lived. About a mile east was New Town, then Wabbaseka, some five miles distant. South of the track in Altheimer were two blocks of white residences ending at the Altheimer High School site, adjoining which was about a six-bedroom house where single female teachers resided. The Altheimer school population in 1941—the year of my graduation—was 143 white students in grades one through twelve. In 1940 there was no senior class; in 1941 there were thirteen of us.

Altheimer enjoyed prosperity while cotton production and prices steadily rose. In 1906, total U.S. production of cotton was over thirteen million bales and the average farm price per pound was 9.6 cents. By 1919, the price had increased to an average of 35.6 cents, driven, in part, by a decline in production by some two million bales. The South's, and Altheimer's, dependence on cotton, however, would become a serious problem by 1920, as production increased to its turn-of-the-century levels while prices plummeted to less than 14 cents per pound.[10] Throughout the 1920s, cotton prices continued to fluctuate in a downward spiral in response to production levels.

For our family, however, disaster struck even before the economic declines of the twenties. In 1918, the influenza pandemic struck the nation. Servicemen returning from Europe following World War I brought this highly infectious disease with them. By October of that year, the entire state of Arkansas was under quarantine.[11] My only sister, Lois Rhene, died just shy of her fourth birthday. I recall my mother singing part of a song throughout the remainder of her life: "Tying on the leaves so they won't fall down, so the wind won't blow them away, for the sweetest girl in all the world is going away that day." By the next spring, the epidemic had claimed over twenty-two million people worldwide. More than five hundred thousand Americans died, including nearly seven thousand Arkansans.[12]

The falling crop prices of the 1920s trapped tenant farmers in a cycle of indebtedness, which escalated as the country entered the Great Depression. Many landowners were also deep in debt after financing land purchases following World War I, only to face diminishing cotton prices. In 1926, cotton prices dropped nationwide to an average of just over twelve cents per pound.[13] Farmers responded by planting more cotton in an attempt to recover some of their operating costs, but the higher production levels led to larger surpluses and lower prices.

During this time, as our family grew to four sons—ultimately, there would be five—my father, with the help of two of my uncles, built our family a new

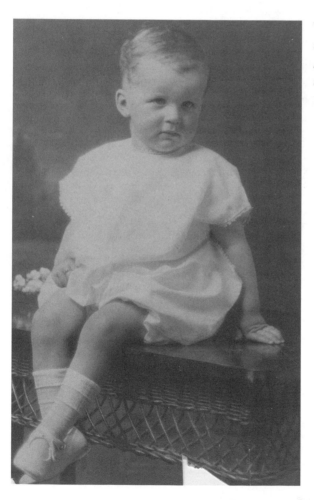

William H. Bowen as an infant in Altheimer, Arkansas, around 1924. *From the author.*

home in 1925. The home stood on a lot on Dixie Street and contained three bedrooms, a living room, dining room, kitchen, and bath. Although heated with three stoves in various rooms, the water pipes often froze in the winter and we boys took our Saturday baths in a number 3 washtub in the living room. The yard, shaded by cottonwoods and a water oak that I planted on my eleventh birthday, included a garden, a chicken yard, and a livestock lot. Unlike many of the houses in Altheimer at the time, our house also had indoor plumbing, although the system was far from admirable by modern standards. In fact the system poured into Flat Bayou, after going through a septic system, so the bayou was something of a cesspool. Despite that fact, I thought the bayou was the greatest arboretum in the world. It was a place where we could fish and hunt and see all kinds of wildlife—all of the species that grow in that part of Arkansas—and it was only about one hundred yards north of our house.

My brothers and I, along with our friends, spent much of our free time around and in the bayou. Once I helped build a flat-bottom boat so we could explore more of the area. We built the boat with great care out of used front porch flooring that was ill-suited for a boat. We put it in the bayou and it went straight down because there was not enough water displacement for it to float. I was about ten or twelve at the time, surrounded by fellow carpenters of comparable age and skill, including my brother Jim, who was about seven. Eventually, we obtained a suitable cypress boat and later, a barge, so we always had transportation through Flat Bayou.

My first venture into the world of work outside the home—where we cut kindling, mowed the yard, raked the leaves, and milked the cow—was carrying water and sharpening axes and hoes on a ditch-clearing effort on our farm in the summer of 1934. This work allowed me to save enough money for two weeks of scout camp at Camp Caudle in Russellville. I went with my cousin, John Rankin, that summer. Our camp adjoined the Illinois Bayou, where the water was amazingly clear compared to the murky waters of our Flat Bayou. I was greatly impressed. Camp Caudle was unique in that one of our challenges was to build our own cabin accommodations. But what can you expect for $2.50 per week?

The next summer, I attended a scout camp at Christian Brothers Academy in Searcy with my friend and neighbor, Bud Clary. In our first weekend at camp, we made a trip to Sugarloaf Mountain at the foot of the Little Red River. From the top of the mountain, we enjoyed a remarkable view of trees and river that made the climb to the top of the Altheimer water

Bill Bowen (in the middle) with his brothers Patrick Mims Bowen (on left) and James Ferguson Bowen (on right), around 1932. *From the author.*

tank pale in comparison. My scouting days waned after a few years as a Lone Scout (a program that allows boys to participate in scouting even if there is no formal troop in the area) and with Altheimer coaches who occasionally served as scout masters and organized formal troops for us.

In 1925, a new Methodist church was built in Altheimer, and we attended that congregation because there was no Presbyterian church in town. My mother was a leader among the ladies' organizations that brought the construction to fruition. My father was also on the building committee, although he was not a member of the church. He resisted the idea of making a public display of his commitment before the entire congregation, so, although he supported the church his whole adult life, he was not an official member until shortly before he died, when the minister and district superintendent confirmed him.

My father, together with two partners, Louis Altheimer and Willis Clary, founded the ABC Store—"Come to the ABC Store: Always Better and a little Cheaper!"—and he also shared ownership of the Altheimer Cotton Gin. As a child, I worked in the store and cotton gin at various times. In the store, I stocked shelves, served customers, and was also assistant butcher. The store had two front doors. The one on the east side of the building opened into the "dry goods" department, where we stocked women's dresses, overalls, and other items. On the west side were the groceries. In another room, we sold feed, seed, and fertilizer. When I worked as a butcher, we sold mostly pig feet and neck bones with the meat pretty much taken off. We also had round steak and it was always the same. It was never broiled because it was not a good enough cut. It was cooked with a sort of gravy and quite often we added tomatoes and okra. I loved it. I distinctly remember in the Navy when I first ate a grilled steak, I did not think they had cooked it properly.

I also ran the gristmill at the gin on Saturdays in the fall. There we ground whole grain corn into cornmeal. My day began early—my first duty of the day was to make sure there was enough kindling for my father to start a fire in the living room stove. I learned early on to make sure I cut the kindling the night before because, if not, my body was roused and I would go out in the dark and cut kindling. My tasks also included going to the ABC Store every Thursday to get twenty dollars in cash. We used the money for household expenses and paid the cook and laundress each a dollar a week.

After school, my brothers and I and our friends played sports: six-man football, basketball, softball, and baseball. We also wrestled and boxed some. Our home was sort of an assembly point for all the activities. Life was not all fun and games for us, though. The Altheimer School, under the direction of Ms. Ruth Suits, educated and disciplined all of us and instilled in us a sense of belonging. Determined that Altheimer's children receive a full education, she took a personal interest in each child's welfare.

Ruth Pipkin Suits came to Altheimer in 1923 as the superintendent. That was the same year the new all brick, two-story Altheimer School was built. The campus included a "teacherage" that housed single female teachers. The school housed elementary grades on the ground floor, and high school classes, an auditorium, and a library upstairs. Under Ms. Suits's leadership, the Altheimer School thrived. Latin and English grammar were taught to the point that an Altheimer High graduate could regularly test out of freshman English in Arkansas's four-year colleges. She never failed to earn the school an "A" rating among the state's then more-numerous school districts. Every Wednesday morning, we had a schoolwide assembly in the auditorium. Ruth Suits led the student body in prayer and the national anthem, and made announcements. She stood like a Marine sergeant—erect, shoulders back, head up—and her stentorian voice reverberated throughout the building.

In 1939, a new gymnasium was built by the Works Progress Administration and named Suits Hall, after Ms. Suits. The gym became the center of the town's social life—the site of our annual turkey supper, as well as periodic school dances. For the dances, we moved a nickelodeon under the eastern basketball goal and, for a time anyway, Altheimer High did have a band of sorts that played at some of the dances.

Of course, this school was for white students only. In 1896, the U.S. Supreme Court ruled in Plessy v. Ferguson that "separate but equal" facilities based on race were constitutional. Those facilities were never equal, however. This case gave rise to another half century of unequal treatment for black Americans. They were seated in the back of buses and trains; they were required to use public facilities for blacks only; and they were separated in the military, in school, and in employment. In the Arkansas Delta and across the South, the prevailing viewpoint was, "Teach a black person to read and you lose a good cotton picker."

In 1939, I visited the Plum Bayou Township voting office in downtown Altheimer where my father was serving as a voting official during the election. I was there when Ed Freeman came to the door. He was my father's right-hand man and was a senior member of the team that operated the Altheimer Cotton Gin, and a senior carpenter in the crew that serviced the gin in the off-season, the cotton house, the cotton bale platform, tenant houses, and other structures of the Elms Planting Company and the Bowen farm. On that day, he motioned me to come to the door where he stood on the sidewalk. He asked to see my father and I asked him why he didn't just come in to the polling place. He said, "Oh no. Colored folks are not supposed to come in the voting places." The efforts to keep blacks from voting obviously worked in Altheimer. My father joined him on the sidewalk and they handled whatever business had necessitated the meeting, while the wall of disenfranchisement was left inviolate.

"Jim Crow" laws translated into separate and unequal public schools in Altheimer, as they did across the South. Classes for blacks were held in substandard facilities apart from the Altheimer School, and typically for a much shorter school year, as schools were closed in the fall to allow students to help pick cotton. This, of course, resulted in minimal educational opportunities for black students—and fewer job opportunities as well.

When I was thirteen, I tried my hand at farming, taking charge of a thirteen-acre cotton crop on what we called Tupelo Break. My father wanted at least one of his sons to farm. My older brother, Bob, worked in the cotton gin and my brother John called himself an "oil horizontal transfer engineer"—big words for working in a filling station and pumping gas into cars. Heavy rains destroyed most of my crop that year and I decided at an early age that whatever I did with my life, it would not be farming if I could help it. By the time the water had subsided the plot was pretty barren and there was a stalk alive about every ten feet. That ended my farming career.

As did many children of the era, I saw the harsh realities of a life tied to the land. One of the first, and most devastating, lessons came in 1927. That year, as cotton prices continued to fall, nature compounded the problems with the worst flood in Arkansas's history. Heavy rains began in December 1926 over the Mississippi River valley. During the first two weeks of the following April, nine inches of rain fell across the Arkansas Delta. The Mississippi and Arkansas rivers reached their capacities on April 13.[14] Shortly thereafter, the Mississippi River levee system failed, causing the Arkansas River to overflow its own banks. Two days later, the Plum Bayou levee near Altheimer broke from the water's force.[15] On April 19, the *Arkansas Gazette* reported that in Pine Bluff and the surrounding area, "more than 100,000 acres were under water from breaks in the Arkansas at England to the south and Plum Bayou levee to the north."[16] That same evening, over five hundred people crowded onto the "free bridge" between Pine Bluff and Altheimer. Rescue workers arrived in boats and erected tents to provide shelter for the refugees. The next day, Army Air Corps pilots flew over Jefferson County to inspect the damage. They reported seeing hundreds of dead livestock floating in what were once towns.[17]

The residents of Altheimer sought shelter wherever they could. Some of the merchants moved to the upper floors of their stores to escape the rising water. Others, like our family, moved to the second floor of the Altheimer School. I remember the water gushing over the sidewalk in front of the school building. For more than two weeks, we sought shelter with others while waiting for the floodwaters to recede.

The effects of the flood were far-reaching. Although seven states suffered damage, Arkansas bore the brunt of the disaster. At its height, thirteen percent of the state lay under water and property losses totaled nearly fifteen million dollars. In all, 127 people in Arkansas died—twenty-five of them from Jefferson County. More than a thousand residents of Altheimer and the surrounding countryside sought shelter in Red Cross relief camps.[18] The flood destroyed miles of railroad track and roads and deposited large amounts of sand over previously rich farmland.[19]

Congress responded with the Flood Control Act of 1928. This act stated that repeated flooding on the Mississippi and its tributaries was tantamount to a national dilemma and that a "comprehensive program of flood works would be paid for entirely by the federal government."[20] A new flood control plan was adopted by the U.S. Army Corps of Engineers as part of this act. This plan directed the extension and enlargement of the levees on the Mississippi, although its tributaries were not included until 1936.[21]

Although devastating in its effect on the economy, the flood did have at least one positive outcome for the children of Altheimer. Because the floodwaters were building up on the bluff side of town as the waters came south down the valley, the Corps dynamited a place in the railroad track between Altheimer and New Town to let the water run through. Where it went through it dug a hole that we used to call the "trustle"—mispronouncing trestle, a railroad bridge. That's where we learned to swim—in that muddy water about five feet deep.

In spite of the widespread devastation, hard times were only just beginning. A severe drought in the early 1930s, coupled with the Great Depression, affected the entire nation. Rural areas, such as Altheimer, were especially hard hit. The stock market crash of 1929 signaled the beginning of the Depression for most of the country, but rural areas did not feel its immediate impact. Fluctuating cotton prices of the late 1920s affected Altheimer's economy more directly. Cotton prices fell to a low of 9.46 cents per pound in 1930.[22] By 1931, production peaked at sixteen million bales, causing the 1932 price to decline to a disastrous 6.52 cents per pound. At the same time, foreign cotton production increased, thereby diminishing the global market for American crops, causing heavy losses for the nation's farmers.[23]

Again, nature did not cooperate with the farming interests. No rain fell during June and July of 1930 and in August the temperatures averaged highs of over one hundred degrees. Farmers could only watch as their cotton crops and home gardens burned in the late-summer sun. Production declined as much as seventy percent in some areas. The heat also took its toll on other crops, such as corn. The loss of corn was especially significant, since it meant farmers could not feed their livestock.[24] Cotton prices did not rebound in the face of lower production because the drought did not affect all areas of the nation equally. In addition, the worldwide demand for farm commodities dropped in response to the ongoing global depression. Arkansas produced the lowest cotton yields since 1923. On the other hand, South Carolina, Georgia, and Florida harvested their best yields in several years. These states benefited from the dry weather's effect of limiting the boll weevil's threat.[25]

President Herbert Hoover told Arkansans, as well as those in other devastated states, that they would have to handle the situation alone. Hoover, like the majority of Americans, believed in the virtue of self-reliance and was therefore reluctant to extend federal assistance to farmers.[26] Unfortunately, organizations such as the Red Cross were still recovering resources and funding after their relief efforts of 1927 and could offer little help. Unlike the flood, the drought was not confined to an isolated area. It was a nationwide disaster. Despite reports from field workers that help was desperately needed, the national Red Cross director was reluctant to diverge from President Hoover's stance. He too expected local Red Cross chapters to depend on local volunteers and state funds and only under the direst circumstances would the national organization provide assistance.[27]

By 1931, 96 percent of Arkansas's sharecroppers depended on free food from the Red Cross. Their diet consisted of corn meal, beans, and flour. Many sharecroppers became ill with pellagra, a disabling disease caused by malnutrition. Finally, Hoover approved a program to distribute seed and grain to the farmers of Arkansas, but not for the use of their starving families. Hoover did not approve of using federal dollars to provide food for people, but he did agree to a federally funded program to feed livestock.[28]

I remember one child, Hollis Moore, who lived in a "shotgun" house. A hand pump in the back yard was the sole source of water and a privy supplied the "facilities." The house was narrow, and appeared even narrower because it was on about a twenty-five-foot lot with similar houses on either side of it. They were called shotgun houses because it was said that you could shoot a shotgun from the front porch to the back and never hit anything. There were no screens on the porch, and I cannot recall screens on the windows or the two doors, although I cannot imagine living with the swarming mosquitoes from Flat Bayou and Wabbaseka Bayou without screens.

Hollis's father achieved some notoriety and a police record when he joined Squawly Hewitt in a robbery attempt of the Sing Company. They entered the store through the skylight. It was located between Doc Talioferro's drug store and the general store operated by J. S. McDonnell Company. The heist was poorly planned and executed, as the would-be robbers overlooked the fact that the Sing family lived in the back of their store and, upon hearing them enter, apprehended them at shotgun point.

My memory of Hollis's house is faint, not just because of the passage of time, but also because my parents discouraged me from visiting. Hollis came over to our house after school almost every day to make a peanut butter sandwich and drink a glass of milk. He was a year older than I was, but we were in the same grade. He typically wore a ragged pair of overalls and went barefoot, even in the chilly days of fall. At school, we often raced to the swings during recess in the south schoolyard. One day, I jostled him as we raced for the last available swing and I beat him to it. He hit me in the face with his fist and I instinctively hit him back, knocking him down and leaving a rapidly swelling mark on his cheek. It hurt his feelings—it hurt mine, too. I shared the swing with him that recess period and we must have made amends because he came by the house for his glass of milk and his peanut butter sandwich that afternoon. Hollis, his house and family are haunting reminders to me of the grief and devastation of the Depression.

President Hoover's delayed response to the crisis eventually tarnished his political career. His hard-earned humanitarian image, so carefully cultivated from his sympathetic response to the 1927 flood as secretary of commerce, was severely diminished. Political opponents criticized his handling of the relief efforts by discussing his willingness to feed "jackasses, but not starving babies."[29] Franklin Roosevelt's determination to use federal resources to help those in need stood in direct contrast to Hoover's restrained approach.

Supporters propelled Roosevelt into office in 1932 on the promise that he would use federal resources to create "a new deal for the American people."[30]

The New Deal response to the devastating cotton-price situation was to initiate a program of parity payments for farmers. Many viewed overproduction and large surpluses as the key to low crop prices. The plan for increasing prices was to lower production and stabilize the amount in surplus.[31] The Agricultural Adjustment Administration was created as one of the many new bureaucracies of the New Deal era to deal with the problems of intense suffering caused by the ongoing Depression.

The basic plan called for farmers to plow under one-fourth of the new crop, or about ten million acres nationwide. In return, farmers received parity payments from the AAA ranging from seven to twenty dollars per acre, depending on the average yield per acre of the destroyed crops.[32] The planners initially feared that the majority of farmers would be unwilling to destroy growing crops, but the very real possibility of five-cent cotton in 1933 encouraged many farmers to comply. One mantra of this era was "with five cent cotton and forty cent meat how in the world can a poor man eat?" I remember a man in our community, John Washington, a Bowen tenant farmer, who named his twins—born during this time—Parity and Subsidy, in recognition of this program.

In 1934, Congress passed the Bankhead Cotton Control Act. This act forced more farmers to comply, as it placed a heavy tax on growers who ginned more than their allotment. This prevented growers who did not limit their production from gaining too great an advantage over farmers who did.[33] The program was moderately successful in that cotton prices in 1933 did rise to 9.72 cents, but the changes created by this system forever altered labor patterns and social interaction.

One of the primary criticisms of this plan, which emerged rather quickly, was its inherent unfairness to tenant farmers. The payments were made directly to the landowners, who were responsible for distributing the proper proportion to the tenants on their land. While some New Deal administrators may have realized the devastating effect of decreased production on tenants and gin operators, they proceeded with the plan anyway. Landowners received parity checks and did not always distribute them equitably, creating problems for tenant farmers in the area. Some even withheld part of the payment to cover the debts the tenants already owed the landowners.[34]

The Depression affected the residents of Altheimer in a number of ways. Many people who had previously left the rural areas for industrial jobs returned, simply because they could grow their own food. This "back-to-the-land" movement resulted in approximately 184,000 new farmers arriving in Arkansas in 1932, most of whom rented the land because they could not purchase it. The Haymon family of Altheimer used their farming skills to provide for themselves:

> We had our gardens and we had our sweet potato patches . . . Mr. Collier would plant a great big field of peas and we would go out there and pick peas . . . and we lived good. We raised our hogs. We had our own meat. We had our cows, had our own milk and butter . . . we wasn't lacking for nothing but clothes.[35]

The Resettlement Administration sponsored an experimental communal farm at Lake Dick, near Altheimer. Under this system, volunteer families were supplied with new frame houses with indoor plumbing and access to a specified acreage on which they raised cotton and selected cash crops. Additionally, each had a garden and livestock and there was a communal cotton gin with other appropriate farm services. Lake Dick featured some eighty houses and six community buildings on 3,669 acres of land.

At Altheimer School, we benefited from this experiment in the form of new talent for our six-man football team. The Lake Dick families supplied

The Altheimer football team in the fall of 1940. Coach Wooley is on the left. Bill Bowen is standing in the back row, third from the right—No. 63. *From the author.*

No. 63 Bill Bowen, fall 1940. *From the author.*

the Miller boys, Bob and Bill, as well as Kenneth Cook, Bob Lancaster, and Bob and Jake Rawls. At about the same time, Gene Lyon and his family arrived from Ohio. His father was a corn expert and added his talent to the growing Elms Farming Company. W. T. McBurnett, son of a rural mail carrier, moved from the neighboring town of Sherrill to Altheimer. Our eleventh and twelfth grade classes gained this athletic talent just as a new coach, John Woolly, arrived in Altheimer and just as the school finished its new gymnasium. The construction of Suits Hall allowed us to play indoor basketball for the first time. Previously, the basketball court was outdoors and was always filled with worm mounds after a rain.

Coach Woolly arrived in Altheimer with a plan for six-man football and an enhanced basketball program. He believed in training and no bad habits— no smoking and, it went without saying, no drinking. Six-man football was briefly popular in rural middle America in the late 1930s and early war years. As I recall, there were about twelve to fifteen schools in Arkansas that fielded teams including Arkansas City, Drew Central in Monticello, Gould, White Hall, Watson Chapel, Des Arc, Marvell, and Crawfordsville, among others.

The game featured a center and two ends and a three-man backfield—two halfbacks and a quarterback—and a smaller playing field, which was forty yards by one hundred, instead of fifty by one hundred yards on a standard field. The rules also required a clear pass, not a handoff, in the backfield before the ball could be run across the line of scrimmage. Of course, a regular pass play was alright, too. Our team consisted of Toppy McBurnett and Kenneth Cook at left end, Paul Bryson and Jim Walt in the center, Bob and Bill Miller at right end, J. B. Pierce at left halfback and Gene Lyon at right halfback. I was the quarterback and Billy Mosenthin and Bob Lancaster rotated positions from the backfield to the line.

Our team had a spotty record that first season, losing badly to Gould and barely prevailing against less-well-trained teams. The next year, 1940, was a different story. With a much better trained and conditioned team, Altheimer won all of its games and played for the state championship against Crawfordsville, the eastern division champion. We spent the night before the game in the Nobles Hotel in Blytheville. Like most of my fellow teammates, I had never spent the night in a hotel. To our surprise, we learned when we arrived that the Crawfordsville coach argued that the six-man rules should not apply and therefore, no pass was required in the backfield before the ball could cross the line. This changed our game substantially. After much argument, Coach Woolly gave in and, without any practice in eleven-man rules, we did the best we could in the game.

In Crawfordsville we confronted the biggest line of the year. Their center weighed at least 250 pounds and it was difficult for us to run against him. On defense, he could be in our backfield as soon as we snapped the ball. In spite of the new rules and sheer size of the opposing team, each side scored three times and the game was tied at the end of the first half. Crawfordsville scored twice in the second half, however, and won the game. We still believe we would have won that game if we had played with six-man rules. Still, our efforts resulted in players being named to two All State positions, one honorable mention, and one, Kenneth Cook, was selected as a *Boys Life* All-American honorable mention. Coach Woolly went to Pine Bluff to coach in 1943 and then joined the U.S. Navy as an athletic officer. After the war, he was recruited by the Greenwood, Mississippi, high school team to lead its athletic program. He was so good, he was chosen as Mississippi's Coach of the Year at least twice.

Although aware of the New Deal administration's cooperative farming experiment at Lake Dick, most of Altheimer's families continued to battle the Depression's effects without government assistance. Like many families, however, ours suffered tremendous economic loss. By the end of the 1930s, my father had lost most of his land and business interests. He avoided bankruptcy, but at a high cost—in fact, he sold 420 acres of land for a pittance to C. E. Spann in 1934. He had about 2,000 acres going into the depths of the Depression, and ended up with 160, plus the home. The store was gone, the larger farm was gone, and the cotton gin ownership was essentially gone. Refusing to enter bankruptcy, my father continued paying on his debt into World War II.

About this time, Ben J. Altheimer, a lawyer in Chicago and Pine Bluff—and a relative of the Altheimer for whom the town was named—began acquiring substantial land holdings in the area. It was his good fortune to persuade Richard S. "Dick" Barnett Jr., newly returned home from Washington and Lee University, to manage his properties. Dick was immediately successful at the new Elms Farming Company. My father was the gin manager and managed a house and farm building repair crew, which still left him time to attend to his Tupelo Break farm.

Altheimer High School Senior Dance, 1940. Bowen is in back row, second from left. His date, seated in front of him, is Frances Mosenthin. *From the author.*

My father also busied himself in service to the community and school. He served as a member of the Altheimer school board, and during the latter part of the 1930s and into the early 1940s, served as president of the board. He also became mayor of Altheimer in 1950 and served in that capacity until he died in September 1956. My brother, Robert, succeeded him—as the Elm's gin manager, on the school board, and as mayor from 1959 until 1978.

I graduated from high school in 1941 in a senior class of thirteen students. My two older brothers had already begun attending college. Robert alternated attending the University of Arkansas at Fayetteville with working odd semesters selling Continental cotton gin equipment, while John attended Monticello A&M (later the University of Arkansas at Monticello) under a work-study program. Our parents encouraged us to get all the education we could even though they could not afford to pay for it.

After graduation, I spent the summer of 1941 working at the Kroger grocery in Pine Bluff to save money to attend Henderson State Teachers College (now Henderson State University) in Arkadelphia the following fall. I worked all summer to save about fifty dollars, twenty-five of which was for tuition and the rest was for books and the first month's room and board. I hitchhiked to Arkadelphia to enroll in school, as this was our only way of affording travel in the aftermath of the Depression. I waited tables in the Henderson dining room, at the restaurant on Highway 67 down the hill, and at the coffee shop in the Cunningham Hotel. I also worked in the cattle auction barn on Saturdays. I made enough to pay my room and board and had a little left over for Saturday night. I did not finish my third semester at Henderson. As it did for so many others of my generation, World War II intervened.

Chapter Two

Becoming a Navy Fighter Pilot

I was sixteen in the summer of 1939 when I joined the Civilian Military Training Program at Camp Robinson, in North Little Rock. I volunteered for the basic course for thirty days. We were taught the elements of shooting the 1903 Springfield rifle, marching, and bivouacking and living in National Guard tents. Operated by the War Department under the authority of the National Defense Act, the camp's objective was to:

> bring together young men of high type from all sections of the country on a common basis of equality and under the most favorable conditions of outdoor life; to stimulate and promote citizenship, patriotism and Americanism; and, through expert physical direction, athletic coaching, and military training, to benefit the young men individually, and to bring them to realize their obligations to their country.[1]

My first rifle was in a box of six, covered with cosmolene (a petroleum-based packing product used to inhibit corrosion) that had been packed in 1919 at the end of World War I. The guns had been stored for twenty years. I'll never forget seeing that beautiful rifle covered in cosmolene.

I became interested in the camp through my early fascination with World War I aviation and from reading magazines like the *Lone Eagle* as a child. I attended the camp again in the summer of 1940 and completed the Red Course (the four courses were Basic, Red, White, and Blue and young men could attend only one camp each year) that provided training in Infantry, along with advanced instruction in the areas covered in the Basic course. While none of us received pay for our service, we were reimbursed five cents per mile for travel—which meant about six dollars for my round trip from Altheimer. In 1939 we wore World War I look-alike uniforms. They changed to khakis plus a sun helmet in 1940. The program ended when the draft began in 1940.

On December 7, 1941, I was returning from a dance in Fayetteville with a carload of Henderson classmates when we learned of the Japanese attack on the U.S. fleet at Pearl Harbor. The next day the U.S. declared war on Japan. Soon after, Japan's ally, Germany, declared war on the United States. Students at Henderson, like others elsewhere, immediately began to leave school to join the armed forces. In late May 1942 my college roommate, Robert Stephens, and I decided to join the U.S. Navy V5 aviation program. I became interested in this program because of its War Training School, in which cadets learned to fly in light aircraft at the Arkadelphia municipal airport. I loved airplanes as a child, more so after Charles Lindbergh's visit to Toney Field, just east of Pine Bluff. As a kid, I built model planes and regularly read two magazines—about World War I and air combat—that I had to hide under my bed because my mother did not approve of such a waste of time.

Because I was barely nineteen, I needed my parents' permission in order to enlist in the Navy. My mother knew how much I wanted to join, but nevertheless tearfully declined to sign the permission form because she already had two sons serving in the war effort. My brother John was in Dutch Harbor in the Aleutian Islands with his National Guard unit, and Bob was serving with the Army Air Corps, learning to maintain aircraft after his poor eyesight barred him from the Army's flight program. John had been involved in an incident at college in which fifty or so students entered the Fine Arts Building late one night and took an unpopular professor from his office and threw him into the fishpond in front of the building. The school president, Marvin Bankson, accepted voluntary withdrawals from John and two other students to resolve the matter, thereby ending the threat of expulsion for other students. Although Bankson later persuaded my brother to return to school, John's unit was called into active duty. On January 6, 1941, I drove him to Pine Bluff to join a friend for a ride to Monticello. I never saw him again.

In late summer 1942 the war heated up on several fronts. While German submarine attacks in the Atlantic all but isolated England, bitter fighting erupted in North Africa and German forces pushed the Russian front nearly to Moscow. Meanwhile, the U.S. was left to fight the war almost alone on the Pacific front, resulting in a significant confrontation with the Japanese Navy in the Coral Sea. There the U.S. stopped Japan from invading Australia and while it was a strategic victory, the U.S. lost the *Yorktown* carrier and the *Lexington* was badly damaged. In addition, Japanese Naval Order 17, issued in late May 1942, directed that country's fleet to attack U.S. forces in the vicinity of Midway Island. The same order directed two Japanese carriers and support units to attack Dutch Harbor, the principal location of American forces engaged in the defense of the Alaska territory. During the Battle of Midway (June 3–6, 1942) U.S. naval forces sank four Japanese carriers and one cruiser, while losing only one American carrier and one cruiser. This was a significant victory for the outmanned U.S. forces, and many consider it the turning point in the war in the Pacific. Control of Midway (1,100 miles northwest of Pearl Harbor) removed any immediate Japanese threat to Hawaii.[2]

The Japanese fleet consisted of an experienced force of eighty-eight warships with the goal of luring the crippled U.S. Pacific Fleet to its destruction. Armed with superior radio intelligence, the U.S. contingent of twenty-eight surface warships sped past Midway and were waiting for the Japanese attack.[3] U.S. forces also repelled the attack at Dutch Harbor and diverted the Japanese troops to Attu and Kiska, at the extreme western end of the Aleutians. They were driven out in May 1943 during the Battle of Attu, the first island confrontation of the war.

After the battle at Dutch Harbor, John and his battery of the 206th Coast Artillery of the Arkansas National Guard moved from the mainland to a tiny island at the harbor's entrance called Hog Island. Conditions there were brutal. On these islands:

> the cold winds from the Bering Sea meet the warm air masses and currents flowing across the Pacific. Their interaction produces the williwaw—winds of high velocity—and dense fogs, rain, mists, and snow, making life miserable for the foot soldier. Those who served in the Aleutians . . . will never forget the treeless terrain and the extreme weather, the poor visibility, icing damage, frostbite, and other hazards of occupation.[4]

On October 19, 1942, while attempting to save supplies on the temporary dock, John and James Allen, from Helena, were washed out to sea by large waves caused by a williwaw, and drowned. Sgt. John Weese, watching from a distance, described the scene.

John jumped on the debris with the cable but the wave action caused him to lose his balance and fall in the water on the side away from the beach. He was wearing his boots and a heavy lined parka and once he went under he never appeared on the surface. All around were help-less to do anything.[5]

Another fellow soldier, David Alspaugh, wrote in his diary:

We lost one of the best men that has ever been in the battery today. John Bowen was drowned down on the beach this afternoon trying to save some of our dock that was about to float off. Sgt. Allen of G Btry [Battery] also lost his life in attempting to tie the dock down . . . John was, without a doubt, one of the finest lads I have ever known.[6]

Two months later, on December 2, Billy Nichols from Hot Springs and I joined the U.S. Navy in New Orleans (my first trip outside of Arkansas) where we were inducted into the Navy V5 Aviation Program. Congress had lowered the draft age to eighteen, so I was able to join without my parent's permission. My brother Pat died of a ruptured appendix six days later. In a letter to her niece, Mildred Priddy of Russellville, my mother extended Christmas greetings, but stoically did not mention the family's losses in 1942, including her own sister's death earlier that year.

I waited eight months until August 2, 1943, before being called for active duty. In the meantime, I took a job at the Pine Bluff Arsenal as a junior chemist. My job was to measure and weigh sodium palmate, from which napalm bombs (mixed with gasoline) were made. In operation by late 1942, the arsenal contained three separate areas: a manufacturing area for incendi-ary bombs, a chemical manufacturing area where agents for toxic gases were produced, and a storage area for chemical agents and weapons. At its peak production capacity in 1944, the arsenal employed nine thousand civilian government employees and 450 military employees—both men and women, blacks and whites.[7]

In early August 1943, I arrived in Troy, New York, to attend Rennsalaer Polytech Institute (RPI), the nation's oldest engineering school. There were some three hundred cadets each from the Eighth and the Second Naval dis-tricts (from New York and Connecticut) there. I roomed with James Blevins of Little Rock, and sought out the company of others from Arkansas. Despite a difference in accents, the class work, athletic program, and Navy indoctri-nation brought us together as a team. We were issued GI clothes—khakis, black shoes, and caps—and were granted the authority at our own expense to buy a Navy dress uniform. Strictly a ground school, with intense physical conditioning, the cadets' studies included U.S. Naval history, aircraft identification, principles of flight, dead-reckoning navigation, and meteorology, among others. At our first class, we were told to look around and understand one of three would be washed out of the program. By the time we finished all six phases of training, two of three had been washed out.

Upon my arrival at RPI, I called home as my mother had insisted. I reached the Altheimer switchboard, operated by the Garrett family. When Mrs. Garrett heard the long-distance operator announce the call from me she replied that she thought my mother was out in the yard because she had not answered a previous call. She volunteered to call our neighbor, Mrs. Sachs, and ask her to look in the chicken yard and tell my mother to come to the phone. Mrs. Sachs left immediately to check and soon my mother came to the phone, out of breath, to take the long-distance call. Modern communication can hardly work as well.

I completed three months of ground school and physical training at RPI before being sent to War Training School (WTS) at the University of South Carolina in Columbia. I enjoyed returning to the South; our first meal upon arrival consisted of fried okra and black-eyed peas. My new roommate, Walter Barbu from Brooklyn, New York, thought the meal was fish and beans, in observance of the Catholic tradition of eating fish on Friday.

Ground school was more advanced in this assignment and we began flight training at Owens Field in downtown Columbia. The planes were Taylor Craft, forty-horsepower, high-wing, single-engine tandem two-seaters. Each cadet put on a shoulder-strap seat parachute for all flights. We had minimum instruction in the art of bailing out, but it was a comfort to have the parachute. After only eight hours of training, I successfully completed my first solo flight on Friday, November 13, 1943, in airplane number thirteen — my new lucky number. The next day, my engine quit at three thousand feet over the Congaree River, north of Columbia. I made a "dead stick" landing in a field, luckily missing all of the tree stumps scattered throughout. The plane was not harmed in the landing.

After completing sixty hours of training, we received another twenty hours of flight time in a Navy-built N3N biplane, which had a 250-horsepower radial engine. Mistakes, such as landing downwind, were punished by making the cadet march through the airplane parking area with a parachute strapped on his back. Landing downwind added the wind speed to the normal landing speed, making the landing trickier and faster. Fortunately, most of us managed to avoid this embarrassment.

We next attended preflight school at the University of North Carolina, Chapel Hill. My Arkansas friends Tom Aycock, Allein Beall, and Ward Rosen, who had taken WTS training in New York, rejoined me in North Carolina. There, we endured intense athletic training and ground school training, but no flying. The curriculum was expanded to include celestial navigation and more refined dead reckoning navigation training. We learned to plot a take-off from an aircraft carrier and return while the carrier was in motion—all without radio communication or electronic navigation equipment. The athletic training program included boxing, wrestling, basketball, swimming, track, football, and gymnastics. Our instructors included a wide assortment of former all-Americans and Olympians, among them "Red" Vaught of Ole Miss fame.

In May 1944, we transferred to the Bunker Hill Naval Air Station in Indiana. There we received primary training in the Stearman N2S biplane known as the "Yellow Peril." As another pilot described it, these planes "could be flown through acrobatic maneuvers that would disintegrate a fighter, [and] they could be dropped to a landing from a stall twenty feet in the air."[8] My first flight was with an instructor up to ten thousand feet. We broke out of nearly solid cloud cover to a beautiful blue sky and a carpet of white clouds. I still remember the awesome view. In order to prepare for duty on an aircraft carrier, all of the training flights included proper carrier landing procedures, and a full stall, three-point landing where the plane's wheels and tail touch down simultaneously. The approach anticipated coming downwind on the port side of the service runway. At the end of the runway the pilot would begin to turn, which put him at the landing end of the runway as he rolled out of the 180-degree turn. This procedure was in contrast to the procedure of the Army Air Corps, which used square turns and a fairly long straightaway to the landing strip. The Army Air Corps flew to the strip—the Navy dropped the plane in at a full stall.

We flew eight out of every ten days, weather permitting. The ground school training also continued, with the addition of simulated flight in a Link Trainer—a mechanical cockpit with all of the instruments of an airplane. The Link Trainers simulated flight in almost all respects.

Aerial acrobatics were an important part of the training at Bunker Hill. One test included "S" turns and slips to a small circle which, in addition to the full stall landing, helped teach us exactness in approaching the small landing zone on the strip. Other aerial maneuvers included loops, split "S's," chandelles, stalls, spins, and rolls, among others. Although our practice area was clearly marked on aviation maps, Army planes occasionally intruded into the area. In one such incident, I came out of a series of rolls only to encounter a B-17 bomber in a full turn, trying—successfully—to avoid a head-on collision.

We soon completed primary training and were selected to continue to advanced flight training at Pensacola Naval Air Station in Florida. This was a coveted assignment as NAS Pensacola was the birthplace of naval aviation prior to World War I. It was the site where pioneer aviators honed their craft at the dawn of carrier aviation. We also continued basic training at the Saufley Field Naval Air Station near Pensacola, and ultimately advanced to single-engine training at Barin Field in Foley, Alabama.

After formation training at Saufley Field, we attended instrument school at Whiting Field, a few miles inland from Pensacola. Here we performed turns, climbs, and modest acrobatics while flying "under the hood," in which a canvas curtain separates the pilot from the outside world and he is left with only the instruments by which to guide the plane. This was an unsettling experience and was a phase of training where a good percentage of fellow cadets were "washed out." The successful cadets learned to maintain altitude, make turns with a needle and ball indicator, and climb and descend with instruments alone. By the end of instrument training, only about 25 percent of the cadets from our original class remained.

In August 1944, I read an article in *The Saturday Evening Post* that brought home how dangerous aerial combat could be. The author interviewed Lt. Ira C. "Ike" Kepford about his experience being pinned in by three Japanese fighters for twenty-five terrifying minutes. After shooting down two fighters near Rabaul, Kepford found himself boxed in by three other planes. He pushed his Corsair to the limit to try and outrun them, but they stayed right with him, flying just above the water and denying him any room to maneuver away. If he turned in either direction, the Japanese fighter pilots would have a direct shot at him, and he could not drop below them because they were too close to the water. Finally, in danger of running out of fuel and causing high speed damage to his engine, Kepford turned suddenly to the left (the side with only one enemy fighter) and outmaneuvered the Japanese pilot. He avoided the enemy fire and the Japanese pilot's wing hit the water and cartwheeled the plane into the water. Kepford then had a large enough lead on the other two planes so they gave up the chase. Emotionally and physically drained from the experience, Kepford managed to land back at base where the doctor gave him a shot of "medicinal" brandy and enough sleeping pills to render him out of service for a day or so.[9] I never forgot this description of combat and, in fact, I still have a photocopy of the article.

We began final training at Barin Field, on the east shore of Mobile Bay in November 1944. It was called "Bloody Barin" by Walter Winchell in 1944 after a dozen or so fatalities occurred the prior year. While there, we five Arkansans flew together as a group. We had cloth Razorbacks on the back of our flight jackets. After take-off, the leader would announce over his radio, "Whoo Pigs! Rendezvous over point able!" Quite often, the airfield tower operator would respond, "You Razorbacks get off the air!"

At Barin Field my fellow cadets and I flew SNJ's, which featured a 550-horsepower radial engine, retractable landing gear, two thirty-caliber machine guns, and could house bombs under each wing. This aircraft, called the AT-6 by the Army, was the advanced trainer for the Allied forces. Advanced training with this aircraft included bombing and strafing (machine gunning) of water targets in Mobile Bay, formation and instrument flying, fighter tactics, night flying, and field carrier landings. Field carrier landings were said to separate the men from the boys. The pilot would circle the landing strip in slow flight—two to three knots above stall—so that he could drop the plane in at full stall in about a twenty-by-fifty-foot designated landing area. Formation flying, especially at night, involved precision flying designed to place the pilot safely close to the lead plane.

In March 1945, we began our final twenty hours of flight training at Chevalier Field in Pensacola. There we flew the SBD Douglas Dauntless—the same type of plane used at the Battle of Midway in 1942. We received our commissions as ensigns and were designated Naval aviators on May 1, 1945. With my training complete, I initially was assigned to instructor duty, but traded this assignment for a fighter billet, or assignment, with an acquaintance of mine from New Jersey. This fellow cadet secured the help of another friend, a WAVE, who handled the necessary paperwork. After a week of leave, we returned to Florida and the Deland Naval Air Station. There we joined a combat team and trained in fighter tactics, field carrier landings, gunnery, and combat techniques in simulated air-to-air gunnery, navigation, and instrument flying.[10]

At Deland, we flew a "souped up" version of the Grumman Wildcat, the FM-2, made by General Motors. It was nicknamed the "Fertile Myrtle Deuce." The plane's 1,250-horsepower engine propelled it at about 350 miles per hour. It weighed 7,200 pounds (nine thousand pounds loaded) and featured four fifty-caliber machine guns—two on each wing—and carried about sixty gallons of gasoline in a fire-resistant plastic tank, located just under the pilot's seat. It also featured manual landing gear and vacuum-operated wing flaps.

That summer our combat team began air-to-air gunnery. Our targets were nylon sleeves, about two and half feet in diameter and thirty feet long. Our fifty-caliber bullets were different colors so each hole in the sleeve could be credited to the correct pilot. To achieve a passing score, we had to hit the target at least 10 percent of the time. We towed our own targets. To become airborne with a target, the tow rope and sleeve were placed in front of the plane—about one hundred feet or so ahead—to allow the pilot to get airborne before the tow rope picked up the sleeve.

We used four types of gunnery runs: a split S, which began some two thousand feet above the target where the pilot would dive directly down on the target; a high side run above and typically to the right of the tow target; a run that began even with the target; and one that started about two thousand feet below the target. Our guns were zeroed in at about one thousand feet so as to converge and concentrate the fire. We had to be in position to shoot some 1,200 to 1,500 feet away in order to optimize the concentration of fire.

During our last month at NAS Deland, we had some thirty hours of gunnery training. The tow plane and other members of the combat team would head east out of Daytona Beach some one hundred miles into the Atlantic Ocean. The tow plane flew about twelve thousand to fourteen thousand feet. We used short bursts of gunfire to conserve ammunition and were over the target area for a total of about one and a half hours on each gunnery training mission. In real combat, a trailing shot would be the most desirable, but it was unavailable in practice because of the certainty of hitting the tow plane. On at least one occasion, a frustrated pilot—and poor marksman—fired from the tail position and hit the tow plane. Needless to say, he was washed out of the program.

The antics we engaged in were dangerous. "Tail chasing" was routine. In tail chasing, you get just under and right behind the front airplane and it leads the team through turns, loops, and what have you.

In June 1945—on Father's Day—one of our fellow pilots, William Ducharme, was killed when his plane crashed after a simulated combat session. I was leading the flight down from twelve thousand feet at about 250 knots, well within guidelines. Bill Ducharme was stepped down two planes on the right behind me, and I looked back just as he turned it into a split S, pulled it through and went straight down and never pulled out. We don't know what happened, of course. He went some eight feet into the ground so the airplane didn't show any detail of what had happened.

In July of that year, five members of the training squadron—including me—crashed. I was the only survivor. One pilot lost a wing when he hit a tree that turned the plane sideways and he hit another tree, which took the canopy and his head off. Two other accidents were field carrier landings gone wrong. My crash occurred on the takeoff from Red Base. I was the fifth man in the combat team on this particular flight. The lead takes off into a slow turn to the left, the next a little tighter turn, and by the time the fifth man takes off, it's a very tight turn. I had just gotten airborne and the wheels up— we had to manually roll the wheels up. At about four hundred feet over the Indian River, the engine stopped. I had just closed the canopy and was looking down at the river on the left, not wanting to go there. It was too shallow to go in—the plane likely would have flipped and I would have drowned. So I made a 270-degree turn and landed on the west side of the river in timber that was about sixteen feet tall. I hit trees with my right wing and my left wing at about the same time and the impact stopped me in brackish water and mud about hip high. I jumped out immediately because I didn't know if the plane was going to explode. Nothing happened, so I climbed back in and called the tower. Within a few minutes a weasel amphibious tank came to get me, but by that time I had walked out to the river's edge.

The only injury I received were blue marks on my shoulders, chest, and lap where my seat belt and shoulder straps had restrained me, and a knot in the middle of my forehead where I hit the gun sight immediately in front of me in the cockpit. After a visit to sick bay, I flew again that night under the theory that it's good to get back onto a horse after being thrown. The report of my crash listed 100 percent operational failure as the cause—not pilot error. I think a previous rough simulated carrier landing might have jarred something loose, causing the engine to fail. I certainly was fortunate to have survived the accident.

The five destroyed planes were lined up on the base flight line to serve as a grim reminder of the dangers of combat training flight.

Other pilots, of course, heard about plane crashes. As another pilot said, "In Florida in 1944, one dive-bomber pilot died every day. We heard about them at dinner . . . the account of every crash was embellished with details: how the plane buried itself in the bull's-eye, how the wreckage covered the target, how the body was gathered up in a bushel basket and sent home in a coffin that had to be loaded with engine parts to give it sufficient weight."[11]

Bill Bowen (standing, second from right) with fellow fighter pilots at NAS Deland in Florida, June 1945. The other pilots are: First row (left to right): Ward Rosen, Harold Mongovan, E. L. Milner, and Tom Aycock.

Second row (left to right): James M. Blevins, William Ducharme (who died in a plane crash on Father's Day, a few days after this photo was taken), Bill Bowen, and Allein Beall. *From the author.*

After completing our training at Deland, our combat team was ordered to report to the Naval Air Station at Glenview, Illinois, for carrier qualification. NAS Glenview was about twenty miles north of Chicago on Lake Michigan. All of our previous flights were ground landings. We trained to land properly in the correct amount of space, but not on a ship until we arrived at NAS Glenview. From there, our orders directed us to report to NAS Los Alamitos, near Long Beach, California, to be assigned to Fighting Squadron 98—a fighter replacement squadron for the Pacific fleet. Aycock, Rosen, and I arrived in Chicago in a 1941 Packard convertible. In early August, Aycock and I were ready for actual carrier landings on the USS *Sable*, anchored at Navy Pier in downtown Chicago. Beall had been assigned to NAS Corpus Christi for night fighter training.

Onboard the USS *Sable* on August 10, 1945, Aycock and I stood on the catwalk on the starboard side of the deck and watched as another pilot attempted a landing on the ship. He began to land, as he had been signaled to do, but then evidently had second thoughts and attempted to take off again. Unfortunately, his tail hook had already caught and he crashed back down to the flight deck. One wheel of the plane came off and flew between Aycock and me. I still remember Aycock's saucer-sized eyes, which were to be evident again that morning as he and I went up to qualify.

I was on the catwalk as Aycock attempted his first takeoff. As he made his preparations, the pin in his right rudder pedal gave way. The rudder pedal of the typical carrier plane was adjustable to accommodate varying leg lengths. Pilots needed to hold full right rudder to combat engine torque on the short takeoffs required for carriers. Unless the pilot maintained a hard right rudder, the plane would skid to port. I watched Aycock as he ran his engine up, brakes on for the takeoff. As he did this, the spring-loaded pin in his right rudder gave way and the torque from the revving engine caused his plane to skid across the port (left) side and off of the carrier deck. I next saw him as he cleared the water and low deck line and started around for his first landing attempt. As he landed, he looked at me with eyes again as big as they were earlier that morning when the wheel came between us.

I followed Aycock. We each were expected to make eight landings. I did not experience any trouble on take off and made nine quick landings before the landing signal officer waved me to a stop. We celebrated that night, unaware of the successful bombings of Hiroshima and Nagasaki on August 6 and 9. A week after the Japanese accepted unconditional surrender on August 14, 1945, Aycock, Rosen, and I continued on our trip down Route 66 to NAS Las Alamitos between Long Beach and Los Angeles, detouring long enough to witness the sunrise over the Grand Canyon. At the Harvey House Restaurant we had a big breakfast—our appetites having been whetted by a little bourbon we drank awaiting sunrise. Aycock ordered kippered herring, which he claimed was on the menu at the Aycock Bus Stop in Forrest City. It was clearly less alluring to him at the Grand Canyon—he tried to eat it, but couldn't get it down.

Upon our arrival at the naval air station in California, we confronted what seemed to me to be an eerie peacetime environment in which many more people were interested in leaving the service than staying in. We were expecting to qualify at night on the USS *Ranger* CV-4, the first U.S. carrier built from the keel up. The Marine unit commander, Major William H.

Enfield (Rosen's brother-in-law), told us we were fortunate not to have to qualify on that carrier at night, because of the high fatality rate.

None of us expressed our feelings aloud, but we regretted that our long, intensive training would not be put to use. However, we took part in a large, arrow-shaped formation flight out to Catalina Island to welcome home a battle group from the Pacific Theater. The battle group responded by tracking the planes with their guns. It was an eerie feeling to look down the muzzle of multiple antiaircraft guns—even though in friendly hands. Our sense of loss at not having been in combat probably was tempered by that experience.

We sometimes flew to the Naval Air Station at Salton Sea, located in southeast California, between the Imperial Valley to the south and Coachella Valley to the north, for dive-bomber training. The base was 245 feet below sea level and was extremely hot. I later learned that it was 130 degrees at times. Pilots had to wear gloves to get in and out of their aircraft because of the hot exterior. Fortunately, it was a short tour.

At North Island NAS, San Diego, we entertained ourselves occasionally at a bar in the Del Coronado Hotel, located on the beach near the air base. At dinner there one evening, Admiral "Bull" Halsey, commanding admiral of the Pacific Fleet, and some of his staff entered. The admiral walked up to our table and shook hands all around, saying, "hello, son," just like he might have greeted new pilots on his carrier. I later learned that one of his staff members, a black man, had been refused service that evening by a bartender from Mississippi. Halsey had the bartender fired that same night.

One evening in Los Angeles, we visited Hollywood and went to the Brown Derby for dinner. The four of us, Aycock, Mongovan, Rosen, and I, first had a drink or two and then we asked the waitress for menus. The prices were high and Rosen ordered braised beef tips—the cheapest item on the menu—which he said he wanted medium well. At this point, our waitress, who had been patient with our behavior and had observed us for some time, said, "I know you boys are from Arkansas because I have been listening to your conversation. I'm from Oil Trough, and braised beef tips ain't nothing but hash—It's the same here and it's all cooked the same." We settled back for a little hash and continued to enjoy our dinner.

Our last duty station, beginning in late summer 1945, was at the North Island NAS with the Ferry Squadron Three. The squadron's role at this time was to fly stockpiled airplanes from the West Coast to bases inland, including Clinton, Oklahoma. There, the aircraft were either stored or, more likely, dismantled. It was an appalling waste of some of the best airplanes we flew during World War II. In December, Rosen and I volunteered to fly two "war weary" Hellcats to Minneapolis for donation to an American Legion post there. My plane displayed numerous Japanese flags on its side—indicating considerable combat experience—and was said to have had an engine freeze at six hundred flight hours. In addition, the cockpit heater did not function properly. This was not a problem in San Diego, but by the time we reached Minneapolis, the cockpit temperature was twenty degrees. While en route, Rosen and I flew through Fayetteville and "buzzed" Old Main on the University of Arkansas campus.

Navy recruits Jim Bowen and Tom Lyon arrived at this same time at the San Diego Navy Operating Base to begin two years of training. Jim ended his Navy career on the destroyer tender USS Dixie in China. My brother was discharged in the fall of 1947 and he hitchhiked home. He already had a year at Hendrix College under his belt, although he had only been sixteen when he went, and he and Tom returned to Arkansas and graduated from the university in Fayetteville—both beneficiaries of the GI Bill.

Before leaving active duty, I tried out a couple of planes that I had not had the chance to fly during the war. I flew an SB2C torpedo bomber over Point Loma, a few miles up the coast from the air base, and, although I conducted a thorough preflight check, my engine faltered on takeoff and I barely cleared the point. Not heeding this lesson, I also flew a F4U-5 Corsair—the newest fighter in the Navy—and I didn't even read the handbook. I just said, in the spirit of the times, "where do I put my feet?" So I climbed to ten thousand feet over San Diego Bay—rolled it and then put it into a loop. I didn't have enough airspeed to make a complete circle and I dropped through into an "L," which meant that I was heading straight down toward San Diego Bay. As I tried to pull out, I developed a mush (lost lift), and I went right down to the water's edge before I pulled up. En route back to North Island NAS, my radio was barely operative and the next thing I knew, I had landed wheels up at the end of that flight. The attitude was such at that time that no one even questioned me about it or noted the event in my logbook—much to my pleasant surprise.

Aycock, Beall, and Mongovan had elected to leave the Navy in the fall of 1945. Rosen and I stayed on until the beginning of the spring semester in 1946 before leaving for Fayetteville. We were discharged from active duty in January 1946. I accepted an invitation to join the U.S. Naval Reserve. This involved weekend training once a month and two weeks of active duty every year. I was assigned to Fighting Squadron 791 located at the Millington Naval

Air Station near Memphis, where I flew from Fayetteville every month while attending the University of Arkansas. In June 1950 I transferred my duty station to NAS Anacostia in Maryland with Airwing Staff 66. I served there as an intelligence officer while working for the U.S. Tax Court and the Department of Justice in Washington, D.C. At NAS Millington, our squadron commander was "Happy" Campbell of Helena and my fellow pilots included Charles Harper of Little Rock. Within two weeks of my transfer to AWS 66, my former unit in Millington was called up for active duty in the Korean War and was assigned to the USS *Boxer* in the South China Sea. I missed both World War II and Korea by the luck of the draw.

After my return to Little Rock in 1954, I served as an intelligence officer under the guidance of the Eighth Naval District in New Orleans. My associates there included Phillip Dixon, George Hartje, Hubert Barksdale, and Robert McHenry, leaders in the Arkansas Bar Association. I remained with that unit until the end of the summer in 1963, completing over twenty years of service in both active duty and reserves. On my last training cruise in 1963, at the Alameda Naval Air Station on the east side of San Francisco Bay, I participated in a secret briefing on the emerging conflict in Vietnam. It included an Inchon-like plan—similar to MacArthur's amphibious landing of Joint Task Force Seven at Inchon Harbor, Korea in 1950—for an attack on Hanoi in North Vietnam. My experience in two and half years of active duty and seventeen and a half years in the reserves were significant events in my career. I was able to fulfill every boy's dream of flying, much of my education was paid for, and I made lasting friendships that I continue to cherish today. My biggest disappointment was not having the opportunity to apply over two years of training toward fulfilling my role to help fight World War II.

In the spring of 1983, newly reelected Arkansas Gov. Bill Clinton appointed me state chairman for the Arkansas Employer Support Committee for Guard and Reserve (ESGR). This national organization, created by presidential decree in 1972, with affiliate offices in all fifty states, three territories, and the District of Columbia, was chartered in 1973 to support the guard and reserve as full partners in the total force concept of the armed forces. This came on the heels of termination of the draft in mid-1973. The stated purpose of the ESGR was to bring the guard and reserve in as equal partners with regulars in the total force. It was made up of volunteers, served by a paid staff and a national office in Washington.[12]

In addition to its goals of making a seamless fighting force, the ESGR worked to foster public understanding and employer support of the role played by reserve forces. In 1975, a national ombudsman office was created to mediate conflict between employers and employees at loggerheads over call-up to active and/or training duty. The U.S. Department of Labor supported the effort and, in particular, supported the ombudsman program. Each state office had a Department of Labor expert assigned to its committee. On the twenty-fifth anniversary of the national office of ESGR, there were some 4,200 volunteers in place, served by the full-time staff.

In 1983, ESGR held its national conference in St. Louis. We met there again the next year where we were addressed by then secretary of defense Dick Cheney. In the summer of 1991, the members of the Arkansas staff and air guard, under the leadership of Adjutant General Jack Ryan, flew to the Panama Canal in a C-130 to visit the scene of conflict leading to the capture of dictator Gen. Manuel Noriega. The following year, we flew a commercial airline to NAS San Diego, and then flew a Navy plane 150 miles out to sea to the carrier USS *Carl Vinson* to observe carrier qualification of all of that ship's squadrons.

In early June 1992, Adjutant General Ryan arranged a C-141 flight for members of the 206th Coast Guard Artillery Association of the Arkansas National Guard to Anchorage, Alaska. There we changed to a C-130 and flew to Dutch Harbor to celebrate the fiftieth anniversary of the battle with the Japanese forces at that site. The next year, Ryan and I met with then President Clinton in the East Wing of the White House, where he presented us the original of a presidential decree giving the name Arkansas Beach to the beach on Hog Island at Dutch Harbor—the beach where my brother and two of his fellow guardsmen lost their lives.

President Clinton appointed me National Chairman of ESGR in September 1994. I served in that capacity for a four-year period until November 1998. In the summer of 1998, I flew to Frankfurt, Germany, with the assistant secretary of defense for reserve affairs and the national chairman of the American Legion. From there, we flew on military aircraft to Tuzla, Bosnia, to visit Base Camp Eagle. There U.S. troops shared peacekeeping responsibilities with NATO forces located in Bosnia. All Base Camp Eagle service personnel carried weapons with live ammunition at all times. Each day at 5 p.m., the commanding officers of U.S. forces met via video with NATO and Russian forces to discuss the day's events. On our second day there, paratroopers from the nearby Russian base camp entertained us with a remarkable display of hand-to-hand combat and parachute jumping efficiency.

That fall, at the last national meeting I attended as chairman, the executive committee of ESGR was briefed by the commanding officers of all U.S. forces. Standout comments included: 1) the total force concept was seamless and in place—that is to say the guard and reserves had been melded into regular forces so as to comprise a national force of three million men and women, 47 percent of whom were in the guard and reserves; and 2) our weaponry was so advanced that U.S. forces controlled the night and had no peer in firepower. This latter point was proven in Kosovo in 1999 when, with 37,000 sorties by aircraft, we wrecked the hostile establishment, never flew lower than 15,000 feet, and lost no personnel in combat.

As a going away present, the president invited the national office of ESGR to the Rose Garden, where he greeted us and spoke. That same weekend, at the Pentagon, acting under secretary of defense Charles Cragin and Mack McLarty from the White House awarded me the Secretary of Defense Outstanding Service Medal for my tenure with the ESGR.

Chapter Three

Learning to be a Tax Lawyer

I attended Henderson State Teacher's College in 1941 and 1942, leaving to join the Navy in November 1942. After returning from the service in January 1946, I entered the University of Arkansas at Fayetteville and took classes in the spring and summer semesters. I received some credit for my military service and my attendance for three months each at Rennsalaer Polytech Institute in Troy, New York, the University of South Carolina, and the University of North Carolina, and was able to enter the university's law school by the fall.

Constance Wanasek, a third-year student and temporary employee in the registrar's office, enrolled me and we became "pinned" that fall. A year later, on August 31, 1947, we married at St. Mark's Episcopal Church in Fayetteville. I knew right away she was the one for me.

I attended classes under the GI Bill, which paid for my tuition, fees, and books, and provided a seventy-five dollars per month stipend. This amount increased to $105 after we married. The GI Bill, or officially the Servicemen's Readjustment Act of 1944, was passed to help the country reabsorb returning veterans. The opportunities afforded by this bill fundamentally changed American life as millions of returning servicemen sought college educations and prepared themselves for a standard of living unknown and unavailable to most of their parents. These young ex-GIs were "anxious to make up for years lost to the gods of war, tedium, and terror—with similar stories they soon wanted to forget. Life was waiting; the days of dying were over."[1]

Connie attended Muskogee (Oklahoma) Junior College for two years before transferring to Fayetteville. She had graduated the previous June and worked as secretary to the dean of the School of Agriculture. Her salary of $110 per month gave us a combined income of $215 monthly. In 1947, this allowed us to live in relative comfort in a small house on Lindell Street, just three blocks from the university campus.

Not having taken any previous classes that required essay answers to test questions, I was at a disadvantage on entering law school—and my first semester's grades reflected that difficulty. However, Connie often joined me at the law school library, just south of the student union. I recall discussing my progress in contract law that first semester with my professor, Joe Covington. Covington observed Connie as she exited the student union, en route to meet me at the library. Covington told me that I needed to choose between her and contract law, in order to succeed in the class. Despite the admonition, I stayed with Connie as well as contracts and managed to pass the class.

I was in law school when Silas Hunt, the first African American to be admitted to the law school program, entered the University of Arkansas in the spring of 1948. Hunt was the first black student to attend a white southern university since Reconstruction.[2] Hunt graduated as his class salutatorian from Washington High School in Texarkana, Arkansas, and enrolled at Arkansas AM&N (now the University of Arkansas at Pine Bluff) in 1941. Like so many of us, Hunt's college career was interrupted by World War II. He was seriously wounded at the Battle of the Bulge while serving in Europe. He returned to Arkansas and graduated from AM&N in 1947. The next year, Hunt applied for admission to the University of Arkansas law school and was accepted on a segregated basis.[3] I was acutely sensitive to the racial issues surrounding Hunt's enrollment because of my childhood in a segregated society. I was also supportive of Hunt's admission for the same reason. Hunt attended segregated classes in the law school's basement, but he was not alone for long and because his teaching was individualized, some white students began to join him and pretty soon the façade of segregated education was broken. Indeed, some white students attended Hunt's individualized lectures in the basement because they felt they received better instruction in the smaller class. Unfortunately, Hunt was unable to complete his first semester due to problems resulting from his service-related injuries. He died three months later in a veteran's hospital in Missouri. Although Hunt did not complete his semester, his admission opened an important opportunity for other African American students who followed.[4]

I graduated from law school in the spring of 1949 and immediately took a summer job in Pine Bluff with the Rowell, Rowell, and Dickey law firm. As a veteran, I did not have to take the bar exam. I began my first job that summer with no salary but the expectation of being paid for my completed work at the end of the summer. My "office" doubled as the waiting room for African American clients—segregation still being alive and well in the South. I enjoyed the work. One of the firm's clients was attempting to dam a 640-acre section of the Wabbaseka Scatters for a duck-hunting facility and landowners up and downstream objected, asserting that it would impede the flow of the Wabbaseka Bayou through the wetland area. I worked on the case all summer and the firm successfully negotiated a settlement with the landowners, allowing the duck club owner to keep his facility. I was pleased when I received a check in September for $2,250 for my services, an amount equal to a year's salary when I was in law school.

Before I was released from active duty, I had signed up for the Navy Organized Reserve and immediately upon returning home, I joined VF 791, a reserve fighter squadron, at the Naval Air Station Millington, just northeast of Memphis. My service involved being picked up by a Navy transport plane either in Fayetteville or Little Rock once a month for a long weekend of training—or "weekend warrior" duty. In addition, like today's reservists, I served two weeks' active duty each summer. This "reserve cruise" every summer turned out to be our family's only vacation through 1963, when I had completed twenty years of reserve service. Connie was patient with my reserve commitment throughout the years and we enjoyed some of the two-week training trips.

In the fall of 1949, I returned to school to begin graduate studies in tax law at New York University. Former UA law school dean Robert Leflar had chaired a seminar for judges at NYU and encouraged me to attend the tax law program there. Connie supported the idea, so I traveled to New York to register for school and find a place for us to live. My last flight with the Navy was in an advanced trainer called the SNJ. I flew it from Naval Air Station Millington to NAS North Philadelphia, got on a train and went to New York, enrolled in classes, found accommodations, and returned that same day. I flew back via Kentucky, where I hit a squall line and had to stop in Lexington to allow the storm to blow over before finally landing back in Memphis.

We arrived in New York in early September, but Connie did not care for the temporary housing that I had secured, so we moved to a third-floor walkup at 108 Montague Street, next door to Brooklyn's Bossert Hotel. It was a half block from uptown Brooklyn Heights and a half block east of a promenade along the East River. There we discovered that our landlord had once lived in Pine Bluff, Arkansas.

The head of the graduate tax program at New York University was Gerald Wallace, a one-time special assistant to the U.S. Attorney General, assigned to the Appellate Section of the Tax Division in Washington, D.C. He befriended me and by mid-fall 1949, hired me as his graduate assistant. With this job and Connie's employment as a secretary for the Home Life Insurance Company, we had the resources to enjoy some of New York's nightlife. After receiving my summer pay from Rowell, Rowell, and Dickey, we celebrated by attending *South Pacific*, a premiere play in midtown New York, and enjoying dinner at a fancy restaurant near the theater. Mary Martin starred in the play as the "little girl from Little Rock."

In May 1950, I began considering my future job prospects. I visited a friend, Clarence Thomas, in Washington, D.C., and the next day I interviewed with the United States Tax Court, the U.S. Treasury Department, the Internal Revenue Service, and the U.S. Department of Justice. Judge Bolon B. Turner of the U.S. Tax Court, formerly a Little Rock lawyer and partner of then Rep. Brooks Hays, offered me a job as one of his two law clerks. I accepted and began work for the judge upon graduation in June 1950.

Connie and I moved to a garden apartment in a Clarendon, Virginia, development called Colonial Village. Nearby was Community Methodist Church, which we joined. At day's end we could hear the sound of "Taps" at nearby Arlington Cemetery and we were only about a mile and a half from the Memorial Bridge across the Potomac River at the Lincoln Memorial. Connie found a job with the National Lumber Manufacturers Association on DuPont Circle in Washington and with our new affluence we bought our first car, a standard 1950 black Chevrolet from Smart Chevrolet Company in Pine Bluff. It cost $1,607 and we commuted from Arlington to downtown Washington.

I chose the position with Judge Turner because I knew I would have ample opportunity to hone my writing skills. The U.S. Tax Court was created by Congress to provide a forum in which taxpayers could dispute proposed tax deficiencies as determined by the commissioner of the Internal Revenue Service. The Tax Court has the authority to hear tax disputes where taxpayers can have their cases heard before paying the full amount, as opposed to district court, where they must pay first. While the court is located in Washington, D.C., the judges travel and conduct trials all across the country.

Turner required his clerks to research and write the findings of fact and draft opinions, which he would then review and finalize. In one case, I declined a deduction for a taxpayer who testified that he gave $150 per year to his church but he had no proof. Judge Turner told me that testimony was also evidence and he believed that the taxpayer deserved the deduction—an interesting experience about the importance of testimony. Turner was a taciturn person with whom I developed little rapport. The learning experience was helpful, however, because he relied on his law clerks (Boyd Cypert of South Carolina was his other clerk) almost entirely to draft the facts of the case and he relied on our suggestions for disposition and memoranda to make his decisions. This gave us ample opportunity to express ourselves and to learn in the process.

During this time, I joined an informal organization known as the Arkansas Association. It was made up of federal and congressional employees with an Arkansas background, including former Rep. Brooks Hays's son, Steele, Senator John McClellan's daughter, Mary Alice McDermott, and her husband Buddy. After a little less than a year working for Judge Turner, I transferred to the office of U.S. Tax Court Judge Clarence V. Opper, and routinely joined the judge, his law clerk, Arnold Hoffman, and Steele Hays for weekly lunches at O'Donnells in downtown Washington. Judge Opper was an Ethicist from New York—and from a Jewish background. Hoffman was a practicing member of the Jewish faith. Steele, at the time, although Baptist, was studying a splinter faith of the Presbyterian church. We discussed life in the District, including Congress, Senator Joe McCarthy, Mrs. Roosevelt, and Cardinal Spellman, and the controversies they sparked.

In early winter 1950, Connie realized she was expecting and on Friday, July 13, 1951, Cynthia Ruth arrived—all four pounds, twelve ounces of her. She was in an incubator for two weeks before we could bring her home. Connie quit her job and from then on our lifestyle revolved around Cynthia and the other children who were to come.

In June 1952, I began working in the Trial Section of the Tax Division at the U.S. Department of Justice. My title was Special Assistant to the Attorney

Bill and Connie Bowen with daughter Cynthia in front of Connie's sister's house in Ponca City, Oklahoma, December 30, 1952. *From the author.*

General and I was assigned cases involving federal taxation issues in U.S. District Court. By the fall, I was assigned my first case in Great Falls, Montana. I received the file the Friday before the trial, which was set for the following Monday, and I flew all night to arrive in Great Falls on Saturday morning to prepare for the case. That morning, I met the U.S. Attorney, Krest St. Cyr, who told me that the trial had been postponed until Wednesday, giving us two additional days to prepare. I had never participated in a trial before, nor had I observed one, but by trial time I had read Goldstein's book, *Trial Techniques,* had interviewed our witnesses, and had established a good relationship with St. Cyr.

In the case, taxpayer and plaintiff Mr. Anderson was a farmer who claimed for tax purposes that his wife and son were partners in the business. He was attempting to recover income taxes he had paid for the year 1945. During the war, tax rates could be as high as 90 percent, but if the income was divided among several members of the family, the rate could be reduced to nearly 50 percent. U.S. District Judge Albert Pray ruled against the Justice Department, and the case was appealed to the Ninth Circuit Court of Appeals, where the judgment was affirmed. The district court held that the family members acted in good faith to conduct business and distribute the profits. It confirmed that the members of the partnership received income from the partnership regardless of whether they actively participated in the farming and ranching business.[5] After the trial, U.S. Attorney St. Cyr wrote a letter praising me to the head of the trial section, Andrew Sharp. After receiving the unsolicited letter of praise from the U.S. Attorney, Sharp was quite upset. He called me in and threw the letter across the desk and said, "Have you seen this?" I said, "No." He said, "Young man, you solicited that letter and I don't appreciate it." I'm sure my face flushed and I said, "Mr. Sharp, I had no idea that he'd written it. I did not solicit it and I resent that." I decided that day that I was going to leave the Justice Department at the end of 1953.

For the rest of that year, I continued to try cases in Birmingham, Little Rock, Oklahoma City, Tulsa, Memphis, Jackson, Mississippi, and other areas of the South. I handled a tax lien in bankruptcy court in Pittsburgh, an excise tax case in Columbia, South Carolina, and a nondescript case before Judge Hatch in New Mexico (Judge Hatch was famous for the passage of the Hatch Act in the 1930s while serving in Congress—which governs political activities of federal employees).

In 1953, I tried my first case in Little Rock and won. I was selected for the trial because I was from the area and, after sending attorneys from the North who routinely lost cases in Little Rock, my supervisor decided to send some southern boys down to see what we could do. As an example of southern sentiment against federal tax attorneys, one of my colleagues, Moxley Featherston (later Chief Judge of the U.S. Tax Court), tried a case in Mobile, Alabama, in which the defendant argued that his wife was his partner. However, he had filed written affidavits with the local draft board every six months during World War II claiming he was the sole proprietor and that if he were drafted it would destroy his business. Featherston submitted those affidavits to the jury, which nevertheless ruled in favor of the defendant.

The Little Rock case I handled involved alleged business expense deductions. The taxpayer made a fifteen thousand dollar loan to Rich-Aire, Inc. that became worthless in 1947. He claimed that the debt was a bad debt related to his business of selling refrigerated display cases, or, alternatively, his business of promoting, financing, and managing various business enterprises. As a business debt loss, the amount would be deductible in full from his ordinary income in the year the debt became worthless. On behalf of the government, I maintained that the debt was unrelated to his business and under the IRS code at the time a nonbusiness bad debt that became worthless could only be deducted against ordinary income to the extent of one thousand dollars. The case was submitted to a jury after the three-day trial. The jury held for the government and found that the taxpayer did not regularly engage in either of the alleged businesses and that the bad debt was not related to his business.[6] According to trial judge Trimble, this was the first jury trial win for the government in a tax case in Little Rock since before World War II.

A case I handled in Oklahoma City was the first to reach a jury involving a charge under special Internal Revenue Service legislation prohibiting improper accumulation of surplus in a corporation. The purpose of accumulating surplus by corporations was to avoid paying dividends and having the income taxed first in the corporation and then again as income for the stockholders. In this trial, KOMA, a Tulsa radio station, maintained that it was accumulating net reserves for the construction of a planned FM and television broadcasting facility, as well as the improvement of existing AM facilities. The company paid no dividends and a handsome surplus accrued, which the IRS claimed was accumulated beyond reasonable needs and so accumulated to avoid the additional taxes that would have accrued had this surplus been distributed as dividends to the stockholders. The U.S. District Court and the Court of Appeals, Tenth Circuit, determined that the corporation acted to avoid taxes and not for future construction needs.[7]

However, in a related case, KOMA filed a refund suit and this time the question of unreasonable accumulation of profits to avoid the surtax was submitted to a jury. During the trial, I used a pitcher of water with dollar signs on it to represent the corporation. I then poured the water into several glasses that represented taxpayers. I pointed out that money left in the pitcher would only be taxed one time. If taxed and then poured into the glasses, which represented the stockholders, it would be taxed again in their hands and that was what this statute was designed to make happen.[8] I lost the case and later discovered that one of the jurors had sold insurance to opposing counsel, but was not disqualified. This tax law was later repealed. In my opinion, it was difficult, if not impossible, to enforce and I wrote a memorandum to the Department of Justice to that effect after the trial.

In another case, the same trial judge in Oklahoma City heard my opening statement presenting the question whether the taxpayer, whose farm was on the edge of town east of Oklahoma City, operated the farm for profit or whether it was a hobby. If the latter, the expenses would not be deductible. The judge interrupted me to say, "Mr. Bowen, do you know this taxpayer is a friend and neighbor of mine and that I have a farm adjoining his? Are you telling me that my losses are not deductible because it is a hobby?" I said, "Judge, I don't know your situation, but in this case, that is our position." The judge ruled from the bench after opening statements only—with no offer of proof—in favor of the taxpayer. The Court of Appeals, Tenth Circuit, after a series of similar complaints, including his participating as a defendant in both civil and criminal proceedings and refusing to disqualify himself in pending cases despite requests that he do so, disciplined the trial judge. The Tenth Circuit Court prohibited the assignment of any future cases to him—the effect of which was to leave him on the bench but unable to hear cases, thus prompting him to take early retirement.[9]

While in Washington, Congressman Hays had encouraged me to teach a Sunday school class as a learning opportunity for developing facts and expressing conclusions on sensitive subjects. He reasoned that this would help me in the practice of law. It so happened that our minister at Community Methodist Church in Arlington was seeking a teacher for an adult Sunday school class consisting largely of professionals and couples our age. I accepted and taught this class from June 1950 to December 1953. On a couple of occasions, Congressman Hays taught the class in grand style, confirming his reputation as the best storyteller in Congress.

Teaching Sunday school invited me to express myself on emotional issues of life and religion. It was a demanding endeavor to prepare for the weekly class and appear before professionals and their families. We used an official Methodist text, but we also included events of the day from the Korean War to Senator McCarthy, Congress, and anything else we felt was relevant to our discussion. My conversations with the "Arkansas Association" and Judge Opper helped provide fodder for my Sunday school lessons.

While with the Department of Justice, I took the pro-government side because I believed in what I was doing. As a matter of fact, if I had stayed another year I might have converted to the IRS side. I got out in time not to have been too tainted by that. And later, I turned completely to the taxpayer's side, but my experience in the department served me well. In January 1954, I returned to Little Rock and joined the Mehaffy, Smith, and Williams law firm and began the next phase of my career as counsel for the taxpayer. When I left the Department of Justice my caseload totaled eighty-eight active files.

Upon arriving in Little Rock, Connie and I rented a small house on A Street, where we lived until 1955, when we moved into our new home, a split-level at 53 Pine Manor Drive. I prepared the contract for the construction of our new home and the builder, N. P. Alessi joked that afterward, his initials stood for "No Profit." Our construction funds came from a GI Bill loan with an interest rate of 4.5 percent. Our son, Scott, was born on July 19, 1955, about a week after our relocation. It was a hot summer—made more so because we had installed air conditioning ducts in our new house, but decided to wait and install the cooling unit the next summer to save money. Our daughter Patty arrived on December 7, 1957, completing our family. They were healthy and a joy. Connie ran the house and my days were spent in the office—including Saturday mornings and sometimes Sunday afternoons.

When we arrived in Little Rock, we joined the First United Methodist Church at Eighth and Center streets and became part of a new Sunday school class called the Harmony Class. Because of my prior teaching experience, Reverend Walton invited me to teach this new class. In due course, it became the "Bowen Class" and then the name was expanded to the "Bowen-Cabe Class" to thank Lucy Cabe for her unfailing leadership as our piano player and head of music. I continued to teach this class until about 1980,

Bill Bowen with his wife, Connie, and children Scott, Cynthia, and Patty at the Bay Breeze Resort on Bull Shoals Lake in August 1960. *From the author.*

when the responsibility rotated to other members of the class with me appearing on call from time to time.

When I left the Department of Justice to return to Little Rock and enter private practice, I could not have had better experience in preparation for a tax practice than my time spent in Washington. This time, however, I would be serving the taxpayer rather than the government.

Chapter Four

Building a Tax Law Practice

When I arrived at the eleventh floor of the Boyle Building on January 1, 1954, there were seven lawyers in the Mehaffy, Smith, and Williams firm. I was designated a little corner office at the southeast side of the building. On the twelfth floor were two law offices, and Russell Brown and Company, the state's largest accounting firm, occupied the entire seventh floor. Allan Gates, Arkansas manager for the Penn Mutual Life Insurance Company, occupied most of the fourth floor. The local paper included a small article and picture announcing my arrival and Mr. Gates called and invited me to visit him on my first day in the office. He told me he wanted to put me on a fifty dollar a month retainer and use my services in preparing wills for his rather substantial statewide clientele. This opened many doors for my future endeavors in estate planning.

While I was in Washington, Rep. Brooks Hays had befriended me because of a common Pope County background and my friendship with his son, Steele. Before he was elected to Congress, Hays had served as the National Democratic Committeeman from Arkansas, and he recommended that I pursue this as a way to get involved in Arkansas politics without plunging into it. Shortly after I arrived at the Mehaffy firm, I visited with Pat Mehaffy about this idea because, in part, I had precious little tax work to which to commit my time. He discouraged it, saying that it would dilute my tax specialty and, moreover, that he might want to be Democratic National

Committeeman himself. In fact, he did later acquire the job through appointment by the Arkansas Democratic Party leadership.

The Mehaffy firm's list of clients included the Missouri Pacific Railroad, then in bankruptcy, Little Rock's First National Bank, the Arkansas Contractors Association, T. J. Raney and Sons Brokers, Ben Hogan and Company Highway Contractors, Parkin Printing Company, and the Little Rock Housing Authority. Estate planning was pretty much limited at the time to a one-page will for which no charge was made, with the expectation that it was enough to represent the estate in probate court. There was no tax practice in the firm as such. I was the only attorney in the state at the time with a master's degree in tax law and that, combined with my government tax law experience, allowed me to be one of the first attorneys in the state to specialize in a particular area. Jim Rice, trust officer at First National Bank, and Harry Erwin, a CPA in Russell Brown and Company and a contemporary of mine, invited me to join them in forming the Central Arkansas Estate Planning Council, comprised of lawyers, CPAs, bank trust officers, and life underwriters. It grew into a vital center of estate planning activity and proved to be a good source of business as well as a melding influence of the four professional groups that comprised its membership.

My first important case came in the mid-1950s when Witt Stephens, founder of Stephens, Inc., employed me to pursue a refund of some half a million dollars in Arkansas excise taxes paid under protest in the purchase of controlling stock of the Arkla Gas Company. The purchase was closed in New Jersey, which did not have a franchise tax on the transfer of stock. The plan was to avoid the New York and Arkansas taxes.

The Arkansas Revenue Department took the position that it was an Arkansas business deal and therefore was subject to Arkansas tax. Stephens, Inc., paid the tax. We then filed suit in Pulaski County Chancery Court for a refund. We prevailed in the case and it was affirmed on appeal to the Arkansas Supreme Court in January 1961. According to prior decisions of both the United States and Arkansas supreme courts, the equal protection clauses of the federal and state constitutions barred the state from taxing a domestic corporation doing business both within and outside of the state on that portion of its income derived from sources outside the state.[1]

After the trial, Pat Mehaffy and I sat down to discuss what our fee ought to be. We agreed on ten percent of the recovery, or $55,000—a very large sum at that time. As I rose to walk out, Mehaffy said, "Wait a minute, boy. I want you to deliver the bill to Witt Stephens." I really didn't want to deliver such a large bill, but I did. I sat down with Stephens and he congratulated me—then I handed him the bill. He looked at it and, in good humor, said, "My God, that's a lot of money." Because it involved two well-known organizations, Arkla and Stephens, this was a significant case for our firm and we received much attention following the win.

In the summer of 1954, the executors of the Myers estate in Van Buren consulted me about representation. The Internal Revenue Service had sent deficiency notices to the estate alleging that Myers owed additional income taxes for 1942 and 1943 in the amount of $137,989. The estate did not have the funds to pay the deficiency and then sue for a refund, as required to establish jurisdiction in United States District Court. We risked sending a partial payment of $2,500 per year and filed a claim for a refund followed by suit. The government argued that the estate was limited to two remedies: 1) it could challenge the alleged deficiency in Tax Court without prepaying any portion of the deficiency; or 2) it could pay the entire deficiency and then bring a refund suit for the total amount. District Court Judge John Miller agreed with the motion filed by the Department of Justice and dismissed the case. We appealed it to the Eighth Circuit Court of Appeals, however, which reversed Miller's ruling and held that the estate could also use the remedy of making the partial payment.[2]

After the case was remanded to the U.S. District Court, the government threatened to sell certain assets of the estate to satisfy the unpaid portion of the additional income taxes owed by Myers. The court, however, enjoined the sale of the assets until a trial could determine the tax liability because a forced sale at less than fair market value would produce substantial losses for both the estate and the government.[3] The first trial ended with a hung jury, but we prevailed before the second jury. It was a significant piece of tax litigation involving charges of tax evasion and the right of taxpayers to claim U.S. District Court jurisdiction without a complete payment of taxes.

That same year, I was employed to represent the Reuben Bredlow estate. The decedent owned a large farm in Scott, Arkansas, and was found dead in his office with his head almost blown off. It was a day or two before duck season and his shotgun was just under his chin. The case involved a claim of double indemnity (for accidental death) against New York Life Insurance Company, which had raised the defense of suicide. The insurance company argued that if you are found dead with a shotgun across your body and you have been depressed and the Bible is open on the desk to the Twenty-third Psalm, then it is a suicide. I argued that his Bible was always open to the

Twenty-third Psalm because it was his favorite passage, and that his gun was out because duck season was about to start and he was an avid hunter. I told the jury that even if he had been depressed, he would not have taken his own life because he was looking forward to duck season. I also argued that the strongest presumption of the law is that one would never take one's own life, unless proven otherwise. After two days of trial, the jury held that the death was accidental. Despite that, the visiting district judge granted New York Life's motion for judgment notwithstanding the verdict, overturning the jury's decision. We appealed to the Eighth Circuit and the court ruled that we had presented proof of accidental death and there was sufficient evidence to make the issue of suicide as opposed to accidental death a proper question for the jury to decide.[4] In probate of the estate, Chancery Judge Guy Williams ruled that about thirty cows claimed by Bredlow's daughter and son-in-law actually belonged to the estate. Tom Eisele, now Senior United States District Judge in Little Rock, represented the daughter and son-in-law and the entire family testified on a hearing *de novo* (as if it were a new trial) before the Arkansas Supreme Court that Reuben Bredlow gave the cattle to them, and Judge Williams's decision was reversed.

The Bredlow alleged suicide was a disturbing case to handle. About a week after his death I walked into his office, which had already been cleaned, and I put my hand on a steel shelf and began to fumble with something I thought was an ashtray. I pulled it down and realized it was the top of his skull, blown clean from his flesh, that they had missed in the cleaning. Still, the case opened the door for many more and I soon had more clients than I could accommodate. I employed three more associates in tax and estate litigation to help: Jerry Light, Trip Larzalere, and Byron Eiseman.

In the course of my estate tax work, I handled two cases that involved the assessment of estate taxes arising out of "gifts in contemplation of death." At that time, the law viewed such gifts, if made within three years of death, as creating the presumption that the gift was made with the purpose of avoiding the 55 percent estate tax and were taxed as though still part of the estate. In the estate of John Baxter, a banker and farmer from Dermott, we litigated this question in the U.S. District Court in Pine Bluff before Judge Oren Harris—one of his first cases after being appointed to the bench. It was his first tax trial and he ruled for the estate. In a similar case, I represented the estate of Minnie V. Parkin, where the question involved a gift of stock in Parkin Printing Company, a major Little Rock business. In 1963, Parkin transferred stocks to several trusts for the benefit of her grandchildren. The income from the trusts was payable to the grandchildren for fifteen years, at which time the trusts were to terminate and the property of the trusts distributed to them. Just under three years later, Parkin died and the Internal Revenue Service sought to include the stocks in the trusts as part of her gross estate for tax purposes. The court concluded, however, that Parkin was in excellent health at the time of the transfers and did not transfer the property in contemplation of death—rather, she wanted to increase her grandchildren's investment portfolios while allowing them to use the current income.[5] Both of these cases brought a flood of new estate planning business our way. Although the tax regulations prohibiting gifts made "in contemplation of death" were designed to ensure that people who were dying did not try to avoid estate taxes by giving property away at the last minute, I still felt it was appropriate when such regulations as the three-year waiting period were later stricken from the tax code.

In another estate case, Eiseman and I represented the niece of the decedent, Mrs. Thomas Barrineau, who had given some sixty thousand dollars in securities to several people, including a close friend, her stockbroker, and her lawyer, about six months before she died. After her death, her niece (our client) sued to set aside the gifts on the grounds that her aunt had been unduly influenced by the recipients. The recipients admitted having confidential relationships, but denied any wrongdoing. Many witnesses testified to her strong will, but gave conflicting testimony regarding her mental state. The chancellor in this case found for the people who received the gifts and ruled that, although she was suffering from serious physical problems, she was of sound mind when she made the gifts. The Arkansas Supreme Court affirmed the decision.[6]

In December 1962, my new status as a partner in the firm was formalized with a name change to Mehaffy, Smith, Williams, Friday, and Bowen. When Pat Mehaffy was appointed to the Eighth Circuit Court of Appeals in 1963, we became Smith, Williams, Friday, and Bowen and grew to one of the largest firms in the state.

In 1962, I represented a coalition of the four downtown bank CEOs (from Worthen, Union National, First National, and Commercial National) who opposed Jess Odom's bid to charter a new bank in Little Rock—Capitol National Bank. The then Comptroller of the Currency, who had jurisdiction over the issuance of new national bank charters, seemed willing to grant the new charter. However, Odom, when organizing his earlier insurance company, had been found guilty of civil fraud in the misrepresentation of relevant facts. We agreed that we needed to raise this issue before the comptroller. The bankers drew straws to decide who would be the witness through whom we would present the background data. Finley Vinson of First National drew the short straw and we offered proof of Odom's frailty through Vinson's testimony. We argued that Odom had been found guilty of civil fraud in the sale of insurance stock in the 1950s and that if there were a need for another bank in Little Rock, the spot should be reserved for owner- ship unblemished by a finding of fraud. These arguments were persuasive, and Odom's application was denied. The victory opened the door for me to banking law business, including tax cases in federal court for Arkansas Bank & Trust Company of Hot Springs and First National Bank in Fort Smith.

During this time, the Mehaffy firm represented then governor Orval Faubus. I became involved because I prepared his tax returns for the years 1953 through 1966. An aggressive IRS agent tried to impose an income tax on Faubus on the rental value of the governor's mansion. The local IRS agent proposed a tax deficiency against Faubus for a three- to five-year period, asserting that the fair rental value of the governor's mansion, coupled with the maintenance cost paid by the state, was income to the governor. He arbitrarily assigned a fifty thousand dollar rental value to the mansion and added the eighteen thousand dollar annual expense account paid by the state for maintenance. This added sixty-eight thousand dollar each contested year to the governor's taxable income, which at the time was ten thousand dollars a year.

Governor Faubus called and asked me to represent him in this matter. I joined Senator John McClellan and Ham Moses, who were in practice together as Moses McClellan, and we devised a telegram that we sent to the governors of all fifty states and to President Eisenhower, asking if they had a mansion or similar facility and whether they paid taxes on the fair rental value. Within a week, we received thirty-eight responses, including one from the White House. All affirmed they had housing provided for them and none paid taxes on the rental value. As I understand it, the IRS agent was humbled by the experience, but did stay on with the agency until he retired. The IRS made no further effort to collect such additional taxes from Faubus. Although I did not support Faubus's actions in the 1957 school crisis, I felt certain that the IRS agent targeted Faubus because of it.

My representation of Jacuzzi Brothers, Inc., manufacturers of whirlpool baths and spas, involved family legal matters as well as the types of corporate questions that lawyers employed by corporations as general counsel usually encounter. Upon employment in the summer of 1962, I was handed a family minority stockholders lawsuit filed in San Francisco that had produced a default judgment because of inattention. As I recall, the dollar amount of the judgment was equal to the total capital of Jacuzzi Brothers, Inc.

This began a lengthy confrontation that finally matured into a settlement in the fall of 1967. During this time, I worked regularly with San Francisco lawyer, and later mayor, Joseph Aliotto, with whom I shared the case. An added trust question broadened the base to include a trip or two with him to Washington, D.C., to the Antitrust Division of the U.S. Department of Justice. Aliotto and I always entered the Justice Building from the east Constitution Avenue entrance so we could salute the statue of an Italian leader in Justice during World War I.

After disposing of the family minority lawsuit, Candido Jacuzzi celebrated with a corporate trip to Rome, the family's ancestral home in northeast Italy, and Switzerland. It was a pleasant experience. While in Rome, Connie and I visited the original Alfredos on Augustus Caesar's Circle in downtown Rome. I asked the violin ensemble if they could play "Dixie" and they did—proving that this is, indeed, a small world. We traveled from Rome to the Jacuzzi family home in northern Italy. We stayed for several days, enjoying the scenery and the food, with Jacuzzi waxing eloquent about his family's background at all of our gatherings.

In about 1975, we took a Jacuzzi-sponsored trip to Brazil, ultimately to visit the plant in São Paulo. Before that, however, we flew the length of the Amazon River to a juncture some three hundred miles south and there we visited an Indian village in the outback, finding, to our great surprise, a native playing a battery operated record player featuring Frank Sinatra. The capital of Brazil, Brasilia, was an interesting stop, but not nearly as interesting as Iguacu Falls—the world's largest—in southeast Brazil, near the border with Argentina and Paraguay.

The Jacuzzi plant was in São Paulo, a teaming coastal city of over twenty million people, through which a river of raw sewage flowed in a stream as large as Maumelle River in west Pulaski County. Along the banks were shanties of corrugated metal, cardboard, and plywood, where poverty-stricken families lived—and where their children played.

In 1963, I was hired to represent state senator Q. Byrum Hurst, who was charged with tax evasion. In this case, the IRS, in the absence of adequate record keeping by Hurst, attempted to establish his beginning and ending net worth for the assessment period. The IRS considered the estimated increase in net worth each year as taxable income. It was the same method they used to send Al Capone to prison in the 1930s and they attempted it in Hot Springs with Hurst.

Ray Morris, the manager of Russell Brown and Company accounting firm, was our expert witness and was able to assail the government's computation of tax with proof that some—actually many—of the additions to net income were from nontaxable funds, such as borrowed funds. Specifically, we called Owney Madden to the stand in Hurst's defense. Madden, a Prohibition-era gangster from New York, retired to Hot Springs and eventually ran gambling halls such as the Southern Club, his "infamously posh hangout."[7] Once the gang leader of Hell's Kitchen in New York, Madden previously served eight years in prison for the gangland killing of William "Little Patsy" Doyle.[8] I met Madden in Hot Springs's Anthony Hotel to prepare for the trial. We sat out on the porch on a hot summer day. He was wearing a short-sleeved sport shirt. I could see scars on his arms and across his stomach where his shirt button was open. I said, "Mr. Madden, by way of getting acquainted with you, I notice the scar tissue across your body. May I ask what happened?" He said, "Sure, I was walking across Central Park in the summer of 1932 and this lady came toward me in a black veil, black dress, pushing a perambulator [baby carriage]. When she came alongside, she pulled out a Thompson sub-machine gun, shot me across the body and left me for dead in Central Park." He told me that he decided that day it was time for him to go to Hot Springs to stay and he did. I asked him to wear long sleeves to the trial.

Madden testified to loans he had made to Hurst and, after three weeks of trial and a bruising round of closing arguments, the jury agreed with the Morris calculation and Hurst was exonerated. The trial was exhausting. I spent three weeks staying up until 2 a.m. and then getting up at 6 a.m. to continue preparations. I decided around that time that killing myself wasn't exactly the best way to live and practice.

In a series of cases from 1963 to 1971, I represented Witt Stephens, Arkansas Bank & Trust in Hot Springs, and First National–Ft. Smith in a gift-tax issue. These cases opened the door to a flow of tax representation across the state. In the Stephens case, Witt Stephens had filed refund claims for gift taxes he had paid in 1949 and 1956. In 1962, the IRS agent recommended that the refund claims be disallowed and that an additional gift tax deficiency of $243,174 be assessed against Stephens for tax year 1956. The IRS sent Stephens a letter notifying him that he had thirty days to appeal the proposed deficiency assessment. Stephens understood this letter to be a denial of his claim and filed suit against the government. The government claimed that Stephens's suit was premature, but the District Court held that, while the letter did not specifically say that the refund claim was denied, that was its implication when read in conjunction with the attached agent's report.[9]

In the Arkansas Bank & Trust dispute with the IRS, the bank occupied a building in Hot Springs that was owned by an unrelated partnership. The partnership offered to sell the building and land to the bank, but banking regulations prevented the bank from investing in real estate. Instead, the bank agreed to lease the building for fifteen years, with an option to renew for another fifteen years, plus an option to purchase the building and land during the second fifteen-year extension. The IRS disallowed nearly fifteen thousand dollars in rent paid by the bank on the grounds that it was acquiring an equity interest in the building. The bank paid the deficiency and filed a refund claim. The court held that the transaction was a genuine lease because the payments were equal to the reasonable rental value of the property and ruled in favor of the bank.[10]

In the First National case, the Arkansas Savings and Loan Association Board had denied the application for a charter to do business in Van Buren. The board held that the applicants failed to demonstrate a public need for the proposed institution and failed to show that it would be successful. The Arkansas Supreme Court ordered the board to grant the application, however, citing testimony that no other savings and loan association existed in Van Buren, that ten savings and loan associations were then operating successfully in small cities, and that Van Buren was experiencing unusual growth in building construction.[11]

About this same time, my university friend, Warren Bass, president of the Arkansas State Society of CPAs, named me general counsel for the society. Tax and business opportunities opened wider with this appointment. In addition to my work with Russell Brown and Company, I also represented other CPA firms like Marion Bell, a Fort Smith CPA. He was charged with tax fraud. Typically, he had waited until the last minute to prepare his own tax return for the year in dispute. In fact, because filing extensions were then difficult to obtain, Bell filed returns in 1945, 1946, 1947, and 1949, but failed to document his sources of income, deductions, and credits. Instead of filling in the form, he estimated a figure that he argued was his taxable income (this was the only entry on the form), signed it and sent it in with his check.

He later filed amended returns for 1947 and 1949, and he filed a complete return for 1948, but did so two years after it was due. The IRS penalized Bell for fraud and failure to file and argued that his filings did not constitute a tax return. I argued that he was an honest CPA who made time for all of his clients and did not have time to prepare his own, but he did the best he could to stay within the law. The court held that he did not intend to evade taxes by filing skeleton returns; rather, he was attempting to avoid penalties for late returns. In the absence of fraud, then, the court ruled that deficiencies for 1947–49 were barred by the statute of limitations.[12] We won the case and saved him from the equivalent of being disbarred and unable to prepare tax returns again.

In a similar case with a different outcome, I represented an executive with Daisy Manufacturing Company (now known as Daisy Outdoor Products, maker of air guns, ammunition, and accessories.) Mr. Beaver was charged with failing to file income tax returns from 1956–62. During these years, Beaver often received salary advances from his employer. He maintained that these advances were loans and should not be included in his gross salary when he received them. The IRS argued that the advances were taxable because they were compensation for future services. The Tax Court agreed. The court also found Beaver liable for fraud penalties for his delinquent returns and the court noted that, as a certified public accountant, Beaver was clearly aware of his obligation to file.[13]

In the spring of 1964, Frank Lyon Sr. and Ed Penick offered me senior officer status in Worthen Bank and Trust Company, but I declined because I did not yet feel ready to discontinue practicing law. Later that same year, Max Mitchum of Smackover State Bank, president of the Arkansas Bankers Association (ABA), asked me to become general counsel for the statewide organization. I accepted and found myself immersed immediately in ABA work as well as legal matters and opportunities for individual banks. For example, I organized a bank in Gillett (Arkansas County), which became Planters and Merchants Bank, and was hired to do tax and banking regulation work by some two dozen banks across the state. My ABA duties gave me at least an acquaintance with the leadership of every bank in the state, primarily through attendance at the organization's annual regional and state meetings. As general counsel, I also was at the forefront of planning ABA strategy and testifying before Arkansas General Assembly committees handling banking legislation.

In the late 1960s, I defended a North Little Rock motel owner/operator and his wife, Sam and Jimmie Lou Fowler. Just after the trial began, I discovered that they had failed to report all sources of income to me, besides the motel. It was too late to settle and the jury ruled against the Fowlers. Next came the Humpy Bell case. Bell, a resident of Pleasant Plains, Arkansas, was tried for tax evasion, but the jury held in favor of Bell.

In the early 1960s, Main Street Little Rock began looking westward to expand. Among other reasons, the Little Rock Central High crisis of 1957–58 had discouraged any downtown development. This unrest continued through the sit-ins at the McClellan five-and-dime store and the Blass Tea Room in 1961, both on Main Street. I was employed by some forty-four doctors in the Donaghey Building to help them acquire acreage at the intersection of University Avenue and what would in due course be Interstate 630. We acquired thirty-three acres for three hundred thousand dollars and set about construction of the Doctor's Building—built by the Little Rock Land Company under the leadership of some of the city's prominent physicians, including Drs. Barnett Briggs, Joe Norton, Ted Dillahay, F. R. Buchanan, Jack Brizzolara, and Bud Downs. It was a formidable concentration of medical talent, and when the building was completed in 1963 it virtually emptied the Donaghey Building and much of downtown's medical practice.

Ross Anderson, chairman of the board of Commercial National Bank, died in September 1970. Richard C. Butler, a former lawyer, longtime friend, and president of the bank, began making overtures to persuade me to become president of the bank. From mid-September through mid-December 1970, Butler called or visited me weekly to pursue this effort. Connie and I took our family to Jackson Hole, Wyoming, during the Christmas holidays to get away and come to terms with this opportunity and the remarkable change that it would encompass. I returned home undecided.

In January 1971, I read John Gardner's book, *Self Renewal: The Individual and the Innovative Society,* including a chapter on "repotting yourself." He reasoned that a plant, once repotted, grew stronger and that a mid-life change could do the same for the reader. On the third Friday of January, I told Butler I would come to the bank and was warmly welcomed to the board at its February meeting with the expectation that I would be in the bank as president starting on Monday, May 3, 1971.

The intervening weeks gave me time to close or transfer my practice to Byron Eiseman and his leadership in the tax division. In early 1971, I represented Albert H. Rusher of the Bank of Brinkley, who was in a contest with his lawyer and cousin, James B. Sharp, over control of his bank. This was to be my last trial. We tried the case in Chancery Court in Clarendon and won. My practice was at an end. At the time, we had twenty-nine retained tax clients and were still growing. I agreed to a salary as president of the bank of one-half of my previous year's legal earnings because in my opinion that amount was more consistent with the bank's salary levels.

Chapter Five

Commercial Banking

When I arrived at Commercial National as its president, I found myself sitting at a desk outside Richard Butler's office in the lobby of what appeared to be the lending platform. I sat out in the lobby for a year before moving into the president's office because Butler still occupied it and I wanted to build camaraderie with the staff.

In April 1971, I met Barnett Grace, a lawyer and Certified Public Accountant, who then was with the "Big Eight" accounting firm of Arthur Andersen of Dallas. Grace was a Batesville native whose family I had known through the law firm. I urged him to do what I was doing—to leave his current profession and enter banking. We agreed that Grace would join Commercial National Bank as an executive-in-training in January 1972.

In retrospect, several factors motivated me to become a banker, not the least of which was my then twelve-year-old son Scott's declared ambition to become a physician. I had expected him to become a lawyer and join the firm. Also, heading a bank allowed me to invest in its stock, whereas the opportunity to invest while practicing law was limited. In addition, with twenty-nine retained legal clients and a growing practice, I found myself working seven days a week with little opportunity to do anything else, leaving me unable to respond as fully as I wanted to a call that was equally strong in me: to work in the community with the aim of producing a stronger Arkansas.

In the summer of 1971, a young Yale graduate with Vietnam War experience as a Marine came to see me in my new capacity as Commercial National's president. The young entrepreneur, Fred Smith, gave me a copy of his Yale thesis, which had as its theme the creation of a nationwide air transport system for overnight delivery of packages. It was to be called Federal Express. I took the thesis to the bank's loan committee. The committee members responded that Smith needed investors, not a loan. Undaunted, Smith went to Worthen Bank and Trust Company, where he received a warmer reception and a loan to start his operation with two planes and staff members at Adams Field, the airport serving Little Rock. Subsequently, Smith's need for additional space could not be met by the Little Rock Airport Commission and within a year he moved his entire operation to Memphis, where he moved into airport space vacated by the Tennessee Air National Guard. Smith's persistence was such that he succeeded beyond his most aggressive expectations. At one point, he was the highest paid executive in the United States and FedEx is a fabulously successful company.

Even as I was pondering whether to make this career change, the banking scene in Arkansas was heating up. The state's largest financial institution, Worthen Bank and Trust Company, had established the First Arkansas Bankstock Corporation (FABCO) as a one-bank holding company in 1968, allowing FABCO to engage in activities that were not permissible for banks, such as owning other banks.[1] In early 1970, FABCO applied to the Federal Reserve Bank to convert to a registered bank holding company so that it could bring other banks under its umbrella, with the first being the Arkansas First National Bank of Hot Springs. Ninety-nine percent of the shareholders in the Hot Springs bank already had tendered their stock to be exchanged for FABCO stock by the time it went to a hearing in Little Rock before the Federal Reserve in June 1970.[2] Richard Butler was one of those who testified against FABCO, charging that the move was a back-door way for Worthen to move into branch banking, which was prohibited by state law. This prohibition was a holdover from the Depression. When deposits began to be insured in 1933, the prevailing attitude was that branching was a dangerous activity because it provided more opportunities for banks to make risky loans. Although FABCO and the individual banks whose stock it owned would be separate corporate entities, Butler said, "it controls these banks just as surely and just as effectively and absolutely, as if they were mere branch offices despite the elaborate trappings of separate entities, separate boards of directors and so forth."[3]

Butler went on to predict that if the Federal Reserve approved FABCO's application, the 1971 Arkansas General Assembly would pass a law clearly making such operations illegal, although nothing could be done to wipe out FABCO itself. Butler was correct on both counts: the Federal Reserve approved FABCO's application and the 1971 General Assembly enacted a law that barred FABCO from purchasing the stock of more banks (it held control of the Hot Springs bank and was allowed through an amendment to continue the acquisition of one in Stephens, Arkansas) and blocked the formation of any other multibank holding companies in Arkansas.[4] This battle gave Arkansas bankers a new familiarity with the laws governing holding companies, and nearly two dozen such companies were formed throughout the state in the wake of FABCO's approval. The multibank holding company conflict was but one of the many intramural battles that the banking community would wage during my tenure as counsel for the Arkansas Bankers Association and in my new position as Commercial National Bank president.

Just as the banks could fight, they also could come together when they decided something was in their best interest. For example, the 1973 General Assembly received a bill to authorize banks to establish full-service branch offices, something that had been decried as late as 1971. Until this point, branches could operate only as teller's windows and could not perform such services as making loans.

The bill, which passed after being described by a sponsor as "a settlement" among the banks, allowed banks to establish full-service branches in the city where its main office was located but no closer than three hundred feet to the main office of any other bank. A bank also could establish a full-service branch in any incorporated city or town in its county with a population of 250 or more, if there was no main office of another bank there, or in any *planned community development in the county with a population of 250 or more*. No bank could establish a branch outside the county where its main office was located, and all existing teller's windows were authorized to operate as full-service branches.[5] The planned community point in the bill is emphasized because it came into play five years later in a contest between Commercial National and Worthen with the development of Maumelle.

Leroy Donald, an *Arkansas Gazette* business writer, wrote in January 1978 that observers anticipated a major fight between Commercial National Bank and Worthen Bank and Trust Company over a branch bank in Maumelle "New Town," a planned community west of North Little Rock on which development had begun in 1967. In what has to be one of the better ironies in Arkansas banking history, Maumelle's developer was Jess Odom, the founder and former president of National Investors Insurance Company, whose plan to establish a Little Rock bank I had helped defeat in 1962. The first house in Maumelle was occupied in 1975. Ever-growing Commercial National kept a close eye on Maumelle.

Anticipating the community would reach a population of at least 250 by August 1977, the bank signed a lease agreement with Odom that spring. Under the agreement, Commercial National Bank would not only occupy the first commercial building constructed in Maumelle but would have exclusive banking privileges in Odom's "new town." Commercial National's aggressiveness was made possible in part by the fact that Andy Waldo, the vice president of its leasing subsidiary, also was president of the Maumelle Property Owners Association.

When I started at Commercial National, I thought I knew more about banking than I did. I knew the law side of it, but the operations side and the traffic of money among banks was entirely new to me, so it was a major transition. I sought to remedy this by enrolling in the Stonier Graduate School of Banking, sponsored by the American Bankers Association at Rutgers University in New Brunswick, New Jersey. The school entailed two concentrated weeks of classroom study, seven days a week in June for three years, and monthly correspondence work in between the campus sessions. Participants also were required to produce a thesis on an acceptable subject at the end of the three years. My thesis subject was "Bank Directors' Duties and Liabilities." To further enhance my learning curve, I participated in the sixteenth Assembly for Bank Directors of the Foundation of the South's Western Graduate School of Banking in Mexico City in February 1973.

In September 1974, I was invited to address a meeting of bank directors in Denver sponsored by the Southern Methodist University School of Banking. The subject was banking ethics, and I delivered the speech the same week President Richard M. Nixon resigned. My speech was published under the headline "Required Reading" in the *American Banker,* the daily publication of the American Bankers Association. This led the Stonier Graduate School of Banking to invite me to fashion a case study on bank ethics, which I taught from 1976 to 1998, the last fifteen years in cooperation with Robert Serino, senior counsel for the office of the Comptroller of the Currency. The course was designed to make bank directors more sensitive about their duties to their banks. Serino and I typically were at Stonier at Rutgers (until it moved to the University of Delaware) for two to three days during the first week of the annual June sessions. At first the course was an elective, but it became required for graduation in about its fifth year. Three years after I completed schooling at Stonier, I was named to the school's board of directors.

In summer 1971, while still positioned outside Butler's office, I began a study of all of Commercial National Bank's operations—its staff and its book of business. At the time, Worthen Bank and Trust Company, Union National Bank, and First National Bank were considerably larger than Commercial, which had resources totaling $108.7 million and which jockeyed that summer with Simmons First National Bank of Pine Bluff for the honor of being the fourth-biggest bank in the state.[6] I found Commercial had a reputation of not asking for business and I vowed to turn this around. A year later, a man who was to become governor of Arkansas, Frank D. White, joined Commercial's staff. He was a friend of mine through Chamber of Commerce activities and was a member of my Sunday school class. I persuaded him to take a leading role in selling the bank to new customers. Ebullient and an unquenchable optimist, White ended all memoranda, speeches, and visits with the observation "AFTB"—Ask For The Business.

Each quarter provided an occasion to examine the balance sheets of Arkansas's top banks. Commercial began moving past Simmons until the third quarter of 1972, when the Pine Bluff bank moved into fourth place. My response was to borrow a casket from the Griffin Leggett Funeral Home in Little Rock and place it on the table in Commercial National's board room. I then invited all of the bank's directors and major officers to bury any attitudes of complacency, symbolized by each dropping an artificial flower in the casket. They all responded in good humor and we agreed we were going to have to be more aggressive in going after deposits and in pursuing all reasonable sources of income. We knew we needed to be expansionist-minded instead of being satisfied to be a neighborhood bank. Everybody signed on and I think it was the beginning of an attitude of pursuing excellence and growth as our young team began making its mark on the bank. Commercial National's major achievement in 1973 was a striking growth in assets. The total climbed during the year from $141.7 million to $190.2 million and net income, after all entries, was $911,943, or $3.16 a share, compared with $884,310, or $3.06 a share, in 1972. Stockholders' equity increased to $7.9 million from $7.4 million in the same period.

Although a good year for us, the year also brought indications of change on the banking community's horizon. In an article that appeared in December

1973 in the *Arkansas Gazette* one of my former law partners, William J. Smith, revealed that a drive would begin in 1974 to place a constitutional amendment on the November ballot to allow the legislature to regulate interest rates, a move that to many would be tantamount to removing the prohibition against interest rates above 10 percent.[7]

Economically and financially, Arkansas has never been an easy state in which to conduct business. Manufacturing on a large scale did not even make an appearance in the state until well after World War II had brought the first industrial-type plants to Arkansas. Chronic poverty was reflected in some of the provisions in the constitution under which Arkansas was governed, and the document itself contributed to keeping the state poor. As Leland DuVall of the *Arkansas Gazette* explained, the people who lived in Arkansas in the mid- to late-1800s did not trust banks, and they had good reasons for this. Money values shifted quickly, and bankers usually managed to stay at least one step ahead of their customers. The results were predictable, and the only safe course for the average person was to stay out of the game. For an extended period, the state simply refused to charter banks.[8] DuVall continued:

> The assortment of carpetbagger banks that sprang up like mushrooms after the Civil War employed a variety of tricks, but their best and most profitable maneuver was high interest rates. The need for credit was desperate and chronic and interest rates ranged from 20 percent to grand larceny. When a measure of government was returned to the state level and the Arkansas people began reconstructing their legal framework, they adopted a Constitution that attempted to deal with the then-current problems. One was the matter of interest rates.[9]

The new constitution, adopted in 1874, prohibited usury, which was defined as any credit charge that exceeded 10 percent simple interest.

What looked as if it would be a clean and uncluttered campaign for a constitutional amendment to change Arkansas's usury provision became muddled in 1974 by the success of a bill by U.S. Senator William E. Brock III (R-TN) that would override state usury laws and allow national banks and federally insured state banks and savings and loan associations to charge up to 5 percent more interest than the federal discount rate on business and agricultural loans of $25,000 or more. The bill did not address consumer or home mortgage loans.[10] In August 1974, Brock's bill was amended to the give the legislatures of the three affected states (Tennessee, Arkansas, and

Montana) the right to nullify the Brock bill.[11] U.S. Senator J. William Fulbright, (D-AR), who lost the Democratic nomination for reelection to Dale Bumpers that year, was one of two Democrats who joined Brock in sponsoring the bill.

The Arkansas Credit Requirement Committee, the group Smith represented that obtained some two hundred thousand voter signatures to put proposed Amendment 57 on the Arkansas ballot in November 1974, frowned on the Brock bill. Committee leaders were quoted as saying the law would "fragment" the state's economy by allowing some loans to draw higher interest rates than others. The group also suggested that funds for consumer and home mortgage loans would be more difficult to obtain because banks and other lending institutions would funnel money into more profitable business and agricultural loans. Little Rock lawyer Ted Lamb's group, Public Against 57, issued a statement in October 1974 saying the Brock bill had made the proposed constitutional amendment moot. "From the bankers' viewpoint and according to their own arguments, there can no longer be any justifiable excuse to support Amendment 57, except, of course, simple greed," the antiorganization declared.[12]

The outcome of the balloting was never in doubt, but the size of the defeat of Amendment 57 was shocking to some. Only 13 percent of those who went to the polls voted for the measure, which *Arkansas Gazette* reporter Ernest Dumas said was "the most lopsided vote on a statewide ballot proposal in years."[13] Dumas went on to say that the "best hint of the ultimate defeat of Amendment 57 was the way politicians avoided any association with it." All major candidates for public office, and for many minor offices as well, denounced the amendment. Even bankers and savings and loan representatives in the legislature were compelled to state their opposition. No one wanted to be associated with raising interest rates for consumers.

Meanwhile, an attempt to repeal the ban on multibank holding companies failed in the 1973 General Assembly, but another effort appeared inevitable. In August 1974, the late state Senator John F. Bearden Jr. of Leachville had predicted the 1975 legislature would write some kind of multibank holding company law, and that the only issue would be what restrictions it should contain. The Federal Reserve Board had ruled that insurance was a "closely related activity" in which multibank holding companies could engage, therefore, Arkansas's insurance industry was enraged at the prospect of the ban against multibank holding companies being repealed. "This is unfair competition that we cannot handle," Ron Lensing of the Arkansas Association of

Independent Insurance Agents told a legislative committee.[14] Other witnesses, including Charles T. Meyer Jr., executive committee chairman of Meyer's Bakeries, Inc., and Byron R. Morse of Little Rock, president of Rector-Phillips-Morse, Inc., a real estate and property management firm, told the lawmakers that the shortage of capital was crippling Arkansas economically. Morse said his firm wanted to finance a new Hot Springs shopping center with local money but found the bank's limit to one customer was $350,000 when $1.4 million was needed. A holding company with pooled capital could have solved that problem, he said.[15] The law was not repealed.

That same month, I reported to the legislature's Joint Interim Committee on Insurance and Banking that Arkansas bankers overwhelmingly opposed repeal of the 1971 law barring the creation of more multibank holding companies.[16] Our correspondent bank customer base (banks that maintained checking accounts with us, shared our credit, and sent us customers) almost uniformly opposed the measure. Specifically, a poll conducted by an Arkansas Bankers Association committee that I chaired showed that 154 banks of the 223 that responded said they were opposed to repealing the 1971 law. As a result, both my committee and the association's executive council voted to oppose repeal.

The *Arkansas Gazette* reported that the poll results caused legislators, even those who said they personally favored multibank holding companies with restrictions, to predict chances for repeal were slim, though they expected an effort to do it to be made anyway when the legislature convened in January 1975.[17] The newspaper was correct; the law was not repealed until 1983.

In 1979, the General Assembly was able to agree on only one constitutional amendment dealing with property taxes before it recessed in April. The Arkansas banking and business communities, bedeviled by double-digit inflation and interest rates, were ready with a proposed constitutional amendment that again would give the legislature the authority to set interest rates. When it reconvened in January 1980, the General Assembly agreed to put this amendment on the November 1980 general election ballot.

John F. Wells, publisher of the *Legislative Digest* and the *Daily Record,* had filed suit in December 1979, challenging the "extension" of the 1979 session as illegal and trying to stop the legislature from reconvening. The Arkansas Supreme Court ruled it had no authority to prohibit the legislature from meeting, but three of the justices wrote in their dissenting opinion that they questioned whether any actions taken during the extended session would be legal. Taking this as his cue, Wells filed another suit seeking to void the three constitutional amendments the legislature put on the 1980 general election ballot, including the one on usury.[18] When Pulaski County Chancellor Tom Glaze ruled against him, Wells appealed to the Arkansas Supreme Court, and this time he won. The two amendments that had been considered at the extended session were invalidated; the one on property taxes stayed on the ballot because it had been considered during the regular 1979 session.

The ruling prompted eighteen business groups to organize themselves as the Fair Arkansas Interest Rate committee and successfully circulated petitions to qualify the amendment for the ballot.[19] The amendment provided that the legislature, by a two-thirds vote of both houses, could raise the 10 percent ceiling. It also called for continuing the provision that a borrower paying excessive interest could recover both the principal and the interest, but it also allowed the General Assembly to set a different penalty. Another provision was that regardless of any other penalty, the borrower who had paid excessive interest could recover at least twice the amount of interest he had paid. The amendment also classified a usurious loan as a crime.

Once again, the proposal was defeated at the polls, but this time 44 percent of the voters had supported it—considerably better than in 1974. The *Arkansas Gazette* speculated that the struggle over the amendment had been "lessened somewhat"—at least on the part of the proponents—by Congressional passage in the spring of 1980 of the Depository Institutions Deregulation and Monetary Control Act (unofficially called the Omnibus Banking Act), which preempted state laws in at least two respects:

1) There was no ceiling on interest rates charged on first mortgages on real property; and,
2) A lender could charge interest up to 5 percent above the Federal Reserve's discount rate on business and agricultural loans of $25,000 or more. The discount rate is that charged on loans to member commercial banks by the Federal Reserve Bank.[20]

In October 1980, President Jimmy Carter signed the 1980 Housing and Community Development Act, which contained a rider amending the Omnibus Banking Act so that lenders could charge up to 5 percent more in interest than the federal discount rate on business and agricultural loans of one thousand dollars and up.[21] *Arkansas Gazette* business reporters wrote that since the housing bill passed on October 8, Little Rock banks quietly had been charging as much as 16 percent interest on business and agricultural loans. What this meant was that the small farm or business buyer who wanted to borrow five thousand dollars for a small farm implement would pay up to 16 percent interest. Prior to the rider, banks could not serve the large numbers of small borrowers who wanted to borrow less than $25,000.

Both the business community and organized labor were cast into a state of confusion by the defeat of the usury amendment in 1980 because no one seemed to know what the next course of action could or should be. Would the legislature give the business community the interest rate relief it said it needed so desperately, or would it accept defeat of the amendment by the voters? No one was prepared for what actually happened.

In a four to three vote, the state Supreme Court shocked Arkansas lenders by ruling on December 22, 1980, that the federal Omnibus Banking Act had not preempted the state's 10 percent interest limit in the constitution because loans were not considered interstate commerce that Congress could regulate. The ruling had the potential of negating thousands of agriculture and business loans above one thousand dollars that had been made since Congress changed the law.[22] The court's majority opinion was wrong, and I stated that Commercial National would continue lending money at more than 10 percent. There was clear-cut precedent that money and credit are a part of commerce clearly within the purview of Congress. A week later, the court clarified its decision, explaining that it applied only to real estate development companies such as the one involved in the lawsuit and not to banks and savings and loan associations.[23] Three new justices joined the court in January 1981 and, in mid-February, they reversed the decision, again on a four to three vote.[24]

The state's banking community was unnerved and sharply divided on such issues as whether the law prohibiting multibank holding companies should be repealed and whether branching should be allowed to take place through mergers and acquisitions, but it had no trouble concluding that another try with a new approach should be made to do away with the 10 percent usury limit, even if it had been overridden on business and agricultural loans by federal law until April 1, 1983.

I felt that it was totally unrealistic to tie the generation of capital to a 104-year-old law. I also believed that the Arkansas public was "educable" on the issue. Among other considerations, the banking community's new resolve coincided with my election as first vice president of the Arkansas Bankers Association—as such, I would become the organization's president at precisely the time in 1982 when leadership, cohesion, and organization would be vital to get voter approval if the 1981 legislature agreed to put a usury constitutional amendment on the November general election ballot.

The legislature agreed, of course, and this time the proposed amendment would fix the maximum interest rate for consumer loans at 17 percent with a floating ceiling of 5 percent above the federal discount rate on agricultural and business loans. It also weakened the penalty for charging usurious interest on farm and business loans. The bankers and other financiers turned to the Farm Bureau Federation for support and help, knowing that this group more than any other in the state knew how to organize at the county or grassroots level. The Arkansas Credit Council was formed to promote the amendment in November 1981 and announced its belief that the battle would be won in the trenches, not in corporate boardrooms.[25] Milton Scott, vice president and legislative affairs director for the Farm Bureau, and Jackie Bell, associate director of legislative affairs, were named vice chairman and director of field organization, respectively, for the credit council and began work in earnest in early summer 1982 to put together promotion committees in each of the state's seventy-five counties. Conway automobile dealer S. T. (Ros) Smith chaired the credit council, and I headed the group's executive committee.

At lecterns and in newspaper interviews, we warned Arkansans that consumer credit would dry up if Amendment 60 did not pass. There was no way a bank could lend money at 10 percent when the incremental cost of funds was in the double digits—in the 13 to 14 percent range at the time. I explained that installment loans for bass boats, cars, and the like had all but dried up. Banks, generally, made them only to their best customers and with the hope that Amendment 60 would pass. We warned Arkansans that if the amendment did not pass, there would be no more installment loans by commercial banks. There also would be no "grace period" between Amendment 60's failure and the April 1, 1983, expiration of the federal override laws because banks would start closing out loans immediately. If Amendment 60 failed, we would be a one-armed intermediary taking money in and sending it out of state just like investment bankers. We would be brokers, seeking the best return we could get.

As it turned out, the Arkansas public was "educable," and Amendment 60 passed handily at the polls in November 1982 with 59.39 percent, or 442,325 voters supporting it.[26] Smith, the Conway auto dealer, credited the Farm Bureau Federation, saying, "I don't think we could have done it without them."[27] J. Bill Becker, president of the Arkansas State AFL-CIO and a leading opponent of the proposal, said Amendment 60 benefited from the depressed economy. "People were voting for jobs, but it won't create any," he said.[28] I knew, however, that it would save jobs in any way dependent on the availability of credit.

With energetic and aggressive leadership, Commercial National Bank's entire corporate character was altered—changing from a bank with a reputation of "not asking for the business" to one more ready to take advantage of the changing economic and legal climate. Commercial became the first national bank in the nation to acquire an abstract and title company, and it created an equipment leasing business, primarily for agriculture.[29] When Arkansas changed its law to allow bank branches, we immediately constructed six of them and were the first bank to extend beyond the city limits of Little Rock with the branch at Maumelle in 1978. By the end of the decade, the bank had thirteen branches. Commercial National Mortgage Company even opened a branch in Tulsa, Oklahoma, in 1978.

By 1974, Commercial National Bank had more than doubled in size and had acquired several service-related subsidiaries—the result of an aggressive marketing effort. The formula we had tried to follow had been pretty simple— we trained or hired the best experts we could find in each major field of financial service. Then we created services that people needed and tried to bring those services to our area. Commercial National opened or renovated and expanded three branches in 1974, and it added its fifth subsidiary— Thom-Godwin-Wilson, Inc., mortgage bankers. By early 1975, Commercial National Mortgage Company was prepared to operate three service offices in Pulaski County.

Two hundred of the 260 banks in the state became Commercial National correspondents.[30] CNB became the first bank in Arkansas to offer all three major credit cards—American Express, VISA, and MasterCard—and it created the EasyCheck Card, giving its customers twenty-four-hour access to automated teller machines. Commercial National established a statewide network of ATMs in which twenty banks participated. All in all, 1980 was an exceptionally good year for Commercial National Bank. I always kept an eye on the laws Congress passed, including the Financial Institutions Regulatory and Interest Control Act of 1978 and the subsequent Monetary Control Act, and interpreted what they would mean to and require of us.

On August 20, 1980, stockholders holding 544,591 shares, or 81 percent of the bank's outstanding stock, voted to create Commercial Bankstock Corporation as a one-bank holding company. The one bank, of course, was Commercial National Bank.[31] The owners of 19 percent of the stock (124,290 shares) dissented, and stockholders with 2,905 abstained.

Because of federal law, credit unions and savings and loan associations would be empowered, effective January 1, 1981, to issue a check-like instrument so that the real remaining difference between savings and loan associations and credit unions and banks, which is the establishment of demand accounts served by checks drawn against those accounts, would vanish. Clearly banks had to do something to be ready to meet the new competition, and part of Commercial National's answer was to become part of a holding company. At the time, I explained that the move would allow the bank to have a more effective means of obtaining equity capital and would be able to obtain that capital at a lower tax cost, and have a more flexible corporate structure. As a holding company, we could have a half dozen different bank charters under one roof and we could acquire additional companies, such as abstract companies, to attract different sources of revenue.

Despite the turbulence in the industry and Arkansas's restrictive laws, figures showed that by the end of 1980, Commercial National Bank had become the state's second-largest bank.[32] (Actually, it jockeyed with First National Bank for second- and third-place honors.) The year 1980 was a record in itself with the bank reporting a 56 percent increase in net income to $3.2 million from $2 million the year before.[33] The bank paid out a total of $640,660 in dividends, which was 46 percent higher than in 1979. Deposits were up 15.9 percent to $304.8 million, and loans increased 7.5 percent to $748.7 million. Securities, however, were down 2.3 percent to $42.5 million. Stockholder equity rose 15.7 percent to $19.2 million. The bank's directors had raised the quarterly dividend from seventeen cents to twenty-two cents a share and declared an extra dividend of seventeen cents a share payable January 2, 1981.

The *Arkansas Democrat* reported that Commercial National's resources had risen from $100.3 million on December 31, 1970, to $403.6 million at the end of 1980. Worthen Bank and Trust Company was still the leader with $601 million in resources, but Commercial had surpassed First National at $396.1 million and Union National Bank at $344.3 million. Commercial National also restructured its leadership in March 1981. William H. McLean became senior chairman of the board. I was elected chairman of the board and remained chief executive officer, while Barnett Grace was named president. James R. Cobb was chosen president of the holding company, Commercial Bankstock.[34]

Because of my involvement in the banking industry, politics, and civic and educational endeavors, I tried to keep informed of any changes on the horizon, including the one that came about in 1983 when the Arkansas legislature changed the law to allow multibank holding companies. I, along with forty-four other investors associated with Commercial National Bank began to position the bank for this as early as June when we bought the First National Bank of Russellville. Harold Neal, the Russellville bank's president and principal stockholder, gave me the option to buy control when Neal ran afoul of Comptroller of the Currency guidelines and had to get out of the bank. Four months later, the Federal Reserve Bank approved the application of First Russellville Bankstock, Inc., to become a bank holding company through acquisition of First National Bank of Russellville.[35] After the state law changed, the Russellville institution became a Commercial Bankstock holding.

In 1975, the Commercial National Bank building consisted of four stories and a basement. Reasonably well suited for its modest presence in the banking community, it was still no match for the "behemoths"—Union, Worthen, and First National. A lattice covering on the building's exterior gave rise to its nickname "The Cheese Grater." In good humor, taxi drivers called it the "low building." Norman Farris came by my office one hot Thursday afternoon, shortly after the First National Tower was completed. He motioned for me to join him on the Main Street side of the building. En route, we passed in our entry a sandwich stand operated by a blind man where passerby could purchase cold sandwiches, cigarettes, drinks, etc. On that day, as well as Saturdays in the summer, a farmer's market operated on the vacant lot across the street. An east wind drove fruit flies from the market into our faces. Cattycorner across Second and Main was an empty building that served as the regular meeting place for street people—two or three were there on this particular afternoon—and directly north was the Greyhound Bus terminal.

Farris turned south and pointed to the Union Bank building and noted that its seventeenth floor contained an executive dining room with a reputation for outstanding food. Next, he pointed to the Worthen Bank building, high atop of which was the famous Capital Club, featuring the best in lunches and dinners plus a bar. Lastly, Farris pointed to the new First National edifice and noted the arrival of the Jacques and Suzanne restaurant. He closed by asking, "Bowen, you expect us to compete out of this cheese grater with lunch featured at the corner stand?" His point was clear—we needed at least to study the possibility of constructing our own high rise. Over an eighteen-month period, we explored several possibilities, including proposals from a contractor/builder in Tulsa and from Doyle Rogers of Batesville, who later built the building that now houses the Peabody Hotel and the Stephens Building in Little Rock. In the end, we decided that we really could not afford such a luxury. Later, when Commercial National merged with First National, the "cheese grater" was leveled.

In 1982, we made the announcement that First National Bank and Commercial National Bank, two of the state's four largest banks, would take steps toward a possible merger.[36] William L. Cravens, president of First National Bancshares, Inc., and I issued a joint statement saying, in part:

> The respective Boards of Directors of Commercial Bankstock and First National have authorized negotiations toward the possible merger of the two bank holding companies, and the related merger of their wholly owned, national banking subsidiaries, Commercial National Bank of Little Rock and The First National Bank of Little Rock. The matter is in preliminary negotiation and under active study by the Boards of Directors and executive management of the institutions. We wish to emphasize that no final agreements have been reached.[37]

After pointing out that both of our institutions had experienced record financial growth in 1981, we pledged, "to keep our customers, shareholders, employees and the public fully informed as the proposed merger transactions progress."[38]

If the merger was approved by various government regulatory bodies, it would make the resulting bank the largest in the state. The state's largest financial institution at the time was FABCO (First Arkansas Bankstock Corporation), the holding company for Worthen, with assets of about $1 billion.

Other bankers talked about the possible merger. D. Eugene Fortson, president of Worthen Bank and Trust Company, was quoted as saying, "It is inevitable that you will see combinations of financial institutions like this in the months ahead. We're already seeing widespread merging within the savings and loan industry, and eventually we'll see the bigger banks coming into Arkansas. State lines will not be a barrier." Banking in the 1980s, Fortson continued, "will require larger institutions. Of course, we'd prefer to see growth come through the formation of multibank holding companies rather than mergers, which reduce the number of institutions and lessen consumers' alternatives."[39] Larger financial institutions can make larger loans, and Fortson agreed this was a major reason for the merger under study. A new bank created by the merger could lend as much as six million dollars, which would make it more competitive than the two individual banks in the bidding for major corporate accounts.[40] Edward M. Penick Jr., president of Twin

City Bank, said, "the trend toward bigness is something we see increasing around the country and not just within the financial community. The theory is that operating from a bigger base will improve services."[41]

In addition to being approved by the boards and shareholders of the two institutions, the merger had to pass the scrutiny of at least five regulatory agencies—the Comptroller of the Currency, the Federal Reserve Board, the Federal Deposit Insurance Corporation, the Securities and Exchange Commission, and the Justice Department, which monitors for effect on competition. Of these, the Justice Department was considered to be the most problematic, but its attitude toward mergers had begun shifting recently to favor them.

During a news conference at Trapnall Hall, we announced that our respective boards had agreed to the "equal-partner" marriage in principle with a completion target date of December 31, 1982.[42] I was to be the board chairman and Cravens the president of the new bank. A new name for the resulting bank and holding company had not been chosen yet. The plan of merger was to be voted on by the stockholders at a special meeting on October 19, 1982, and First Commercial sent out its official notices for the meeting August 19, 1982. Although Fortson had been quoted as saying larger financial institutions were inevitable, this did not stop his bank from lodging a formal protest to the planned First National/Commercial merger with the Department of Justice. We found ourselves in a merger fight that included the Federal Reserve, and the completion date was pushed into early 1983. Eventually, the target date became July 31, 1983.

The Federal Reserve had issued an advisory opinion to the Comptroller stating that the merger would be adverse to competition. The opinion was expected because of the Federal Reserve's unwillingness at that point to include savings and loans and other financial intermediaries as competitors to commercial banks. The Comptroller would make the final decision on the merger and was not bound by the Federal Reserve's opinion. On December 3, Deputy Assistant Attorney General Ronald G. Carr in the Justice Department wrote the Comptroller of the Currency that "the merger will have a significantly adverse effect on competition," particularly with respect to commercial loans.[43]

The Justice Department had agreed to review the proposed merger again in early 1983, at which time we pressed the point that two changes in the law affected Arkansas's lending situation. One, of course, was the passage by the voters of Amendment 60, liberalizing Arkansas's usury provision. This encouraged lenders from outside the state to come into Arkansas.[44] I argued that major regional banks in Dallas, Memphis, Shreveport, Tulsa, St. Louis, and Jackson, deterred by Arkansas's previous usury law, would begin calling more aggressively on prospects in the state. The other event providing more competition was enactment of the Garn–St. Germain Depository Institutions Act of 1982, which expanded the lending powers of savings and loan associations, including allowing them to make commercial loans of up to 5 percent of their total assets.

While these were major considerations in the review, it was another turn of events that tipped the scales in favor of the merger—the inclusion of Faulkner and Lonoke counties in the Little Rock Standard Metropolitan Statistical Area (SMSA). This made the home base larger for the Little Rock banks to serve. The opposition to the merger folded when the federal government redefined the SMSA. Yet another factor came into the mix later in the spring of 1983 when the Arkansas legislature repealed the ban on multibank holding companies.

The Comptroller of the Currency did not act right away, however, creating a tense wait for the banks that did not end until approval came through on May 27, 1983.[45] During the previous month, the directors of both holding companies had met and set a ratio of 1.52 shares of Commercial National Bankstock common stock for each outstanding share of First National Bancshares, down from the 1.689 ratio set when shareholders approved the proposed merger in October. As of March 31, 1983, Commercial had 742,144 outstanding common shares and First National had 481,810.[46]

Even with the Comptroller's approval, we had to wait to see what kind of response would come from the Justice Department, which had thirty days to issue a disapproval. June 27 came and went without any action from the Justice Department, and the boards of the two banks announced that the merger under the name of First Commercial would take place at 4:20 p.m. on July 31, 1983, a Sunday, to be effective the next day.[47]

At about 1:30 p.m. on June 28, I received a call from Jackson T. Stephens of Stephens Inc., who invited Bill Cravens and me to his office for a visit. When we arrived, we encountered Mochtar Riady of Jakarta, Indonesia, of Lippo Holding Ltd. fame; George Davis, head of the Stephens brokerage department; C. Joseph Giroir, counsel; and Curt Bradbury, a senior staff member. After introductions were made to Riady, Stephens announced to my surprise that he planned to file a proposal the next morning to acquire not less than 51 percent of the two holding companies. The offer was not coming from Stephens Inc., but from Stephens and his brother, W. R. "Witt" Stephens, and the separate trusts for Jack Stephens's two sons. The offer was to acquire all of the outstanding stock of the two holding companies for cash—$50.16 for each share of First National and $33 for Commercial's or a total deal of $48.7 million.[48] Stephens then called a major Commercial National stockholder, Charles H. Murphy Jr. of Murphy Oil Corporation in El Dorado, to get his reaction to the proposal. To my pleasure, Murphy expressed no interest. Stephens's proposal set the stage for an unexpected episode. For his part, Stephens said later he was "genuinely surprised" by the "emotional and personal" reaction to his offer by the managements of the two banks.[49]

The directors of the merging banks had until July 13 to make a recommendation to their stockholders about the tender offer.[50] We met July 1 and hired The First Boston Corporation of New York and the law firm of Simpson Thatcher and Bartlett, also of New York, to advise us; meanwhile, local newspapers were reporting that knowledgeable stockholders were saying the offer was not high enough.

The next major development occurred Monday, July 11, when Stephens called to tell Cravens and me that two of the principals, his brother and Lippo, were bowing out of the joint venture "to expedite the Federal Reserve's review of the purchase," but that the offer otherwise was unchanged. He retained the option to sell shares to us later.[51] Stephens did not announce this development publicly until 8 a.m. on Tuesday, July 12.

The directors of the two banks met behind closed doors for two and a half hours late that Monday afternoon to prepare a formal response to the Stephens proposal. When we emerged, we had decided to tell the shareholders of the two institutions that the offer was "financially inadequate" and we had a "strong conviction" that ownership of what would be Arkansas's largest and strongest commercial bank should be as widely held as possible by Arkansas investors rather than being the privately held statewide banking network Stephens envisioned.[52]

We also informed Stephens on the evening of July 11 that we would fight the takeover and had drawn up a three-pronged battle plan. First, a lawsuit based on information furnished by The First Boston Corporation and recommended by it and Simpson Thatcher and Bartlett would be filed in United States District Court the next day. Stephens said in his early morning statement on July 12 that the lawsuit would be "groundless and obstreperous," but this was the key to Stephens withdrawing his offer, which he did in a statement released three hours later on Tuesday, July 12. The lawsuit would have charged the Stephens firm with breach of fiduciary duty because Stephens Inc. had been hired to review the books of both banks and assign a value to their stock. In addition, Paragraph 13 of the merger agreement stated that no party to the merger could intrude into its progress, and Stephens, Inc., was a party. Stephens, of course, contended that Stephens, Inc., was not the party making the stock tender, but the two banks would not have had a problem convincing a court that Stephens, Inc., and Stephens himself, who founded and owned the investment banking firm, were one and the same.

The second point in the battle plan was a counteroffer by the management of Commercial National and First National to buy all the shares in their institutions owned by the Stephenses at the price they had offered. Finally, management had agreed they would not offer to sell any of their stock to Stephens. First National's managers owned 24.20 percent of that institution's outstanding shares, and Commercial National managers held 13.39 percent of its stock.[53]

With Stephens now out of the picture, the merger went forward as scheduled with a ceremony at 4:20 p.m. in Secretary of State Paul Riviere's office at the Capitol.[54] First Commercial Corporation, the new holding company, and its wholly owned subsidiary, First Commercial Bank, emerged on August 1, 1983, with sixty million dollars in capital, $1.1 billion in assets, and twenty-six banks and branches in its corporate fold. Because of the excitement generated by the showdown with Stephens, however, the merger was anticlimactic for all but those directly involved.

The new institution's capital structure allowed it to make loans of up to nine million dollars. The significance of this was that corporate treasurers could not overlook us, as some of the state's largest employers who were not based in Arkansas would now make an effort to do more of their banking business "where they earn their daily bread."[55] In the new institution, Edwin C. Kane, First National board chairman, became chairman of the new holding company and chairman of the bank's executive committee. Barnett Grace, Commercial National's president, became the president of the new holding company and vice president of the bank. Bill Cravens became president of the new bank and vice president of the holding company. B. Finley Vinson, First National's vice president, became chairman emeritus of the new bank and James R. Cobb, president of Commercial National Bankstock, became vice-president. I was the chairman and CEO of First Commercial.[56]

Within a week, Kane announced his retirement.[57] Vinson was named to the vacancy as chairman of the board of First Commercial Corporation.[58]

Stephens subsequently proved the seriousness of his intent to enter the banking business. On Friday, October 21, 1983, he announced a Stephens–Riady agreement to acquire 51 percent of FABCO, holding company for Worthen Bank and Trust Company, First National Bank of Hot Springs, and Union Bank of Mena, for sixty million dollars.[59] Within three months of this, Cravens announced his resignation from First Commercial and in March, took over Worthen's reins.[60]

With Cravens's departure from First Commercial, I was elected president of the bank. Cobb replaced Cravens as vice president of the holding company and remained vice president of the bank along with Grace, who continued as president of the holding company. Vinson received the additional responsibility of chairing the bank's executive committee.[61]

Even before the repeal of the law banning multibank holding companies went into effect September 30, 1983, First Commercial Corporation had moved aggressively to make its first acquisition by offering to buy Morrilton Security Bank, a longtime correspondent, whose chairman was Edward E. Jones. First Commercial offered to exchange 2.11 shares of its common stock for each of the Morrilton institution's 45,000 outstanding shares—a $3.3 million deal.[62] The Gordon brothers, Ed and former lieutenant governor Nathan Gordon, longtime members of the Morrilton bank's board, supported the proposal, and it was approved in January 1984.[63] The Morrilton institution had assets of $31.7 million.

In May 1984, we moved to bring the bank we had bought for that purpose—First Russellville Bankstock, Inc., owner of First National Bank of Russellville—into the fold.[64] This brought in an additional one hundred million dollars in assets. About a year later, First Commercial solidified its position in the Arkansas River valley through a merger agreement with Faulkner County Bankshares, Incorporated, parent of First National Bank of Conway. First Commercial agreed to give 590,000 shares (14 percent of those outstanding) for the Conway bank with its $151.6 million in deposits and $136 million in assets.[65] Robert D. Nabholz, the Conway bank's president, joined the First Commercial board.

In early 1984, the Little Rock financial community became excited about the reported sale of a block of 20 percent of First Commercial's stock, purportedly to the wealthy Murchison family of Texas. If the stock was intended for the Murchisons, it did not get there because it was acquired for $10.8 million by a group of investors led by Charles H. Murphy Jr. Gordon E. Parker, top officer of First United Bancshares, Inc., of El Dorado, was named president of First Commercial Corporation in the wake of the sale and Murphy became chairman of the corporation's executive committee. This move propelled me into the board chairmanship and chief executive officer's position of both the holding company and its principal bank, a situation that existed until Barnett Grace was elevated to chief executive officer of the bank in July 1987.[66] Parker retired in December 1988, at which time Grace was elected president of First Commercial Corporation.[67] By this time, I had reached First Commercial's mandatory retirement age of sixty-five, but had been granted a two-year exemption.

In the period right after the First National/Commercial National merger, I was appointed to the Federal Advisory Council of the Federal Reserve by the Federal Reserve Bank in St. Louis.[68] This assignment involved meeting four times a year with the St. Louis Federal Reserve Bank and with the board of the Federal Reserve System in Washington, D.C., then chaired by Paul Volcker. The 1913 law creating the Federal Reserve System provided for the advisory council, which is made up of one member representative from each of the twelve Federal Reserve banks. I served three years from the Eighth Federal Reserve District on the advisory council and was elected its vice president in the latter part of my final term. It was a remarkable learning experience about the way the Federal Reserve system works.

In early 1987, First Commercial teamed with Northwest Bancshares of Bentonville, owned by Sam Walton and his family, to buy the Security National Bank and Trust Co. of Norman, Oklahoma, which had been closed by the Comptroller of the Currency because it was insolvent.[69] This was the first joint venture for First Commercial and was done to spread the risk. First Commercial invested eleven million dollars to acquire a bank with assets of $205 million that I saw as being in the heart of Oklahoma's growth area despite a cyclical downturn in oil prices. The surprise was not limited to the fact that an Arkansas bank had crossed the border to buy an institution in another state. The nation was in a recession that was so severe in Arkansas, particularly in the agriculture segment of the economy, that some viewed it as a depression.

Shortly afterward, First Commercial reported its 1986 earnings were $8.4 million—down 19 percent from the previous year. The downturn was attributed to a three million dollar securities loss in June 1986 due to theft by a former employee.[70] First Commercial was strong enough to absorb such losses,

William H. Bowen in 1987 as president of First Commercial Bank. *Photo copyright by and courtesy of Jorden Davie Photography.*

and in September 1987, it announced it had offered to buy control of the Security Bank of Harrison in far northern Arkansas for about nine million dollars.[71] The sale was approved four months later.

While waiting for approval of the Harrison bank purchase, First Commercial made a bid to buy the Bank of Cabot. The Bank of Cabot fought back in November 1987, and First Commercial dropped its effort a month later. Demonstrating how transitory the 1986 earnings decline had been, First Commercial announced in April 1988 that its 1987 earnings had grown 37 percent. Much of the growth was attributed to an 18 percent rise in net interest income.[72]

To carry out its strategy of acquiring at least one new bank a year, First Commercial continued on the prowl and in July 1988 came up with the Benton State Bank, an institution with $133 million in assets owned by Benton State Bankshares.[73] The price to First Commercial was pegged at $16.75 million, in cash,[74] and the purchase was completed in December 1988.

A month after announcing the Benton State Bank deal, First Commercial revealed it had reached a $3.13 million stock swap agreement with Citizens Bank of England, which had twenty-one million dollars in assets.[75] *Arkansas Gazette* business columnist James M. Hopkins pointed out this was a way for First Commercial to enter the lucrative, fast-growing Cabot market. Cabot and England are both in Lonoke County, and Arkansas law allowed countywide branch banking.[76] Therefore, it was no surprise when First Commercial Bank of England opened a Cabot branch in May 1989, about four months after the purchase was completed.

Business writer Howard Coan wrote a comprehensive article in the *Arkansas Democrat* on March 19, 1989, in which he said that First Commercial Corporation "doesn't flash or glitter," that its loan portfolio showed almost no lending outside of Arkansas, and that it makes "very few loans above $1 million." Coan asked how analysts rated First Commercial. "Boring but extremely successful," in the words of Henry Coffey, a bank analyst at the brokerage firm of J. C. Bradford and Company of Nashville, Tennessee, which tracked thirty bank holding companies in the South at the time. "That's the way I would describe most well-run banks," Coffey added.[77]

First Commercial, Coan continued, had an "utterly terrific" year in 1988, earning $13.3 million or $2.96 a share, up 15.6 percent from $11.5 million or $2.56 a share reported in 1987. The holding company's total assets had grown from $1.25 billion in 1984, the first full year after the merger, to $1.49 billion at the end of 1988.[78]

First Commercial's success was attributed in part to the fact that so many employees, including management, had a stake in the firm. About six hundred of the company's 2,460 stockholders were employees. I owned or controlled 193,792 shares, or 4.19 percent of the company. The directors and top executives as a group owned 29.37 percent of the 4.63 million outstanding First Commercial shares.

As to the company's aggressive posture on acquisitions, what we looked for in a potential acquisition were quality banks in a stable or growth market at a price either in cash or a stock-for-stock split that did not dilute earnings after the affiliation. Every bank that we acquired fit that category.

A month later, Barnett Grace and I sent a letter to First Commercial's shareholders in which we announced a five-for-three stock split.[79] When the split was completed, the holding company would have 7,717,048 shares outstanding. We also revealed that First Commercial had agreed in principle to allow ABT Bancshares Corporation, parent of Arkansas Bank and Trust Company in Hot Springs, to become an affiliate, adding $294 million in assets that would allow First Commercial to overtake FABCO as the state's largest bank holding firm. Arkansas Bank and Trust was Arkansas's eighth-largest bank, the second-largest state-chartered bank, and Hot Springs's largest. A definitive agreement, under which First Commercial paid twenty-four million dollars in stock for the Hot Springs institution, was reached in July 1989.[80]

Through 1989, First Commercial Corporation posted record earnings of $17.05 million or $2.21 a share—a 26.6 percent increase, which was attributed to extraordinary growth in return on average assets and on stockholders' equity. First Commercial was now a holding company with $1.58 billion in assets.[81] In the five years since the merger, stockholders' equity in First Commercial had been tripled to $150 million.

Not all of First Commercial's growth came though acquisitions, and the firm served notice it would continue to grow internally when it sought, and received, approval from government regulatory agencies to establish the First Commercial Trust Company, to be capitalized at $750,000 through the sale of 75,000 shares of stock valued at ten dollars each, all to be owned by its parent holding company.[82]

I informed First Commercial Corporation shareholders at their annual meeting on April 17, 1990, that I would retire at the end of the year and turn the reins over to the man I had hand-picked nineteen years before—Barnett Grace. I said I would "remain on board" at the bank after retiring as an adviser on mergers and acquisitions, litigation (as a lawyer), customer relations, and legislation.

Shortly after my sixty-seventh birthday on May 6, I became the finance chairman for a campaign that opposed a constitutional amendment planned for the November ballot that would repeal Arkansas's prohibition against "games of chance" and allow a lottery.[83] The prohibition remains in spite of numerous efforts through the years to repeal it. Then, in June, First Commercial became the first financial institution in Arkansas to acquire an insolvent savings and loan association when it paid $1.15 million to buy the assets and assume the liabilities of Home Federal Savings and Loan Association of Memphis, through an agreement with the Resolution Trust Corporation, and converted it and its seven-office branch network into a commercial bank.[84]

I took the lead on this purchase, telling a reporter at the time that:

> Acquisition of this institution provides us with a cost-effective means of entering the Memphis market, which we consider a natural extension of our Arkansas franchise.[85]

The prospect of retirement did not sit well with me. Actually, the word "retirement" literally was making me physically ill, as I came down with a cold and fever after just thinking about the word "retirement."[86] My son, Scott, the orthopedic surgeon, knew what was going on, and told me: "Well, I've got you figured out, Dad. You are a child of the Depression, and you equate personal self-esteem with having a job. And as you think about leaving that job, it upsets you; you become anxious, your immune system works less well, and it breaks down and you catch a cold. What you've got to do," the doctor continued, "is come to grips with the fact that you can retire *to* something, just as you can retire *from* something."

In media terms, perhaps the kindest send-off I received came from independent journalist Steve Barnes, who wrote, "Bowen was the key man in the crafting of a bank that was greater than the sum of its two predecessors." Barnes also made the point to warn Arkansas that I might be "retiring," but I "wasn't engineered to be idle."[87] And I wasn't.

Under Barnett Grace's leadership, First Commercial continued to grow, adding banks in Arkansas, East Texas, and northern Louisiana. By the spring of 1998, First Commercial was $7.5 billion in size and had achieved return on equity and expense control equal to the best banks of its size in the United States. This explains why a number of larger bank holding companies began making overtures to acquire it in 1998. An agreement was reached to merge with Regions Bank of Birmingham, Alabama. The exchange value was $2.65 billion in Regions stock, or more than four times book value.

Chapter Six

Private Sector—Public Service

Shortly after becoming president of the Little Rock Chamber of Commerce in September 1961, I took a hard look at what I was seeing every day as I made my way to and from work at the law firm. What I saw was grass growing up and along the cracks in the pavement of Main Street, which was dotted with empty storefronts. That grass was a symbol of what had happened to Little Rock and Arkansas in the wake of the 1957 Central High School crisis when, faced with a defiant Gov. Orval Faubus, President Dwight D. Eisenhower had federalized the Arkansas National Guard and sent in the U.S. Army's 101st Airborne Division troops to protect nine black students as they integrated the school in compliance with a U.S. Supreme Court order. The city and the state had become pariahs to investors.

I began to ponder what could be done to turn Little Rock and Arkansas around—to make the city and state places where the "best and brightest" high school and college graduates remained to build their lives and communities rather than fleeing as they had been doing. Who would be better than those who had left and succeeded to tell Arkansas what it needed to do to retain their kind? I envisioned persuading these individuals to come home, albeit briefly, and join hands with prominent persons who had not left the state to form a kind of "blue ribbon body" to advise Arkansas about enlarging its industrial and commercial base. Perhaps the returnees, realizing that Arkansas was making a major effort to industrialize and to change its image, would have their companies locate facilities in the state that would provide jobs. I sold this idea to the Chamber of Commerce board and recruited Winthrop Rockefeller and Jack Pickens to cochair the committee to make the arrangements necessary to bring these successful native sons and daughters home to mingle with a handful of leaders who had chosen to remain in Arkansas. The group and the event were dubbed "Arkansans-at-Large."

In an *Arkansas Gazette* article in 1963 Rockefeller was quoted as saying the 1962 event was "highly successful."[1] I recall that the group traveled to Rockefeller's Winrock Farm atop Petit Jean Mountain near Morrilton and visited Hendrix College in Conway. J. S. McDonnell, chairman of the St. Louis aerospace firm McDonnell-Douglas Corporation and an Arkansas native, provided a display in front of the Marion Hotel—where the group stayed—of the prototype of the Gemini capsule that his aerospace company was building for the adventure to the moon that President John F. Kennedy had mandated by decade's end.

The 1963 three-day gathering of Arkansans-at-Large received considerably more public attention. We sent invitations to persons selected from those nominated by chamber members, industrial and financial directors, and from names submitted by persons throughout the state, and over fifty individuals accepted our invitation to visit and "see how things are going."[2] Rockefeller and Pickens again were in charge of arrangements that included a reception at the Top of the Rock Club followed by a dinner at which Faubus and Rockefeller were among the speakers. At the time, Rockefeller chaired the Arkansas Industrial Development Commission (AIDC) and was in a not-so-easy relationship with Faubus. The dinner, however, proceeded splendidly.

On Friday, attendees toured the Little Rock Industrial District, after which they journeyed to Rockefeller's farm for lunch and a tour. I hosted the group at a dinner that night at the Country Club of Little Rock as I had in 1962. Saturday's events, which included a tour of Little Rock University and a visit to the Arkansas Arts Center were made optional so the visitors would not feel guilty if they decided instead to spend the day visiting Arkansas relatives and friends.

A reporter caught up with the group at the Arkansas Arts Center on Saturday, October 19, and made much of the fact that Robert D. Brown was "an interloper" because he had not been born in the state. It was Brown who was quoted extensively, however, because he praised the state warmly, saying his firm, Remington Rand, could not be more pleased with the plant it had opened in Searcy.[3] "Arkansans-at-Large" had at least one salutary accomplishment because J. S. McDonnell located a plant in Melbourne (Izard County). The plant is still there and employs about six hundred people.

In October 1963, Connie and I made our first trip to Europe on the occasion of my service that year as Arkansas chairman for Radio Free Europe—an organization with offices in all fifty states and territories dedicated to bringing accurate, pro-Western news across eastern-Communist Europe. Our task was to assemble supporters who would help finance the Radio Free Europe news service to countries behind the Iron Curtain. A reward for this service was an opportunity for each state's chair and spouse to visit Europe and see firsthand the challenges and efforts of Radio Free Europe.

To prepare for the trip, I read William L. Shirer's *The Rise and Fall of the Third Reich*, which had been published in 1960. It was a definitive account of World War II—the events leading up to it and the aftermath, including the building of the Berlin wall. On landing in Frankfurt, I saw a red Fock Wolfe 190 fighter plane parked on the right side of the service runway, symbolic of the war. In downtown Berlin, we visited the stores and restaurants and were impressed by the city's attractive and vital lifestyle and citizenry. The wall was very much in our consciousness because of John F. Kennedy's famous speech there, in the summer of 1961 when he announced to some five hundred thousand cheering citizens, "Ich bin ein Berliner" (I am a Berliner) as he paid tribute to the spirit of Berliners and their quest for freedom.

Checkpoint Charlie was an entry through the wall in midtown Berlin. We went through it and encountered an unbelievable moonscape of a city—almost no traffic, few stores, and fewer people as compared to the teeming mass on the Allied side. While there, I purchased a Soviet magazine in English that paralleled our *Life* magazine. A major article discussed a bountiful wheat crop that fall in East Germany and the surrounding area. On returning to New York City, we were greeted by an article in the *New York Times* that described a wheat crop failure in Communist Germany, requiring help from the West.

From Berlin we traveled to Munich for OctoberFest. Table after table of food and beer stood under massive tents. The waitresses carried five beer steins in each hand—an amazing feat of hand and arm strength that still impresses me. The first day we employed an English-speaking driver to take us on a tour of the city and asked him pointedly to take us by the famous Beer Hall where Hitler launched his first pogrom in 1923. As we were returning to our hotel, I reminded him of our interest. He refused to answer and we returned to our hotel without having seen this historic part of Munich.

In 1964, I succeeded Raymond Rebsamen as president of the Urban Progress Association. This was a civic group organized in 1959 to promote and support sound regional planning, urban development, and redevelop-ment. This was a critical time in Little Rock as the effects of the desegregation crisis at Central High School were still reverberating throughout the city and state and Little Rock was in dire need of positive programs to bring it out of the crisis—both economically and psychologically. At this time, the Little Rock Housing Authority was initiating the Central Little Rock Urban Renewal Project, which included the entire central business district—the first in the nation to do so—and it attracted the interest of civic and government leaders from around the nation. Automobile access into the downtown area a became major objective of both the Urban Renewal Project and the Urban Progress Association.

Our first challenge was to persuade Rep. Wilbur Mills, chair of the House Ways and Means Committee, to bring the Eighth Street Expressway into the interstate highway system. We had explored the possibility of local funding with a bond issue. It was not feasible. The Arkansas Highway Department lacked the funds to build the expressway, so we looked to federal funding as a possibility. In September 1958, the city of Little Rock had petitioned the Arkansas Highway Commission to designate this corridor as a part of the highway system. The next year, the commission agreed, pending the availability of sufficient funds for the construction. Plans for construction began to move forward in early 1963. The city obtained and cleared much of the right-of-way land under the Urban Renewal Program and the first section, from Dennison Street to Pine Street, opened in 1969.

The Federal Highway Administration turned down the Arkansas Highway Commission's 1970 request to designate the expressway as an interstate, but Congressman Mills was able to secure additional mileage amounts for the Interstate system and the administration notified state officials in November that the route would become Interstate 630, making it eligible for federal construction dollars. This funding, however, brought additional requirements under the newly enacted National Environmental Policy Act. In late 1973, a group of citizens known as the Arkansas Community Organization for Reform Now, angry about the displacement of so many black-owned homes and businesses, filed a federal suit contending that the highway department's environmental impact statement was inadequate and that the creation of an east-west interstate would cause residential out-flight west that would destroy the central part of the city. The federal court agreed in its 1975 decision, but later approved a revised environmental impact statement, clearing the way for continued development.[4]

The Central Little Rock Urban Renewal Project involved selective acquisition and clearance of substandard properties, but the major thrust of the project was the rehabilitation of existing properties and infrastructure. Still, the construction of I-630 was, and to some extent remains, contentious—particularly in the African American community, whose homes and businesses made up much of the affected area. Ultimately, the project solidified the downtown area's position as the business and professional center of the city and state. Nevertheless, it has not been able to curb the movement of retail centers to the west.

As early as 1963, I firmly believed that the key to Arkansas's success lay in its ability to provide a quality education for its citizens. One of the first efforts of the newly organized Fifty for the Future in 1963 was to create a graduate school in Little Rock that would furnish high-tech talent to the Central Arkansas community. Fifty founder Billy Rector and I called on Dr. David Mullins, president of the University of Arkansas, with authority from Fifty to offer a gift of fifty thousand dollars per year for three years to the university to launch a graduate institute. We argued that Little Rock was missing high-tech jobs because of the absence of such a school. Little Rock Junior College, founded in 1927, had evolved into Little Rock University (LRU), but was not graduating the technically trained students who were needed in the metro area. At our invitation, Dr. Mullins studied the proposal for months and in 1965, he and the university board agreed to the Fifty proposal and the Graduate Institute of Technology (GIT) came into being. Unfortunately, GIT never received the support, guidance, and leadership that it needed.

After much student and faculty anguish, the leadership of LRU, the Little Rock Chamber of Commerce, and Fifty for the Future agreed to make a maximum effort to bring LRU into the University of Arkansas system. On January 6, 1969, at the invitation of Grainger Williams, LRU board chairman, I appeared before the education committees of the Arkansas House and Senate in the old Supreme Court chambers of the state capitol. The sole purpose of the meeting was to consider making LRU the University of Arkansas at Little Rock. Opposition emerged largely from legislators whose districts included other institutions of higher learning, but I argued that the benefits to the system outweighed the costs. I told the legislators that if the merger could be compared to a marriage, the University of Arkansas would receive a handsome dowry in the form of the seven million dollar LRU physical plant, comprised of nearly fifty acres of prime land at the south end of University Avenue, education buildings in place, and a student body of nearly 3,400. I argued that this would make the largest contribution ever, up to that point, to a state institution of higher learning, and that "the location of a state university at Little Rock would help attract the kind of 'sophisticated' industries that [would] locate only in urban areas" but that the new influx of jobs would improve the entire state's economy.[5] Ultimately, the legislature agreed and the University of Arkansas at Little Rock came into being with the new fiscal year July 1, 1969. Appointed by Gov. Dale Bumpers, I served as a board member and later, chair, of the advisory board for the new university

I also continued my support for my alma mater, the University of Arkansas at Fayetteville. In 1966, I was president of the UA alumni association. At that time, the corporate community did not feel a need to help underwrite tax-supported institutions such as universities. The next year I served as president of the university's Endowment and Trust Fund—the precursor to the University Foundation—and we undertook to develop support within the private sector to fund a honarary chair at the university. Within the year, we raised $100,000 and formed the first distinguished professorship chair within the Department of History.

Some of my other activities in the late 1960s included service on the board of the Arkansas Arts Center (AAC). I served because I believed in supporting the cultural life of my community, not because I had any skill or knowledge of the arts! From the time of its inception in 1961, almost all significant support for the Arts Center came from Governor and Mrs. Winthrop Rockefeller. Because of their generosity, the AAC was completed in 1963 and offered classes to LRU (and later UALR) students. In 1969, the Rockefellers gave one hundred thousand dollars less than their previous year's contribution in an effort to encourage the AAC to become more self-sufficient, and Mrs. Rockefeller left as president of the board that same year. At that time, private sector pledges totaled approximately seventy thousand dollars. We needed an additional thirty thousand to forty thousand dollars just to stay afloat—even if we discontinued offering classes to UALR students. In 1968, we hired Townsend Wolfe as the center's director. He served a long and successful tenure in that position before retiring in 2002.

I served as AAC board president in 1970–71. Immediately, we stepped up our fundraising efforts. Fellow board members Harry Pfeifer and Jack Pickens agreed to take the lead on this and Dudley Dowell, former president of New York Life Insurance Company, who had recently retired and returned to Arkansas, agreed to approach national companies with investments in the state. In October 1970, we received an estate gift in the amount of twenty-five thousand dollars and we asked the city of Little Rock and County Judge Arch Campbell for seventy-eight thousand dollars and fifteen thousand dollars, respectively. By the end of fiscal year 1971, the AAC had secured sufficient community support to meet its annual budget needs of around four hundred thousand dollars and had been weaned of its dependency from the Rockefeller family. In celebration, an I-beam sculpture was erected in front of the center and dedicated to Mrs. Rockefeller in November 1971 for her ten years of service as the AAC's board president. The sculpture still stands.

In 1970 and 1971, I also served as president of the Pulaski County Bar Association. At the time we met in the ballroom of the Lafayette Hotel. One of my duties was to secure speakers for our meetings. My two best-known speakers were Associate Justice of the U.S. Supreme Court Byron R. "Whizzer" White, and Gen. William Westmoreland, the former commander of American forces in Vietnam, who led the United States through a major escalation of the war. Westmoreland's appearance was greeted by a negative press editorial because of the growing unpopularity of the war.

Meanwhile, even though the original Arkansans-at-Large program lapsed in 1964, for me, the idea did not die. After becoming president of Commercial National Bank in May 1971, I wasted no time persuading the bank to sponsor an organization to be made up primarily of native Arkansans who had become major successes outside the state, with a few acknowledged in-state business leaders. I wanted to give Arkansas's sons and daughters a chance to come back and see what was going on in the state and make a contribution where possible. They were not paid for their service, and they would convene at their own expense but be treated like royalty once here. It would be called the National Advisory Board of Commercial National Bank, but would advise all Arkansas—not just the bank—and be independent of the financial institution. The time the group would spend together was cut to a day and a half, with Saturday devoted to an optional trip to Fayetteville to see the Razorbacks play or another leisurely pursuit if there was no University of Arkansas football game. Only one tour was included in the organizational meeting agenda held on Friday, November 19, 1971—that being aboard the *Border Star* for a look at part of the recently completed $1.2 billion McClellan–Kerr Arkansas River Navigation System. The board never elected any officers; I was the convenor and, assisted by a bank executive secretary, made all of the arrangements. The National Advisory Board was and remained unique.

Throughout Arkansas's history, black and white people alike poured out of the state looking for opportunity elsewhere. There was a drain of talent as many of our brightest young people sought their fortunes beyond our boundaries. Evidence of the out migration from Arkansas was the advisory board members who achieved prominence outside the state. However, they joined the Arkansas members in an abiding affection for their native state and a willingness to share their experience and expertise to help Arkansas achieve a quality of life and economic well-being that incorporated the best of their collective wisdom.

Each year the members convened in Arkansas and were briefed authoritatively on the Arkansas economic and demographic scene. The exchange produced a "critical mass" of innovative ideas.[6] We expected many benefits to flow from these annual exchanges. The board adopted the following goals at its initial meeting:

- Ideas for industrial growth should be shared with private and public agencies concerned with the particular problem at hand;
- Information respecting specific ventures, e.g., relocation of corporate headquarters in the Southwest, could be shared and pursued;
- Pitfalls associated with industrial growth experienced in cities served by Board members would be made known and hopefully avoided; and,
- Through annual meetings and periodic correspondence, the Advisory Board was expected to be a clearinghouse of innovative ideas for maximizing employment, insuring equal opportunity, accelerating urban renewal and development, controlling and abating pollution, broadening support of culture and the arts, achieving an improved balance between agriculture and industry and promotion of better rapport and cooperation of business, labor and government.[7]

The issue the board chose as the focus of its 1972 meeting was: "What is the quality of life and living in Arkansas, and how can it be improved and preserved?" Both the 1971 and 1972 NAB reports emphasized a theme championed by the Democratic lawyer from Charleston, Dale Bumpers, who had unseated Gov. Winthrop Rockefeller in November 1970—that it wasn't so bad Arkansas had missed the industrial booms that brought big steel to Pittsburgh, the automobile industry to Detroit, the aviation industry to the East and far West, and the growth of heavy industry dependent on burning coal and other polluting fossil fuels. Because these waves had missed Arkansas, the state had minimal industrial pollution and urban blight. This meant Arkansas could focus on "doing it right" while seeking to grow.

Bumpers himself was the principal presenter at the meeting. Five representatives from his cabinet provided the details within their specific areas of expertise. With the aid of the public relations/advertising firm that held Commercial National's account, now known as Cranford Johnson Robinson Woods, I wrote the printed 1972 board report. The document consisted of short summaries of facts as the presenters had given them and photographs of Arkansas's environmental beauty. It stated the board had reached this consensus:

> regardless of statistics, Arkansas has a most envious style of living. The state's clean environment, low population density, vast and unspoiled stretches of nature and hardy, individualistic people make Arkansas unique in a land of growing social unrest, over-population and pollution. Arkansas' envious style of living also includes an economy that has grown remarkably over the past decade. Rather than compare Arkansas' economic growth with that of the nation, board members pointed out the more important comparison between Arkansas today and Arkansas 10 years ago.[8]

The two recommendations that evolved from the board's discussion were:

> Arkansas' future must be built on two foundations: preservation of her present lifestyle and improvement of her economy in commerce, industry and government . . . this future must be built through long-range, management-by-objective planning for the coming century.[9]

The environmental movement was at full throttle nationally in the early 1970s, and land-use planning was part of the "rage for reform" to clean up the country and prohibit future pollution and despoliation. The board's 1973 meeting was devoted to exploring the issue at both the national and state levels. U.S. Senator J. William Fulbright (D-AR) briefed the board on Senate Bill 268, "Land Use Policy and Planning Assistance Act," and predicted some form of legislation would pass regarding land development. Governor Bumpers discussed the findings of his Advisory Committee on Land Management and his views on the importance of long-range planning in Arkansas. I fell back on my legal experience to talk about the constitutional protection of private property from government acquisition without just compensation, and how the perception that a landowner had unshackled rights to do what he pleased with his property was and always had been at odds with the law.[10]

In its 1973 report, the board congratulated Bumpers on his efforts and said it "heartily concurs . . . there is a pressing need for legislative programs that will balance the rights of the people of Arkansas to private ownership *and* to a viable environment." A sustained effort was called imperative to "inform the people of Arkansas of the importance and urgency of laying out a pattern of growth for the State that ensures this balance. If each citizen can come to see that the goal is to reach a balance between two of his *own* rights, not between his rights and those of someone else—the groundwork for a successful legislative effort will have been laid."[11]

No matter what the subject, NAB members could be counted on throughout the years to voice their beliefs during discussion sessions that Arkansans needed to develop a greater appreciation of the value of education and the state needed to do a better job of educating its children from kindergarten through college. They believed passionately that education was the road to follow to put Arkansas in the American mainstream, yet board members seemed to sense that tackling the broad topic of education would be too much for the group. However, the board did occasionally examine parts of the whole, as in 1974 when it considered the issue of a proposed continuing education center.

The timing of the board's selection of this topic was propitious because the University of Arkansas had just completed a nationwide search and chose Dr. Charles E. Bishop from the University of Maryland at College Park as the institution's new president. Aided by his staff, Dr. Bishop prepared a position paper on the subject of continuing education for board members to study before they convened in Little Rock on October 25. Position papers provided before the annual meeting on whatever subject the board had chosen to consider became a mainstay thereafter.

The 1974 board report entitled, *The People's University—Viewpoints on Continuing Education,* featured another first—dissenting views, presented in writing. The board consensus was that "high priority should be given to construction in Little Rock of a Continuing Education Center to house the leadership of the present growing program and to furnish the springboard from which a continuing education curriculum as expanded could be offered across the State."[12] The board added what it called "a word of caution" that "no equally or more important program should be preempted by the expanded concept and program for continuing education" and that support and aid from private foundations should be pursued after plans for the center and its program were in hand and a base of public support identified.

William E. Henderson, director of the Parks and Tourism Department, made an encore appearance before the board in 1975 to discuss the state's $840.3 million tourism industry and how he envisioned it could grow. The resulting NAB report, *Arkansas Tourism: The Sleeping Giant,* proved to be the board's most popular, in my view. Then Gov. David Pryor said it was adopted as the administration's official position on the subject and a rallying point for the annual "Governor's Conference on Tourism" that he began. The AIDC Bond Guaranty Fund could guarantee up to five hundred thousand dollars in industrial revenue bonds at the time. The board recommended a study to determine if this concept could be expanded to embrace appropriate tourist facilities.[13]

The board's 1976 report, *The Power Shift—Arkansas' Opportunity,* took note of the spectacular growth occurring in the Sunbelt, often at the expense of New England, the Middle Atlantic, and the Great Lakes states, whose industries were moving to warmer and more hospitable climates. Given the amenities of fresh air and water and business-friendly governments and workers, Little Rock and Arkansas were not taking advantage of the demographic shift as they could, the board concluded, and it urged local and state leaders to target specific companies to move their headquarters here. It said:

> a quality personalized and hand delivered report [should] be given to the chief executive officer of select corporations. . . . Partial relocations including regional and subsidiary headquarters are believed to invite special attention. State and local, private and public leadership must join hands in a carefully conceived continuing program of personal visits to decision makers and their staffs in their offices with a purpose of making clear to them that they are wanted in Little Rock and Arkansas.[14]

Arkansas' Water: A Fragile Wealth, the board's 1977 report, contains recommendations more specific in nature than the group was accustomed to giving, but Gov. Bill Clinton said years later that the state took them seriously and attempted to implement them.[15] Some of them were implemented, but the state is still struggling with others. For example, as the board suggested, the state developed a comprehensive, statewide water management plan, and the riparian legal doctrine, which governs who can use water from a stream, was modified so that under certain conditions water can be transferred from one river basin to another. Two other issues on which the board made recommendations apparently remain intractable, and for that reason bear repeating. They are:

> Ground water supplies are being depleted rapidly in the Grand Prairie and in South Arkansas. In addition to employing alternate irrigation methods, Arkansas farmers should start meaningful planning now to substitute surface water supplies for ground water and not wait until a crisis develops. Non-point pollution, especially agricultural runoff,

constitutes a major problem in Arkansas. State leaders involved in "208 Planning" must recommend a plan of education/persuasion, economic incentives, police powers or a combination of the three in an effort to get farmers to adopt and practice conservation treatment programs.[16]

The Arab-dominated Organization of Petroleum Exporting Countries (OPEC) learned how to manipulate the Western world in 1973–74 by curtailing oil production to force up prices. OPEC's actions, coupled with the energy-guzzling lifestyles of Americans, had created a "crisis" in the United States. Long lines formed at service stations to purchase gasoline and diesel fuel, the prices of which had skyrocketed at the pump. Everyday conversations revolved around energy—whether there would be enough to sustain the American economy, especially now that the higher costs had begun pushing the inflation rate into double digits. The National Advisory Board decided it wanted to take a look at Arkansas's energy situation at its 1978 meeting.

A comprehensive report emerged, one that touched on nuclear power, coal-fired electric generating stations, the "hard" and "soft" paths to energy self-sufficiency, lignite, solar, biomass, reuse of solid waste (methane gas, among other products), wind, and geothermal energy sources. This led to the board's conclusion that:

> Conservation, promoting more efficient end-use energy equipment and developing renewable energy resources should be pursued to the maximum extent possible, while recognizing that these routes— without the traditional natural gas, oil, coal and nuclear—will not keep the United States economically healthy or maintain the standard of living that the people demand. And contention that the "hard" and "soft" paths are mutually exclusive or that one is preferred over the other should be rejected vigorously.[17]

The board urged the state to promote development of its known lignite seams in southwest Arkansas as a potential power plant fuel. This idea stayed alive for a few more months until it was proven that the British Thermal Unit content in Arkansas's thin lignite seams was too low to make it cost-effective to mine and transport. As the former president of Arkla, Inc., Sheffield Nelson, eventually told a legislative committee, Arkansas's lignite was no more than "high grade dirt."

A new decade was approaching, and the board elected to forego a specific topic at its 1979 meeting, instead opting for a comprehensive examination of where Arkansas stood and what it needed to do to progress during this period. I returned to preparing the materials presented to the board with help from a consultant, Dr. Charles Minshall, senior scientist at Battelle Memorial Institute in Columbus, Ohio.[18] The board also heard assessments from Arkansas's two senators, Dale Bumpers and David Pryor, and from its young governor, Bill Clinton. Another innovation on the board's part was holding a news conference midway through the meeting to explain its purpose, its study topic, and to announce any conclusions it had reached to that point.

The board was impressed with the progress statistics showed Arkansas had made during the 1970s, and it did not hesitate to say so in an upbeat report:

> Given the economic development momentum achieved by Arkansas in the '70s, its remarkable quality of life, state and local governments which do and, as a matter of law, must live within its [sic] financial means, a work force willing to put in a day's work for a day's pay and ready to learn new skills, its location in the path of growth and development, a mild climate featuring four seasons, and its energy resources only exceeded by the contiguous states of Louisiana, Texas, and Oklahoma, it is expected that Arkansas will be in the forefront of the nation's economic progress during the new decade.[19]

Also drawing accolades from the board were Clinton's revamping of the Industrial Development Department into the Economic Development Department and his selection of James Dyke to put the agency on a new and more vigorous course. Dyke, educated at Yale University and the University of Arkansas Law School, was operating a substantial building-supply business when Clinton tapped him for the job. Dyke gave the board an intensive, in-depth study of the Arkansas economic scene.

The year 1980 was a banner one for the National Advisory Board. I announced at a news conference in April that year that the Commercial National Bank board of directors in October had voted to make a hundred thousand dollar gift to a permanent fund in the NAB's honor. In the interim, three NAB members provided unsolicited gifts—one hundred thousand dollars from J. S. McDonnell's foundation, fifty thousand dollars from Charles M. Kittrell and fifty thousand dollars from Charles Murphy's foundation.[20] The three hundred thousand dollars would capitalize a tax-exempt scholarship fund to help able young Arkansans attend any accredited college or university in the state in hopes they would remain in Arkansas after graduation.

I expected the endowment to produce thirty thousand to thirty five thousand dollars in interest annually that would go into grants to pay the tuition, fees, books, and room and board of students who would attend Arkansas colleges and who were chosen by a fourteen-member governing board on the basis of academic performance, leadership, and college entrance test scores. I explained at the news conference:

> Significantly, this distinctive board meets at the individual expense of its members. Their only reward is the hope and belief that their study and presence and their report are meaningful to Arkansas. The board of this bank has looked for some time for a way to express appreciation to this distinctive leadership.

Mark Bonner of Little Rock, Lynne Hays of Pine Bluff, and Larry Locke of Arkadelphia were chosen in 1980 to be the first recipients of NAB scholarships.[21] The scholarship program lasted until the NAB disbanded eighteen years later, though the bank kept its commitment to students who were in the midst of their college educations on NAB grants. During the life of the program, eighty-one students received full or partial scholarships or cash awards. After the NAB disbanded, the $340,000 principal came under the bank's control, which made the interest available in grants to teachers wanting to improve their skills.[22] The state adopted the NAB's intent in establishing the scholarship program as its own, and in the mid-1990s, began making a series of grants available to high school graduates to attend in-state colleges and universities, both public and private. The Governor's Distinguished Scholars program rewarded high school students who scored at least thirty-two on the American College Test (ACT) with free tuition, fees, books, and room and board. By fiscal year 2002, the state was spending $34 million on three types of scholarships for high school graduates electing to remain in Arkansas for their post-secondary education.

In 1981, the board's chosen topic was *Aging in Arkansas,* a choice prompted by 1980 federal census findings that Arkansas' population had grown nearly 19 percent during the 1970s and that it ranked only behind Florida in the percentage of its residents who were seniors. However, a substantial socio-economic gap existed between retirees who had moved into northwest and north Arkansas from northern states and native Arkansas seniors. Virtually all of those who made verbal presentations before the board at its October meeting were advocates for the elderly, but the panel chose to focus more on where the research pointed. For example, the board said Arkansas did not need to spend resources promoting itself as a haven for retirees from the north because their migration would happen anyway as a result of the state's low property taxes, a climate with four distinct seasons, and the attraction of such recreation-oriented planned developments as Bella Vista, Fairfield Communities, Cherokee Village, Horseshoe Bend, and Hot Springs Village.[23] The board also was cautious about "skewing" Arkansas's demographics— that is, becoming so "top heavy" with retired seniors that younger people would see no place for themselves and their futures and leave.

Surveys by various academic institutions and agencies showed that, contrary to many expectations, Arkansas and its people enjoyed a positive image, internally and externally. This image did not hold true with businessmen across the country who viewed Arkansas as being weak on education, lacking a skilled labor force, and lagging in economic development efforts. The National Advisory Board decided to probe this dichotomy at its 1982 meeting, at which the headline speaker, Pulitzer Prize-winning historian C. Vann Woodward, a native of Vanndale (Cross County), applauded the effort, saying the NAB was:

> showing a rather unprecedented candor, frankness and realism in its sponsorship of the study, *Images and Realities of Arkansas.* Instead of platitudes too often encountered, we are confronted with Facts— instead of images, with realities. It is bracing to see the boldness with which the favorable image of the state at home and abroad is contrasted with the objective realities in public and higher education, appropriation per student, salaries of faculties, basic health services, per capita income and state taxes.[24]

In its conclusions, the board observed that Arkansas's best images, internally as well as externally, were generated by the state's natural beauty and the friendliness of its people, which some call "lifestyle." This was more than a recognition of what the surveys found because it also reflected statements often heard at NAB meetings from some envious members that, in contrast to the residents in the larger cities in which they lived, Arkansans seemed "happy" and relatively stress-free. The board went on to say it would be "unwise" to destroy either the state's natural beauty or its "lifestyle," but "it would be equally ill-conceived . . . not to build on them to achieve a better life, economically and culturally, for the state's residents."[25]

Nationally, the board responded, "technology-based industries accounted for much of the growth of jobs in the manufacturing sector over the last decade and will continue to be the major job generator."[26] This marked the first time the NAB spoke at any length about what became its mantra—that Arkansas must position itself for the new information age. The most significant location factor for technology-based industries is highly skilled and available technical personnel. Therefore, the NAB concluded, Arkansas should concentrate on modernizing its education. The board became enthusiastic about the growth potential for Arkansas represented by the location of the National Center for Toxicological Research (NCTR) in Jefferson County between Little Rock and Pine Bluff and applauded the legislature's creation of the Arkansas Science and Technology Authority (ASTA) to provide state help for basic and applied research within its boundaries.

I was elected vice chairman of ASTA at its organizational meeting on July 6, 1983.[27] Governor Clinton convened the group and echoed the NAB when he said he was convinced Arkansas had to do a better job of "developing its science, technological and research resources and capabilities if we're going to have economic growth and the job mix we need."[28] A dispute about the scope of ASTA's role arose immediately between the agency's newly elected chairman, Dr. Ron Hart, administrator of NCTR, and Dr. Joe Nix, a chemist on the Ouachita Baptist University faculty. Hart's view was expansive; Nix's was narrow, with the research focus being to assist scientists at existing state colleges and universities. Nix's view ultimately prevailed.

My position at ASTA gave me access to some of the state's and nation's leading thinkers on technology in economic development, and I brought some of them forward at the NAB's meeting in October. Frederick Coe, president of Research Triangle Park Foundation and owner of the renowned high-technology research complex, told the NAB how a University of North Carolina professor suggested that a research facility be developed on 4,500 acres located "in the middle of nowhere" between his campus and those of Duke University and North Carolina State University. In 1959, the three universities organized the foundation, the private sector raised two million dollars, and the land was purchased at $248 an acre. After several fallow years, then North Carolina Gov. Luther Hodges talked IBM into locating in the park as its first major occupant. Another key development was the foundation's decision to donate 509 acres to the federal government so that it would locate the National Institute for Environmental Health Sciences in the park. A "critical mass" was achieved by the mid-1970s that allowed the park to pick and choose among institutions and industries wanting to locate there. Coe told Arkansas to "sharply look at your strengths. Find out to whom your strengths will appeal and then go after them."[29]

The board found that one major national research facility and four institutions with substantial research programs and/or potential were located within thirty-five miles of each other in Central Arkansas—NCTR, the University of Arkansas for Medical Sciences (UAMS), the Veterans Administration Medical Center, the University of Arkansas at Little Rock (UALR), and the Graduate Institute of Technology (GIT). The proximity and the complementary nature of their research created the potential, the board saw, for the development of a biotechnology research corridor in central Arkansas. Four steps were recommended to develop this potential, the fore-most of which was that by all means at its disposal, Arkansas should foster a partnership for future economic growth among government, the private sec-tor, and academia. The board also warned Arkansas that success would not be achieved easily, nor would it occur overnight, in part because competition from other states already was intense and would become fierce. Not even to try to develop the potential, however, would be to squander yet another opportunity to move Arkansas into the nation's economic mainstream. The ASTA board, in collaboration with the Arkansas Housing Development Authority, hired Belden Hull Daniels, president and counsel for Community Development, Incorporated, of Cambridge, Massachusetts, and undertook, with the support of the governor's office, some serious economic develop-ment planning that resulted in major reforms during the 1985 legislative ses-sion. Among the changes at ASTA were the establishment of research, technology transfer, business incubator, and seed capital investment pro-grams, and a substantially larger budget.

When the board convened in October 1984, the nation was in the throes of a recession that was rugged in Arkansas, particularly for agriculture. Manufacturing plants were closing and moving out of the country; farms that had been in families for generations were being sold. Experts ranging from Daniels to Walter Perlestein, vice president for venture capital of Merrill Lynch in New York, offered their views about what a chronically poor rural southern state could do about what had been the missing link forever in its economic fabric—the availability of capital.

In response, the board made nine specific recommendations, including these two:

> In today's economic climate, it would be folly for the state to continue
> to focus on luring manufacturing plants from other regions. The evi-
> dence is irrefutable that small business has been generating the new
> jobs in America for several years and will continue to do so. A height-
> ened recognition of this is needed in Arkansas, and the state should
> adjust its policy accordingly so that its principal support goes to build-
> ing on existing resources to expand current businesses and create new
> ones. Only small businesses—a lot of them—will be able to take up
> the slack caused by closing mills. This is the time for Arkansas to put

aside its historical suspicion of public-private partnership to establish a publicly supported, equity-oriented capital corporation that has job creation as its principal purpose. It should be capable of assisting existing businesses with expansion financing, furnishing leveraged start-up funds for new businesses, and providing help for agriculture, especially ventures looking to develop new processing procedures and plants. The Board recognizes that Arkansas will insist, rightly so, that rigorous accountability procedures be woven into the fabric of this corporation.[30]

Early that same year, I was captivated when I came across a formula devised by Sir Robert Thompson, a British guerrilla war expert, to explain those instances in history of individuals or nations that have been victorious although it appeared they were vastly inferior in numbers and resources to their foes or competitors. Thompson's formula was Manpower + Applied Resources x Will = National Power. I began mulling how this formula could be applied to Arkansas and asked the NAB to consider the matter at its 1985 meeting.

The board spent much of the time at its October meeting evaluating the manpower and applied resources components of Thompson's formula. But it concluded that the most important element in the formula and the one in which Arkansas was the weakest was will, which also can be defined as leadership. Leadership is a subjective matter and could not be evaluated statistically or objectively as all of the board's previous topics could be. In the limited time of one session, the board agreed it could not deal adequately with such a subject and took the unprecedented step of deciding to convene again in April 1986.[31] At this meeting, new member Robert H. Dedman noted that Texas did not rely exclusively on its elected politicians to provide leadership, as Arkansas seemed to do. In Dallas, he related, business and professional leaders had been able to set aside their competitive and personal differences to work together for the community's improvement and development. He said they realized that, "a rising tide raises all ships." In other words, Dedman told his colleagues, "Perhaps we have seen the enemy—and it is us." Another board member, William P. Stiritz picked up on this and suggested that Sam Walton, known as the country's wealthiest individual, convene a meeting at a "neutral location" of about a dozen of the state's foremost business leaders to "thrash out" what could be done to move Arkansas forward economically. After some cajoling, Walton agreed.[32] Walton convened two private meetings in 1986 of business leaders such as Charles Murphy, Don Tyson, Jack Stephens, Jerry Maulden of Arkansas Power and Light Company, and Thomas F. "Mack" McLarty, then head of Arkla, Inc. As reported by *Arkansas Gazette* columnist John Brummett, the goal was to bring together the state's business leaders under Walton's volunteered leadership to bring about "a concerted co-operative effort to speak with a single voice of leadership for the state's business community . . . [to develop] a reasoned and achievable long-range agenda for the state's economic progress; . . . [and] a credible, professional, influential and generally apolitical component of the state's efforts to attract industries and other businesses to locate here," among other goals.[33] When the board's 1985–86 report was released in January 1987, it contained Walton's report to the panel on the Arkansas business leaders' activities. Even though Walton's group officially adopted the name of the Arkansas Business Council, Brummett nicknamed it the "Good Suit Club" and the name stuck.[34]

The NAB devoted the bulk of its October 1986 meeting to hearing from representatives of business / government / academia partnerships that were functioning in other states, specifically New Jersey, Minnesota, and California. Thomas M. O'Neill, executive director of the Partnership for New Jersey, stated repeatedly "there is no single pattern that you can take from other states and impose on yours; it must reflect the character and particular needs of your state." O'Neill also warned, with the NAB's agreement, that "the business community has to pay its dues by taking on more altruistic projects. You must not give the impression of being self-serving."[35] Dedman summed up the board's view by saying the Walton group should take this on and be altruistic to achieve credibility.

Although generally unknown at the time, the die had been cast because the business council already had decided its top priority was to rewrite Arkansas's tax code to be more business friendly and get it passed by the 1987 General Assembly. The group, which hired Archie Schaffer III (nephew-in-law of U.S. Sen. Dale Bumpers, D.-AR) as its executive director, succeeded with the tax code rewrite, but this had the effect of tainting the group's credibility from the outset in the eyes of some.[36] The business council did accept a suggestion from the NAB that it concentrate its efforts at first on education because it was the greatest obstacle to improving Arkansas's economic environment. The council divided into three groups to study education.

Harvard University political economy professor Robert B. Reich's fear that America was in danger of becoming a bicoastal economy through the depopulation and policy neglect of its rural interior alarmed many and gave the National Advisory Board a fresh opportunity to examine Arkansas's economy, which was in better shape in 1988 than in 1984.[37] For example, Arkansas was not losing population and its unemployment rate was below the nation's, but its per capita income had stalled at 76 percent of the country's. Reich and other academic presenters outlined extensive recommendations on transportation, communications, technology transfer, retraining, and other education needs to the NAB for "saving" rural America.[38] The result was the board's most strongly worded annual report to date, one in which it declared:

> Arkansas must look to itself and build from within if it is going to be anything but a doormat for the country—a sickly Southwestern stepsister. Self-reliance, yes; retrenchment, no. It is time for Arkansans to break bad habits—to bury the 'them against us' mentality that has made Central and Northwest Arkansas lethargic about the state's overall crisis and for the rest of Arkansas to end its envy and animosity toward Little Rock. In short, it is time for Arkansas to make the effort with the realization that a rising tide raises all ships, . . . The grace period is ending for Arkansas to position itself to achieve economic parity in the 21st Century. There is considerable evidence that Arkansas is continuing to use the shotgun rather than the rifle approach to target its future. This will not get the job done. Arkansas must marshal its will to capitalize on its strengths.[39]

The board's frustration that both the National Center for Toxicological Research and the Arkansas Science and Technology Authority were languishing was palpable. The report noted that Dr. Donald E. McMillan, professor and chairman of the Department of Pharmacology and Interdisciplinary Toxicology at the University of Arkansas for Medical Sciences (UAMS), had been asked recently why there had been no movement to create a "critical mass" of biotechnology industries in the vicinity of NCTR. He replied candidly that it probably was because UAMS and the University of Arkansas at Little Rock (UALR) were only "fair" institutions, largely as a result of inadequate state funding. The UAMS faculty, he continued, was too busy supplementing weak state support by treating patients to have the time and inclination to conduct the kind of quality research necessary to complement NCTR and help attract a critical mass. The board responded with a series of recommendations that revealed it felt Arkansas was on the right track in transportation and communications but was woefully behind in education, retraining, and research.

After two years of study, in September 1988, the Arkansas Business Council Foundation released its eighty-eight-page report on Arkansas education from early childhood through the post-graduate levels.[40] In October, Walton, Murphy, Tyson, and McLarty briefed National Advisory Board members on the findings and recommendations of the study. The board responded with a strong and enthusiastic endorsement of the council's recommendations for reform and accountability at every level of public education in Arkansas.[41] Board member Dr. Mary L. Good praised the report, saying it provided a plan of action rather than being the typical study that would be relegated to the dark corners of a bookshelf.[42]

Although it was difficult to single out particular points in the council's massive study, the NAB said there was special merit in two of the findings: that administrative costs are excessive because Arkansas has too many school districts, which should be reduced, and that the state should emphasize early childhood education because it has a substantial number of disadvantaged children. Arkansas subsequently did the latter under the Clinton and Jim Guy Tucker administrations, but consolidation, then as now, is perceived to be such a political death sentence for any public official who even utters the word that it often is referred to in hushed tones as "the 'C' word." In 1991, the *Arkansas Gazette* reported the business council remained interested in school consolidation but avoided the subject in the 1990 state election to "avoid entanglements with political races."[43] In fact in 2005, school consolidation remains a difficult topic for politicians and business leaders alike to address.

In its conclusion, the NAB noted Arkansas has "a long history of antagonism between business and government and therefore finds it difficult to accept the concept of private/public partnership."[44] This was the time the state needed to try the approach, however, "because the motivation for educational reform and restructuring public schools is likely to flag" otherwise. As the NAB said its report showed, states from the most conservative (Oklahoma and Indiana) to liberal (Minnesota) had done "a remarkable job" of overcoming the attitudinal obstacle to progress, and "it is time for Arkansas to do as much."

The board went on to recommend and urge that the Arkansas General Assembly enact legislation chartering an Arkansas Enterprise Center as a nonprofit, independent private/public partnership, and provide up to five hundred thousand dollars annually on a dollar-for-dollar matching basis with the private sector for its operation. The center's principal mission, the board said, should be to develop a five-year state economic strategy, taking particular care "to preserve and enhance Arkansas' quality of life by making it an integral part of the bottom line."[45] Although it recommended the center be established by legislative authority, the board said its credibility would be diminished if it were dominated by any branch of the state government.

At the same time the NAB concluded that a private/public partnership would be beneficial for Arkansas, Governor Clinton was promoting the establishment of a Commission for Arkansas's Future to provide some long-range planning for the state. Efforts were made to coordinate the board's recommendations with a bill the governor included in his 1989 legislative program to create a commission using the funding approach the NAB suggested. The law creating the commission was enacted, but no state funds were appropriated. The Governor's Emergency Fund and private businesses provided what limited funds the commission had at first. As the years fell away, the lightly regarded agency accomplished little and was abolished by the 1997 legislature.[46]

Meanwhile, I continued to ruminate about a 1985 Winthrop Rockefeller Foundation finding that Arkansas needed a way to develop and disseminate research-based public policy information. The NAB met in 1989 and heard John M. Hills, vice president for external affairs of the Washington-based Brookings Institution, report there were some two hundred research organizations in the United States with annual budgets of one million dollars or less that did essentially what he thought the NAB and I had in mind for Arkansas. Once again, the board felt the subject was too important to be handled in one sitting and agreed to convene at a special meeting in spring 1990 to look closely at three smaller, independent, nonpartisan research organizations that might provide a model for Arkansas.[47]

Hillary Rodham Clinton, then the First Lady of Arkansas, welcomed the NAB back to Little Rock in April with an eloquent plea for help. She said Arkansas had become trapped on a plateau "because we haven't been able to piece together a coherent group to tell us how to do better—how to make mid-course corrections." The Arkansas Business Council had played a major role in keeping Arkansas's education reform from regressing, she said, but neither her husband, the governor, nor the council had succeeded in advancing it. "We haven't been able to follow through . . . because we don't have a critical mass of an intellectual community—public or private—able to tell us how to follow through. We need some place with some resources to help us . . . to let us know how we can take our energy and intelligence and harness them more effectively," she said.[48] After Mrs. Clinton's welcoming remarks, the board turned its attention to learning all that it could about the operations, accomplishments, and problems of Research Atlanta, Inc., the Texas Research League, and the Denver-based Center for the New West. Even before the presentation on the latter, the board had become so convinced that Arkansas needed an organization similar to those operating in Atlanta and Texas that it voted unanimously to recommend, support, and take action to establish a nonprofit, strictly nonpartisan fact-finding entity for Arkansas.

The NAB spent its entire October meeting defining goals and recommending criteria for an Arkansas Research Center with guidance from two resources—officials from the North Carolina Center for Public Policy Research and the Texas Research League.[49] Most of the members' concerns focused on how the center would achieve and maintain credibility for conducting and publishing totally objective research. The board also heard a warning from the North Carolina resource that the choice of an executive director for the center would be the most critical decision made. The North Carolina center had three executive directors before it found the one that could do the job.[50]

According to its 1990 report, the board concluded the center should have a three-year funding commitment of five hundred thousand dollars a year with $350,000 being the level at which it should be incorporated, an office established, and a search for staff begun. All funding should come from private businesses, individuals, organizations, and foundations with none from government. The board asked me to chair the committee to organize the center even though it knew I would be retiring at the end of the year as chief executive officer of First Commercial Bank. In my letter in the report, I revealed that McLarty and Charles D. Morgan Jr. were moving forward with an organizing committee of statewide leaders and had a goal of having the center fully staffed, funded, and operating by the third quarter of 1991.

After I retired from First Commercial Bank, the NAB elevated me from convener to board member and elected me its chairman. The board considered several issues and made recommendations at its 1991 meeting, but the principal business was a progress report on what officially had been named The Arkansas Institute—A Center for Public Policy Research.[51] We had raised one million dollars in cash and pledges from about one hundred individuals as the center's initial endowment. With interest, we expected this amount to cover the first three years of the center's operations.

I recruited Walter Smiley, founder and retired chairman of Systematics, Inc., a New York Stock Exchange–listed company and forerunner to Alltel, Inc., to be the organizing chairman of the center's board of directors—a group of fifty-two that was completed and announced in December. The board's membership touched all bases in terms of regional representation, ethnicity, gender, and interests. McLarty was the organizing board's vice chairman.

Smiley introduced the NAB to William Halter, thirty, a Stanford University Rhodes Scholar who was returning to his native North Little Rock to be president of The Arkansas Institute. Among other posts, Halter had been chief economist for the U.S. Senate Committee on Finance.[52] He confessed he was faced with evaluating "a tremendous quantity" of high-quality resumes from persons wanting staff positions at the institute and that the number of potential study issues was "endless." Smiley warned the NAB that the institute faced an immediate challenge, which eventually may have contributed to its demise—Governor Clinton's race to win the Democratic nomination for president. To avoid jeopardizing the institute's independence and credibility, Smiley said, "we must avoid getting caught up in the Clinton campaign, and we are making extraordinary efforts to see that the perception [of being linked to it] is not there." This was a "mission impossible," however, because Clinton had tapped me to be his chief of staff in the governor's office and McLarty was one of Clinton's closest advisers. The major problem in the eyes of some was that the presidential campaign was so intense it sapped our small, southern, rural state of the energy, leadership, and finances needed to accomplish anything else of significance. There also were those who thought Clinton's election put him in a position to "fix" Arkansas's problems.

Within six months, Halter had been dismissed in a salary dispute with Smiley, and an interim president guided the institute from its office at 620 West Third Street in Little Rock until the board hired Wayne I. Boucher of Riverside, California, in 1993.[53] Boucher certainly seemed to have the credentials for the job, having spent thirty years in policy analysis. The Michigan native had worked for the RAND Corporation, the Institute for the Future, The Futures Group, the Center for Futures Research at the University of California, and Benton International, a management consulting organization in Los Angeles. He also had been deputy director and director of research for the National Commission on Electronic Funds Transfer during the Ford and Carter administrations.[54]

In an interview some five months after he took the job, Boucher told the *Arkansas Democrat-Gazette* that, as a "think tank":

> you want to be independent intellectually. You want to be independent financially. You must have the opportunity to, in the grand sense, question the very nature of the problems as they are given to you. What's the appropriate way of tackling the real issue? That's the question. A think tank is the one that has the freedom to take that stance.[55]

I will say that Boucher was not the right man for the job. There are many who consider hiring a non-Arkansan for such a sensitive post a mistake, but my principal complaint at the time was that Boucher was too much the "futurist" and not rooted in the "here and now" of a state he did not understand. Dr. John Ahlen, president of the Arkansas Science and Technology Authority, believed the institute could not have survived as a pure research organization but needed partners to design action plans and implement research results.[56] On at least two occasions, NAB members robustly discussed whether the institute should stick to research or be an advocacy group as well; they never reached a consensus.

When the NAB convened in First Commercial Bank's boardroom in October 1992, most Arkansans were in a state of suspended animation as they watched their governor criss-cross the country, waging a credible campaign against a sitting president for the world's greatest political prize. Would Clinton make it? If so, what would it mean for his native state? The answer to the first question would be the only one known by the time the board published its annual report. And when Clinton won, the NAB decided to dedicate its 1992 report to him.

Against this backdrop, the board turned its attention to analyzing where the state had been historically, where it was in 1992 in terms of population, economics, governance, infrastructure, and education, and what its future could be. Its findings reflected concern about the Delta and the need for cooperation to pry the region from its economic depression, an assertion that Arkansas must continue to reform its education systems, and that the institute should make assessing the state's research posture one of its first missions.[57] In September 1993, the Institute published a report titled *Federal R & D Expenditures in Arkansas: Today's Realities, Tomorrow's Options,* in which Richard A. Huddleston found that in 1990, Arkansas ranked forty-third among the fifty states and the District of Columbia in the amount of federal research and development funding received ($85.7 million, excluding R & D plant). Only 14 percent of the amount went to industry while about 61 percent went to federal agencies located in Arkansas.[58] In June 1993, the institute announced that eleven new members had joined its board, bringing its size to fifty-six. Aside from the release of the study on Arkansas's position in federal research funding, this was the last publicity the institute received, and it eventually faded into oblivion.

In 1993, the board tackled the question of what Arkansas could and should do with all the potential the panel had identified through the years, particularly now that it had a native son in the White House. There appeared to be no consensus among Arkansans themselves about what they wanted their state to do or be.[59] Did the state need additional vehicles or tools to help maximize its potential? Specifically, should Arkansas become the thirty-fourth state in the country to establish an office in Washington, D.C.? After all, the board was acutely aware the state had tried this before during Clinton's first two-year term as governor in 1979–80, but the endeavor had succumbed quickly to politics.[60] No consensus developed at the board's 1993 session, and it decided to reconvene in April 1994 for further deliberations. The members called for examples of some specific meaningful projects on which a Washington office could prove helpful.

The board found it ironic that the Arkansas Economic Development Commission operated offices in Brussels, Tokyo, Taiwan, and Mexico City but the state had no office in the capital of the United States. It eventually concluded that an office, carefully established with the guidance and support of the state's congressional delegation, could:

- strengthen Arkansas' research and development funding position;
- provide valuable coordination and assistance for such specific projects as the Arkansas Aerospace Education Center, which the Board endorsed, and development of the high-technology biomedical corridor between Pine Bluff and Little Rock, the decade-old proposal for which the Board reaffirmed its commitment; and,
- Help Arkansas obtain additional highway funding once the state decided what it wanted to do in this regard.[61]

Gov. Jim Guy Tucker, who rose from lieutenant governor when Clinton resigned to go to the White House, probably would have followed through with a proposal to establish an Arkansas office in Washington, D.C., but he gave higher priority to trying to modernize Arkansas's 1874 Constitution and finding the funds to repair and upgrade the state's crumbling highways, particularly the interstates.

Tucker told the board that the state government had enough revenues—if spent carefully—to finance all of its needs except highways. With this prompting, the NAB focused on highway funding issues at its October 1994 meeting. In one sitting, the board was no more successful at unraveling the Gordian Knot of highway financing than anyone else had been and had to settle for publishing an informational report that gave an overview of Arkansas's history regarding roads. The report described the needs, as outlined by the state Highway and Transportation Department, for state matching funds to build Interstate 49 as a replacement for U.S. 71 between Alma and the Louisiana line in west Arkansas and for Interstate 69, part of a Canada-to-Mexico corridor that would cut across impoverished southeast Arkansas, and listed funding options the state might consider.

Tucker finally decided on a massive highway bond issue, but the voters overwhelmingly rejected it in January 1996. By this time, however, the people had lost faith in Tucker because he had been indicted by a federal grand jury at the behest of an independent counsel who had been appointed to investigate alleged wrongdoings associated with the involvement of the Clintons in a long-ago Madison County land project called Whitewater. The charges against Tucker had nothing to do with his performance in public office but were related exclusively to business dealings in the 1980s when he was in the private sector. Later convicted, he resigned as governor July 15, 1996. In June 1999, Arkansas voters authorized the Highway Commission to sell up to $575 million in general obligation bonds to rehabilitate about 60 percent of the interstate highways in the state over five years. It is arguable this never would have occurred if Congress had not passed a new transportation law in 1998 that allowed states to pledge future federal aid dedicated to interstate maintenance to amortize bonds.

First Commercial Bank marked the silver anniversary meeting of the NAB by hosting a special event and invited all of the state's former governors, including the one who was president of the United States at the time, to join the sitting governor, Jim Guy Tucker, in addressing the group. All of them appeared in person except for Clinton, who sent a specially prepared video.[62] Former governor Sid McMath, eighty-three at the time and retired from his law practice, had no political considerations to observe, and he brought the NAB members to their feet with an unprecedented standing ovation when he stepped beyond the agenda and addressed the issue of racism with this ringing declaration:

> The right of every man, woman, and child to an equal opportunity and equal chance to do his or her best in our competitive society is the message of America. The dignity, worth and rights of every individual citizen is the secret of America's greatness. If we will accept this idea, this truth in our hearts, confirm it in our minds, teach it in our homes and schools, apply it in our communities and workplaces, we will do more to remove the division between our people than all the resolutions and laws that can be passed by the Congress of the United States.[63]

The governors' presentations about their visions for Arkansas's future stimulated what the board's annual report said was "one of the most vigorous discussions within memory" among the members, but it was not because of substantial disagreements. Rather, there was "immediate and thunderous consensus" that continued improvement of public education must be Arkansas's foremost commitment. Economist Dr. David W. Mullins Jr., son of the late University of Arkansas president, former vice chairman of the Federal Reserve System's Board of Governors and a partner in Long Term Capital Management in Greenwich, Connecticut, summed up the views when he declared:

> We know now how to make economies grow; it's through productivity, and education is the key to productivity. The financial returns for [having] an education are multiplying dramatically because new technology systems are rapidly devaluing low-skill work and widening the gap in wage earnings.[64]

It was not unusual for something said at one meeting to be the catalyst for the subject at the next NAB meeting. In 1995, for example, a subtle difference surfaced among the governors about whether Arkansas should continue low-tech development or emphasize high-tech pursuits and opportunities. Frank White in particular said Arkansas always had been low-tech and should play to this by doing it better than anyone else through more development of value-added processing of agricultural products, including furniture plants that used the state's timber resources. The others, especially Pryor and Tucker, said agriculture should not be neglected but that Arkansas needed to train its people for higher-paying jobs, and this meant high-tech jobs. High technology became the board's 1996 topic, making it the first group in Arkansas to confront and to make an objective, independent assessment of these questions: Does Arkansas have a sufficient base to target industries that intensively use high technology and to foster the development of industries that produce goods and services in either advanced telecommunications or biotechnology or both? If the answer was yes, what did the state have to do to promote this development?[65]

The meeting was awash with information and differing viewpoints until board member Dr. Mary Good, now under secretary of technology for the U.S. Department of Commerce, took the lectern to deliver the keynote speech at the board's traditional luncheon at the Little Rock Club.[66] The former president of the American Chemical Society galvanized the NAB when she declared in part:

> To participate in the high-quality, high-paying jobs of today and tomorrow and to generate significant economic growth . . . [Arkansas] must focus on the acquisition of technology intensive

industries and on the exploitation of its investment in education—higher education particularly—to build indigenous companies with high technology products and research and development activities . . . some might say this approach is too ambitious and Arkansas does not have the infrastructure in place to support it . . . [but the] state must begin to build this base if it hopes to provide its residents an opportunity to share in the fruits of the worldwide market for technology and information-based products and services.

If it did not do this, Dr. Good warned, Arkansas would face a return to "backwater" or "colony" status among the states. "I believe a state that has made as much progress in job growth and poverty reduction as Arkansas over the last 20 years has the momentum and possible mindset to move ahead of other states that started with many more assets," she said.[67]

The board returned to its base beliefs—the points it had made repeatedly for more than a quarter of a century in many different ways—that the businesses and industries Arkansas wants are drawn to areas with strong education and research institutions. The existence in Arkansas of "better-than-you-realize" institutions provides the state with the potential to develop a medical biotechnology cluster in central Arkansas (anchored by UAMS and NCTR). To this, the 1997 board added the potential of an agri-biotechnology corridor developing in northwest Arkansas through the strength of the University of Arkansas. This represents the last time the NAB specifically mentioned the biomedical corridor for which it saw so much potential between the University of Arkansas for Medical Sciences in Little Rock and the National Center for Toxicological Research in Jefferson, north of Pine Bluff.

No such corridor shows signs of developing, and board members were fond of saying among themselves that it was because no "nine-hundred-pound gorilla" ever stepped forward to take the lead as Luther Hodges and Terry Sanford did with Research Triangle Park in North Carolina. This does not mean that no one remembers the concept. As recently as June 2001, Bob Lancaster wrote in his *Arkansas Times* column headlined an "assortment of lesser bests":

Best high-tech corridor that never quite highed, teched, or corridored: The medico-government super complex that was supposed to develop from Little Rock down I-530 to Pine Bluff, anchored by UAMS and the NCTR. Whatever happened to that rascal?[68]

The National Advisory Board revisited the issue of tourism in 1997 at a time when Gov. Mike Huckabee was using it as a tool to promote retirement in the state.[69] The board found that much had been accomplished in twenty-two years because tourists and travelers to Arkansas totaled about eighteen million annually in the mid-1990s and they spent $3.2 billion compared to $840.3 million in 1974. Retired U.S. Senator David Pryor challenged the board in 1997 to help Arkansas "raise its [tourism] game to a higher level." Formally, the board came to one conclusion. Actually, it was a reiteration of a declaration made in the early 1970s—that Arkansas must protect and enhance its natural and cultural resources.[70] Enhancement, the board explained, means an attitudinal change to keep the state clean (less litter) and to recognize opportunities and encourage innovation.

First Commercial Bank was being acquired by Birmingham-based Regions Bank when the National Advisory Board convened in 1998. The meeting became a sounding board for the views and findings of a group of businessmen known as The Murphy Commission that had spent almost three years studying Arkansas state government with an eye toward applying sound business principles where applicable to make it smaller, more efficient, and accountable, and to make the educational system more effective.[71] According to its 1998 report, the NAB was amazed at the effort and time the group had put into the study. In truth, however, the board was not overly impressed with some of the ideas presented, especially those on education that included school vouchers. True to its tradition of remaining positive, however, the board found three of The Murphy Commission's recommendations worthy of endorsement: that the state adopt performance-based budgeting, that it find a form of compensating state employees to reward extraordinary job performance and not just time they had spent on the state payroll, and that it adopt Activities–Based Costing (ABC) accounting.[72]

Hearts were heavy at the meeting. Board member the Rev. John Maury Allin had died, creating a void—one he had filled by tempering the occasional hard-nosed approaches of both presenters and his colleagues with a reminder of their humanity and that of Arkansas's people. Further, NAB members recognized the meeting was to be its last because Regions Bank did not want to say "no" if other states in its service region requested the establishment of similar groups for them. Still others felt the NAB had served its purpose. The board, however, had the luxury of examining issues rationally and purely from the evidence, without having to consider the often strange political permutations that make Arkansas what it is. As James "Skip" Rutherford of Little Rock, a civic leader and public relations company executive, said, the greatest service the NAB performed for Arkansas was "to raise and discuss important issues that otherwise might have been neglected."[73]

As mentioned previously, the NAB had long supported establishment of the Aerospace Education Center. In February 1990, I was named chairman of the campaign to fund the proposed center. Dick Holbert of Central Flying Service was named vice chairman. The center was to be located at the south end of Adams Field, the national airport for Little Rock. At the outset, the Little Rock School District leadership recommended a high school at the site, sponsored by the district. The metropolitan supervisor for the district, Eugene Reville, recommended a combination aerospace high school/aviation museum to the federal court overseeing desegregation compliance in the school district. In March 1989, the legislature passed Act 716 to underwrite a $1.8 million challenge grant and in April 1990, a Little Rock School District millage proposal passed, providing six million dollars for construction of the new school.

In rapid succession, the Arkansas Aviation Historical Society began a $6.5 million fundraising campaign, the Little Rock School District submitted a four million dollar application for a magnet school grant, the Little Rock Airport Commission donated 19.8 acres for ninety-nine years at one dollar per year for the site, and the Winthrop Rockefeller Foundation approved a five hundred thousand dollar grant. By December 1991, private pledges totaled $2,233,197 and public pledges amounted to two million dollars. The Central Arkansas Library System also approved a library branch for the east side of the site. Significantly, an IMAX theater was included in the plan—the only one of its kind in Arkansas. New leadership in the school district decided, after much study and debate, that the district could not justify the expense of a school at the site. The project continued, however, and opened with the library, the IMAX theater, and the museum in January 1995.

In early 1993, I joined Claude Ballard, retired partner of Goldman-Sachs, a major New York brokerage firm, and John Steuri, retired CEO of Systematics Incorporated, in attempting to create an Arkansas-based venture capital company. Over a period of several months, they encountered interest from more than two dozen potential investors, and explored leadership roles in the company with French Hill, most recently a member of President George H. W. Bush's international banking team, and Doug Martin of Stephens Incorporated, a member of the venture capital operation of this leading investment banking firm. Neither overture to these prospective operators matured and by the early fall of 1993, we put the effort on hold.

Meanwhile, in the early 1990s, national trends in health care reached the borders of Arkansas in the form of health maintenance organizations. While the spread of HMOs was not pervasive at the time, providers in the market, such as Baptist Health System and selected physicians in Arkansas, invested in the formation of this venture (Health Advantage HMO). Shortly thereafter, other HMOs entered the marketplace with the American Preferred Provider Organization (PPO) and Complete Health (later acquired by United Healthcare). After market leader Blue Cross/Blue Shield (BCBS) offered competitive bids for a tertiary care facility in Little Rock to anchor its statewide network offerings, competition became intense. Not unexpectedly, BCBS chose the larger facility, Baptist Health, to be its partner. Additionally Baptist Health entered into a joint venture-equity arrangement with BCBS around the Health Advantage HMO product. This joint venture created a powerful adversary—the state's largest hospital system at the time and the state's most dominant health insurance company.

These developments left the number two hospital system in the state, St. Vincent Health System, in a largely defensive position. In a competitive move, St. Vincent solicited bids from national and regional leaders in the HMO market. Finalists in the bidding process were Healthsource Incorporated, Humana, and Complete Health. St. Vincent chose Healthsource of Manchester, New Hampshire, to be its corporate partner in the proposed HMO, Healthsource Arkansas, Incorporated. I was invited to become president of this new organization that would combine St. Vincent's strong reputation with Healthsource's expertise in HMO management and development.

To acquaint myself with the New Hampshire partner and its multistate operation, Connie and I visited New Hampshire in early September 1993. We toured the state from north to south while there for that exploratory visit and spent a delightful weekend at The Balsams, a historic hotel in the White Mountains in extreme northern New Hampshire. From its elevated golf course, we could see Maine, Vermont, and Ontario in Canada. The founder and president of Healthsource, Dr. Norm Payson, was a Dartmouth-educated physician with considerable experience in operating a California HMO created by Kaiser Permanente. Healthsource had operated HMOs in several eastern seaboard states from New Hampshire to Georgia. The organization was well known for its joint-venture partnerships with flagship health systems in "secondary" or rural markets, such as Arkansas. Arkansas was to be the first partnership for Healthsource west of the Mississippi River. My comfort level with the corporate direction of Healthsource at the time was good. The company was led by a corporate board composed entirely of physicians and the organization was focused on states similar to Arkansas, such as South Carolina, New Hampshire, and Maine. I was impressed and returned home committed to undertaking the job of CEO of the Arkansas joint venture working with the leadership of St. Vincent and, of course, Healthsource.

I came aboard knowing that HMOs were designed to reduce the employer's cost of healthcare for employees. I soon learned that the mechanic was to reduce cost by contracting with a few doctors in specialized areas to whom this HMO's business would be referred and from whom reduced charges would be imposed in exchange for having the employees directed to them for health care services. This was a national trend, which was making inroads in Arkansas in the early 1990s. Ideally, the HMO would be able to meet all employer health needs within cost constraints that would contain employer health care costs, supply adequate health care services for the employees, and do so at a profit for the HMO.

The Arkansas leadership included the talent of St. Vincent Infirmary— specifically Joe Timmons and John Ryan. Terri Schilling, a rising star in the managed care industry with an accounting background, came to us by way of Healthsource. In total, the fledgling organization had seven employees. Our first task was to secure regulatory approval from the Arkansas Insurance Department as a licensed Health Maintenance Organization. This was achieved in the fall of 1993 with an initial approval to market HMO products in seven counties in central Arkansas. On January 1, 1994, Healthsource Arkansas enrolled its first HMO client, some four thousand employees and dependents of our partner, St. Vincent.

To afford Healthsource Arkansas a running start, we agreed to buy a well known third-party claims administrator in Arkansas, Spradley and Coker, Inc. (S&C), to help implement the sale of group health plans to employers. S&C clients were primarily self-funded, with HMO products offered as optional plans in a very competitive marketplace. The idea was two-fold: give Healthsource an immediate market presence with S&C's fifty thousand members and provide Healthsource with, as described by Norm Payson, a "conveyer belt strategy." This meant that PPO clients of S&C would be moved from the loosely controlled PPO product into the more tightly steered HMO product offered by Healthsource. If successful, this would generate a huge top line revenue stream and create synergies for profit making. However, it became clear over time that the conversion strategy was flawed.

Most of the S&C clients were in a loosely managed PPO because they wanted to be. They did not want network restrictions and benefit limitations and tight medical management restrictions. Ironically, the popular national insurance products today are PPO products, due to the same trend we saw in Arkansas with S&C—tighter networks and benefit limitations.

The major competitor for Arkansas's HMOs was BCBS, with its partner, Baptist Health of Little Rock. Additionally, there was an emerging effort sponsored by the University of Arkansas for Medical Sciences campus called QualChoice Arkansas. Our employee numbers grew, but our profit expectations narrowed and it became clear to our doctors and health care providers that HMO profitability depended upon reducing medical expenses as well as patient services.

By the end of its first year of operations, Healthsource Arkansas HMO was targeting rapid growth of its network and membership on a statewide basis. The organization boasted contracts with roughly twenty hospitals and over 1,500 physicians. The job of staffing at Healthsource Arkansas entailed employment of experienced healthcare talent to sell the services and see that the obligations of healthcare were met.

St. Vincent's impressive reputation and statewide outreach with sales guidance from Jim Spradley and Daryl Coker got the company off and running and by the end of 1994—a period of less than eighteen months from when the company started—Healthsource Arkansas had approximately one hundred employers signed up serving seventeen thousand employees under contracts, plus two thousand participating doctors.

Although Healthsource Arkansas flourished from an enrollment standpoint, finances were not growing proportionately. This was due primarily to the market driving premiums. Arkansas had some of the lowest premiums in the country while being one of the two most "unhealthy" states in the union—not a good mixture for insurance risk/profit. Healthsource, however, continued to grow. By July 1995 we had enrolled 23,000 members and had 135 employees doing business in nearly thirty counties.

To combat a struggling bottom line, a strategy emerged with which I was uncomfortable. This was to enroll as few doctors as possible in a given market with the understanding that their patients would receive limited services in order to circumscribe charges against the HMO and thus enhance its profitability. Many of these provider network limitations were part of a national and local trend in the business and were imposed in response to actions by competitors such as United Healthcare and Prudential. Still, my uneasiness about this conflict was heightened by the concerns of doctor friends, many of whom had been clients of mine, and the impact that it was expected to have on their practices.

A major reason for Healthsource Arkansas's decline was the fact that the company, from a corporate perspective, became too concerned with the bottom line. This stems from two fronts. First, the major contract in the major city in Arkansas (Healthsource and St. Vincent) was largely unfair to St. Vincent and created animosity within the partnership. The second was the motivation of Healthsource to clean up its books in anticipation of a corporate merger with a larger national insurance firm, CIGNA, which reduced financial and strategic support for the venture. That latter factor was out of the control of local management.

By mid-spring 1995, the matter was resolved for me when UALR chancellor Charles Hathaway invited me to serve as dean of the law school for two years beginning in July. I said yes and began working toward a smooth transition for new leadership of Healthsource by June 30. In 1997, Healthsource and its subsidiaries were acquired by CIGNA for $1.7 billion. By 2000, the company announced it was leaving Arkansas—a move that left the state with just five HMOs. Today, very little of Healthsource or HMOs exist in Arkansas. Fewer than ten percent of Arkansans receive their insurance benefits through the model today.

In the mid 1980s, group health plans averaged 20 to 25 percent annual cost increases. The entrance of PPOs and HMOs reduced the increases to single digits, but at the cost of limiting patient choice. While more insurers have gone back to the practice of providing more options, costs continue to increase for individuals and businesses alike. This trend will inevitably result in greater cost shifts to employees and more employers reducing or even eliminating coverage for their workers.

After I left Healthsource in early 1996, the Little Rock School Board appointed Cora D. McHenry and me to serve as cochairs of a citizens' committee to study and recommend changes in the district's school desegregation plan. Our charge was to review the district's court-approved plan and suggest modifications to the board. Given the long periods of litigation, previous negotiation attempts between the parties involved in the lawsuit tended to "deteriorate into arguments and little was accomplished."[74] Our job was to provide realistic recommendations for improving the quality of education for all children, promote stability in the school district, and continue to improve parent and community support for the schools. With a lot of hard work on the part of all participants, we issued a report that recommended a broad vision and strategies for improving the schools. A subsequent court-approved plan incorporated many of our suggestions and recommendations.

My strong support for education extended to a private school, Philander Smith College—a historically black college—where I chaired a capital campaign beginning in 1999. My fellow campaign members included such educational, civic, and business leaders as Shelby Woods, Alice Abson, Bishop Janice Riggle Huie, Robert Shoptaw, Robert Birch, Doyle and Raye Rogers, Bishop Steven Arnold, and John Riggs IV. The committee also included members of the college's board of trustees—Sherman E. Tate, Elijah Harris, Charles Donaldson, and Charles Stewart—along with then Philander Smith president Dr. Trudie Kibbe Reed and Dr. Stephen J. Schafer, dean of institutional advancement. Our goal was to build a new twelve million dollar library for the college. The campaign reached an unprecedented goal of $30.5 million in April 2002. So far, the campaign has successfully raised funds to build two new buildings (the Donald W. Reynolds Library and Technology Center and the Harry R. Kendall Science and Health Mission Center), renovate another (the gymnasium, which became the new Sherman E. Tate Student Activity Center), and provide funding for three endowments, two building maintenance funds, and a faculty and staff salary endowment.

My experience in facilitating communications with such entities as the participants in the school desegregation lawsuit led to my being asked to do the same concerning the politically challenged merger of the Little Rock and North Little Rock water systems. By successfully bridging the divide of interests and equity, the cities were able to forge a consolidation agreement—a first in Arkansas's history for water systems owned by different municipalities. While the merger initially posed legal and civic challenges, it ended up providing a "win-win" situation for the central Arkansas area. The entity, Central Arkansas Water, is a core partner in a regional initiative to secure a needed future water source for the area.

I remember a framed quote that stood prominent in Gov. Bill Clinton's office that read, "The way to save your soul is through public service." I've always believed that—not only to save individuals' souls, but also to save the community's soul. I strongly believe that it is up to each individual in the community to do his or her part to help make it a better place for all. This belief was one reason why I agreed to join the governor's staff when he asked.

Chapter Seven

Governor Clinton's Chief of Staff

William Jefferson "Bill" Clinton, who had been Arkansas's governor continuously since January 1983, either really did not know whether he would seek reelection or was just being coy in late 1989 and early 1990, because no amount of cajoling could get him to disclose his plans. This left journalists scrambling for "news," such as the article the *Arkansas Gazette* published based on interviews with some of Clinton's close friends. Each of them said Clinton could win reelection but some were not certain he *should* run. For example, then state Rep. David Matthews of Springdale was quoted as saying:

> I think Bill Clinton has a great chance to be president of the United States in the late 1990s because I think by that time the nation will have come around to his thinking on what we must do for education in this country. But by staying governor, he leaves himself open to mounting problems and potential failures in Arkansas—with the legislature, primarily.[1]

There was no lack of individuals who wanted Clinton's job. Thomas C. McRae, president of the Winthrop Rockefeller Foundation, already had announced his candidacy for the Democratic nomination, and Attorney General Steve Clark was ready to run and would have if he had not self-destructed because of the lies he told to support use of his state credit card for personal business. Then there was Jim Guy Tucker, who had said in September 1989 that he was considering running either for governor or to regain the seat in the U.S. House of Representatives from the Second Congressional District that he held for one term in the mid-1970s. This was the "sure" seat Tucker had given up to wage an all-out battle for the U.S. Senate in 1978, only to be defeated in the Democratic primary runoff by Gov. David Pryor.

On February 19, 1990, Tucker called an afternoon press conference at the Legacy Hotel. With wife Betty and their two daughters at his side and fifty supporters in the room, Tucker announced he would seek the Democratic nomination for governor. "I think he's had a good 10 years as governor now, and I really think that's long enough," he said of Clinton.[2] On the same day Tucker's announcement appeared in the newspapers, the results of the season's first poll were published. Of 246 potential Democratic voters surveyed, 68 percent said they would vote for Clinton, 20 percent were for Tucker, 7 percent for McRae, and the remaining 5 percent were undecided.[3] Of 160 potential Republican voters who were polled, 53 percent favored U.S. Rep. Tommy Robinson of the Second Congressional District, who had switched parties mid-term, and 40 percent were for Sheffield Nelson, the former president of Arkla, Incorporated. Clinton reportedly felt strongly that the state had to be "saved" from Robinson, and such poll results could only have strengthened this resolve.

Tucker represented a formidable opponent for Clinton. Harvard-educated with dimpled good looks, Tucker began his political career at age twenty-seven with a victory as prosecuting attorney for Arkansas's largest judicial district—the sixth, comprised of Pulaski and Perry counties. A mere two years later, he was elected state attorney general and served two two-year terms in a position that he used to build a reputation as a consumer advocate. When U.S. Rep. Wilbur D. Mills retired in order to recover fully from the alcoholism that had disgraced him, Tucker campaigned indefatigably for the seat and defeated five other Democrats without a primary runoff.

Tucker was always a man in a hurry, and he took on two other Democrats in 1978 for the seat that had been held until his death the year before by the powerful veteran of the Senate, John McClellan. The two Democrats were then Gov. David Pryor and then U.S. Rep. Ray Thornton of the Fourth Congressional District. Thornton was a nephew of W. R. "Witt" and Jackson T. Stephens. Most pundits were expecting a runoff between Pryor and Thornton. They were wrong; the runoff was between Pryor and Tucker, and Pryor won.

Tucker was not from a wealthy family and fretted constantly about being in debt. He entered private law practice in Little Rock and did not surface again politically until 1982, when Clinton was trying to stage a comeback as governor after being ousted from the job in 1980 by the stunning win of Democrat-turned-Republican businessman Frank White. The 1982 Democratic primary was crowded, and Tucker placed third with 23 percent of the vote in a field of five behind Clinton and Lt. Gov. Joe Purcell after conducting a campaign that left him $250,000 in debt.[4]

Tucker then concentrated on becoming financially secure as a senior partner in the law firm of Mitchell, Williams, Selig, and Tucker, where he represented such blue-chip clients as Arkla and Arkansas Power and Light Company. He also went into real estate, buying apartment buildings that he converted into condominiums, among other projects, and followed his attorney wife's lead into what was then just a promising new technology—cable television. Mostly on personal loans, the Tuckers expanded a fledgling cable operation in Pulaski County's Crystal Hill area into an empire ranging from the Dallas–Fort Worth area in Texas to Florida and finally to Great Britain. The venture made the Tuckers multimillionaires.[5] Unknown to the general public, Tucker also spent much of this period fighting for his life against two genetically based diseases, one of which cost him his colon and brought with it the likelihood he one day would require a liver transplant to survive.

John Brummett, political columnist for the *Arkansas Gazette,* wrote that Tucker's announcement, even in the absence of knowing Clinton's plans for the presidency, "does change the complexion of the race for governor. No longer can Clinton expect to coast to the general election." Tucker later said he was trying to "psych" Clinton out of running for reelection.

Less than two weeks after Tucker's announcement, Clinton stood on a platform before some five hundred cheering supporters in the state Capitol rotunda and said he would seek another four-year term as governor even though "the fire of an election no longer burns in me."[6] He acknowledged that having a Tommy Robinson in the governor's office was a frightening prospect to him, but explained that "in the end, I decided that I just didn't want to stop doing the job."

Reporters made much of two points: that if he won another term and served it out, Clinton would eclipse Orval Faubus as Arkansas's longest-serving governor (Faubus served six two-year terms, 1955–67; in 1984, Arkansas voters adopted a constitutional amendment giving constitutional officers four-year terms), and the only person who knew Clinton's decision before he announced it was his wife, First Lady Hillary Rodham Clinton.[7]

Within the month, Clinton named state Rep. Gloria Cabe, D-Little Rock, as his campaign manager, the first time since 1982 that he had someone other than Betsey Wright in this position.[8] In early February, Cabe had endured press criticism for running up a bill of nearly seventeen thousand dollars in 1989 for travel and other expenses as Clinton's nonpaid education aide.[9] As conditions later proved, neither her role in Clinton's campaign nor as his education aide would endear Cabe to Tucker.

Tucker appeared undeterred by Clinton's reelection announcement. On an hour-long, paid political broadcast on twenty-five radio stations across the state on March 3, Tucker said the sales tax on groceries was regressive but was a "necessary evil" because the estimated $125 million it produced was a huge percentage of the state's annual general revenues. But he also complained the state government was bloated with some two hundred million dollars in wasteful spending that he pledged to eliminate with better management.[10] He made headlines again in mid-March when he proposed creating a basic or "meat and potatoes" group health insurance pool for the estimated five hundred thousand Arkansans who lacked health insurance because they could not afford it individually and their employers did not offer the benefit.[11] A few days later, Tucker had lunch with twenty-four members of the Little Rock Club, a group of central Arkansas leaders who perceived an anti-development, anti–central Arkansas bias in the legislature. Tucker declined to criticize the General Assembly, saying its members were "hungry for executive branch leadership they can work with to solve these problems." He repeated what was becoming the theme of his campaign—that Clinton was putting the state's problems on the back burner while he pursued national ambitions. "You've got to stay here and tend shop. You've got to be governor all the time," Tucker insisted.[12]

Tucker was calculating; his remarks were timed to coincide with Clinton's visit to New Orleans, where he was being elected chairman of the Democratic Leadership Council. The council was formed in 1985 to steer the national party away from the more liberal positions voters rejected when they chose Ronald Reagan to be president in 1980 and 1984 and George H. W. Bush in 1988. As expected, the council was dominated by southern Democrats who considered themselves to be moderates or conservatives.

On his election as chairman, Clinton declared victory in the council's quest to steer the party toward a new and moderate national philosophy. "I think it's fair to say the battle's over and we won . . . [the council must] move beyond the old liberal-conservative debate, and a lot of our policies have both elements," he was quoted as saying.[13] Long acknowledged to be a "policy wonk," Clinton went on to tick off the liberal and conservative elements in a litany of council proposals such as welfare reform and expanding tax credits for the working poor.

As a die-hard Democrat, I watched these developments with growing consternation. A political blood bath was shaping up—one I feared would do great harm to the party and to the state. I was not close to Tucker but had been friends with Clinton since the young law professor had come so close to unseating Republican U.S. Rep. John Paul Hammerschmidt in the Third Congressional District in 1974. I had contributed to Clinton's campaign in that race and made calls and contributions on the candidate's behalf when he ran for and won the attorney general post in 1976 and governor in 1978. I also stood in for Clinton at a major Jonesboro campaign function in 1982, when the young Democrat was intent on retaking the governor's office from Frank White. White attended the event, but Clinton had a conflict. I had sensed from the day I met the "man from Hope" that he had his sights set on the White House and I viewed the Rhodes Scholar as the one person in Arkansas who had the education, experience, intelligence, and capability to reach the Oval Office.

As my concern grew, I turned as I often did to a long-time friend and former law partner, state Senator Ben Allen, a Democrat who had represented Little Rock in either the House or Senate since 1967. Together we decided to visit Clinton to see if he would allow us to explore the possibility of trying to persuade Tucker to run for lieutenant governor instead of governor. The lieutenant governor's seat was open because the incumbent, Winston Bryant, was running for attorney general.

Clinton approved the overture, and when we returned to our offices, I called J. W. "Buddy" Benafield, a wealthy businessman and Tucker's best friend, while Allen telephoned Maurice Mitchell, a Tucker law partner. We regarded both Benafield and Mitchell as good friends and knew they would be the best conduits for relaying our offer to the candidate. We argued that Tucker could not beat Clinton but that he could win the lieutenant governor nomination "without any real opposition," and we offered to restore the money Tucker had spent on his gubernatorial bid so far if he would agree to withdraw.

It was just a matter of days before Allen and I had the answer we were seeking. At about 8 p.m. on March 26, Tucker faxed a five-paragraph statement to news organizations in which he said that staying in the race against Clinton "would result in a highly divisive campaign, one that would be counter-productive to the best interests of our state and my party, at a time when Arkansas needs unity, not turmoil."[14] He said he would file instead as a Democratic candidate for lieutenant governor. The statement went on to say that in seeking the office of lieutenant governor, Tucker hoped he could be "a positive force in shaping public debate and solving the important issues that face us and our legislature." Lest anyone think he would be a rollover for Clinton, Tucker added in what could be seen in retrospect as a warning:

> there is only one requirement for this office and that is that its holder be qualified to serve as governor. I am qualified for that eventuality and will happily use my talents to assist whomever the next governor may be when he seeks positive change and oppose him when he is wrong.[15]

In a campaign-finance report, Tucker said he had collected $85,309 for his bid for the Democratic nomination for lieutenant governor, which included $15,043 of his own money. I fulfilled my promise to help restore the money Tucker had spent on his race for governor, but as I recall, the amount that I paid him was only about fifteen thousand dollars.

I went into high gear on Clinton's behalf again in early August 1990 when Gloria Cabe and Bruce Lindsey needed help selling tickets to a fundraiser black-tie dinner-dance planned for August 25 at the Excelsior Hotel. Only about fifty tickets had been sold. We put in a call for help to Marilyn Porter of Little Rock. "We made a good team," Porter recalled, telling how I approached contributors on a "friend-to-friend" basis.[16] Together we filled the Excelsior's ballroom, raising about six hundred thousand dollars. It also was the last time Arkansas Democrats had a unified event, Porter recalled.

The primary for lieutenant governor did not unfold as I had envisioned. The field was crowded with seven actual or potential candidates when Tucker filed for the office March 27. Wealthy Little Rock ophthalmologist Dr. Hampton Roy was considered the frontrunner before Tucker announced. Roy revealed he had to reconsider after Tucker filed, telling an *Arkansas Gazette* reporter that, "I'm not scared of a fight, but, at the same time, I don't think it's fair to commit your staff and volunteers to genocide."[17] Roy stayed in the race. By mid-May, KATV-TV, Channel 7 in Little Rock, was reporting its polls were showing a shrinking gap between Tucker and Roy. Tucker still led by a wide margin, but the spread was now 53 percent to 29 percent—down from 55 to 23 in an April poll. "The trend indicates a possible runoff in the seven-candidate primary race," *Gazette* reporter Anne Farris opined.[18]

Tucker's last campaign contributions and expenditures report filed with the secretary of state's office before the primary showed the notoriously frugal candidate had infused his campaign for lieutenant governor with $118,660 of his own money while Roy had put $250,000 out of his own pocket into the endeavor. Overall, Tucker reported total campaign donations of $215,829 while Roy said he had collected $322,984. Both figures include the amounts the men had contributed to their own campaigns. Tucker aide Sherry Walker said her candidate regretted the amounts being spent, "but we felt compelled to maintain a similar presence [to Roy's] on television and radio." She noted "It was Hamp Roy who vowed to spend whatever it takes" to top Tucker.[19] Whether Tucker would win the nomination without a runoff provided one of the dramas on the night of May 29. Although the *Gazette* said he "squeaked" through,[20] Tucker took the nomination with 53.5 percent of the vote.[21] But to do it, according to the reports he filed later, Tucker had to spend $473,788, of which $369,746 was his own money.[22] There was a primary runoff for lieutenant governor on the Republican side, however, and it gleaned some national attention. To save face, Arkansas Republicans had to scramble to make sure that erstwhile neo-Nazi Ralph Forbes of London (Pope County) did not best the party's choice, Kenneth "Muskie" Harris, a thirty-six-year-old black businessman who had been a defensive back for the Arkansas Razorbacks. The party succeeded, and Harris became Tucker's general election opponent while Sheffield Nelson, aided by Democrats who "crossed over" to vote in the Republican primary, stopped Robinson in the gubernatorial primary and set his sights on Clinton in the governor's race.

As expected, Tucker coasted to a win over Harris in November with 494,943 ballots or 73.92 percent of the vote.[23] In the governor's race, except for a last-minute television advertising buy that attempted to brand Clinton as a "tax-and-spend liberal" and frightened the governor's camp, Nelson's campaign really did not get off the ground. The Democrat was assured another four years in office with a solid 57.49 percent to 42.49 percent win over Nelson.[24] Tucker still had a debt of $399,029.36 for the 1990 campaign as late as October 1991, all of which was his money. Legislators, lobbyists, and supporters hosted a fundraiser on November 14, 1991, to help erase some of the red ink.[25]

Clinton's victory catapulted him back into the national picture as a presidential prospect, but he denied he was interested. Mike Gauldin, Clinton's press secretary, said the governor had "made it clear to the Democratic leadership that he is tied to a four-year term" as governor.[26] If so, Paul Barton of the *Gazette*'s Washington bureau observed, pundits in the nation's capital apparently hadn't gotten the word or were choosing to ignore it. Barton went on to quote a Democratic polling expert as saying that many had expected Clinton to have a "tough time" being reelected, and they had to be impressed with the way he "rose to the occasion."

Political columnist Max Brantley examined Tucker's future later in the month, explaining to his readers that the former attorney general and congressman was not about to stop with being lieutenant governor—that he was aiming for governor. Although the lieutenant governor's only constitutional roles were to preside over the Senate when it was in session and to be acting governor when the governor was out of state, Tucker made no secret of his desire to be involved actively in legislation on such matters as education, teacher pay, group health insurance, parole system changes, and roads. From such talk, Brantley wrote, "it's not hard to imagine conflict with a governor [Clinton] jealous of his leadership prerogatives." But the columnist said Tucker had told him he knew who was boss, stating:

> The burden is on me to do my job in such a way that I neither am nor appear to be attempting to upstage the governor. I'm not a 27-year-old politician out trying to influence something for the first time in my life. I'm 47 years old, a success in business and law, with previous success in politics. I'm looking for a high-impact, low-profile job.[27]

As Clinton and Tucker settled in to prepare for the 1991 General Assembly session that would begin in January, I was entering a new phase in my life as I retired from First Commercial Bank.

As late as April 1991, Clinton was still saying he would not run for president in 1992, but his name continued to appear around the nation on the lists of potential candidates. When reporters asked him about this, he said it was because he had "been around" a long time "and because there's nobody out there running."[28] When four or five people enter the race, he said, those who are not running will not be mentioned anymore.

The six-year-old Democratic Leadership Council (DLC) he chaired, often seen as a stepchild of the more liberal National Democratic Committee, was preparing to hold its first convention in Cleveland in May. What Clinton said he hoped would come from the convention was "a set of resolutions and principles that will, in effect, shape the debate of the presidential campaign in '92 and redefine in the public mind what the Democratic Party stands for in a way that will be very positive, but I don't see it as candidate-centered." He went on to describe the DLC this way:

> We're certainly not a status quo group, but we don't believe that government money can solve problems in the absence of personal

responsibility and citizen choice and a commitment to restructuring the delivery system of government.[29]

Considerable fanfare surrounded the approach of the Cleveland session, which journalist Jeffrey Stinson said was "as good a barometer as any of how far the group has come since its creation by [former Georgia Sen. Sam] Nunn and others just months after Walter Mondale's crushing defeat in 1984." Stinson acknowledged that who he called "the charismatic Clinton" was accused by some of using the DLC as a vehicle to launch a presidential bid for himself and was seen by others as being silly if he was not. Whatever else he did, Clinton had managed to focus much of the nation's political attention on Cleveland for the upcoming convention.[30]

Clinton's primetime speech at the 1988 national Democratic convention in Atlanta was such an overly long, universally panned bomb that he and others realized he had no choice but to redeem himself at the DLC convention if he was going to be taken seriously on the national stage. Stinson and others wrote that redeem himself was exactly what Clinton did in a thirty-minute keynote address on May 6 that was interrupted thirteen times by applause and brought the delegates to their feet as he implored them to save their country as well as their political party.[31]

As usual at his best without a TelePrompTer, Clinton said Democrats had to dispel the perception that they overburden the middle class with taxes, are slow to defend the nation's interests with military force, and are frittering away hard-earned tax dollars. He continued:

> We've got to turn these perceptions around or we won't continue as a national party. But that is not the most important issue. The most important thing is that the United States of America needs at least one political party that's not afraid to tell the people the truth and address the real needs of real human beings. That is what we're here in Cleveland to do. We're not here to save the Democratic Party. We're here to save the United States of America.

To dispel old perceptions, Clinton tackled the issue of "family values" this way:

> There is an idea abroad in the land that if you abandon your children, the government will raise them. But I'll let you in on a little secret: Governments don't raise children, people do. And it is time they were asked to assume their responsibilities and forced to do it if they refuse.[32]

The Clinton remarks that opened the convention were reported to be far better received than talks by former Massachusetts Senator Paul Tsongas, the only announced presidential candidate at that point, and the governor of Virginia, L. Douglas Wilder, who was thinking seriously about entering the race. There appeared to be universal acclaim for Clinton's performance, so much so that I knew it was a defining speech, moving the party to the middle of the political road and positioning the Arkansan effectively for the campaign for president that was to come.

Clinton wasted no time returning to Little Rock, and by June quietly had recruited his first presidential campaign staff person, Craig Smith, who had entered politics as former U.S. Senator Gary Hart's Arkansas point man in the Coloradan's abortive bid for the White House. Clinton also rented the vacant ground floor of the two-story building at the southeast corner of Ninth and Chester streets for his headquarters.[33] In mid-July, Mark Middleton resigned from the Mitchell Law Firm to join Smith at the headquarters. On July 16, Clinton finally acknowledged publicly that, yes, he was interested in running for president. It was about this time he summoned me to a meeting at which he asked me to be his chief of staff, replacing Henry Oliver of Fort Smith, who had retired in April after thirteen months on the job. This would free up Jim Pledger, the acting chief of staff, to return full-time to his duties as director of the Department of Finance and Administration. We discussed the time frame—Connie and I already were ticketed for an August cruise for our forty-fourth wedding anniversary to the maritime provinces of Canada, from which we would not be returning until Wednesday, September 4. Clinton called me once or twice during the cruise to touch base.

While asserting "I definitely have not made the decision to enter the race," Clinton announced August 15 that he had resigned as chairman of the Democratic Leadership Council and had authorized the formation of a presidential exploratory committee, a step needed to start raising money for the 1992 campaign that he called a "practical necessity" because he had to know "whether people would contribute if I should run." His long-time lawyer friend Bruce Lindsey was named committee treasurer. Max Parker, the *Arkansas Gazette* reporter who later would become one of Clinton's campaign press secretaries, noted in her article that since May, the Arkansas governor had traveled to such politically important states as California, New York, New Hampshire, Illinois and Texas—"ostensibly to spread the moderate message of the DLC." Now he said it was time to resign as DLC chair because the organization was tax-exempt and could not be identified with any specific candidate.[34]

Tucker was not about to make life comfortable for the would-be president. At Tucker's request, Clinton and his senior staff met with him in the governor's office. Tucker asked that Clinton either resign as governor or take a leave of absence whenever he announced he was running for president. Under the 1874 Constitution, there was no such office as lieutenant governor in Arkansas. The office was created in 1926, and in 1941, Tucker argued, the Supreme Court had ruled in *Walls et al. v. Hall, Secretary of State,* that if an incumbent governor left the state for any amount of time, the lieutenant governor became acting governor with all the powers and duties of the office during that period except, perhaps, that of calling out the militia. (The president pro tempore of the Senate and the Speaker of the House are the next two in the line of succession.)[35] Clinton responded he would neither resign nor take a leave of absence.[36] Tucker was abundantly clear in an interview August 19 while Clinton was in Seattle, Washington, at a National Governors Association meeting that he was ready to run the state if Clinton made a bid for the White House. "The constitution is clear. Either the governor is governor . . . or I am governor. I'm not assistant governor. I'm not chief of staff."[37]

I argued just as vehemently during my tenure as chief of staff that while the powers and duties of governor "devolved" on the lieutenant governor in the governor's absence from the state, the political office continued to be vested in the incumbent governor. Clinton was completing his eleventh year as governor, the last nine having been served consecutively. The boards and commissions through which Arkansas state government business was conducted were made up exclusively of Clinton's appointees, and the governor's staff of some sixty talented specialists with service ranging up "to nine years of unbroken commitment" were his appointees as well. Additionally, the first lady, Hillary Rodham Clinton, schooled in eleven years of duty in that office, an attorney of national repute, a member of the boards of Wal-Mart and TCBY, among other private sector responsibilities, is not expected to abandon her role of first lady just because of select travel by her husband outside the borders of the state.

As early as August, Tucker sent a multipage memorandum to Clinton seeking a detailed response to many issues he saw confronting the state, including his view that a child welfare lawsuit should be "mooted" by agreement—with legislative oversight—so that it would not be "held hostage" by Federal District Court Judge George Howard Jr.[38]

The issue of potential conflict already was front-and-center, though Tucker attempted to play down the possibility. "Wherever possible," he told reporters on August 19, "I'll certainly attempt to coordinate anything I do with the governor. I'm going to be working with the staff of the governor's office on a regular basis." But state Republican Party cochairman, Sheffield Nelson, the former Clinton gubernatorial opponent, predicted a power-sharing agreement between the two Democrats would be hard to work out, in part because Clinton's staff was so loyal it was disinclined to do anything for anybody but him. Tucker also disclosed in his August 19 interview that he already had met with Dr. Terry Yamauchi, head of the troubled Department of Human Services, to discuss changes at the agency. As to appointments, Tucker said he did not have a long list of people he wanted to name to state boards and commissions, but that as acting governor, he might make "independent appointments" after consultations with Clinton's staff.[39] As time would reveal, he would make independent appointments even without consulting Clinton's staff.

Connie and I returned to Little Rock from our cruise at 4 p.m. Wednesday, September 4. As soon as the airplane landed, I called and then met Clinton at the Governor's Mansion to discuss the impending assignment. Clinton waited until 9 a.m. Friday, September 6, to inform Tucker of my appointment during a private meeting of the two at the mansion. Clinton told me that Tucker "exploded" at the news and accused the governor of trying to "sandbag" him. Late in the day, Clinton authorized the release of a written statement announcing my appointment as his executive secretary, more often referred to as the governor's chief of staff. Clinton said:

> When I announced the reorganization of my staff a few months ago, Bill Bowen is exactly the kind of businesslike manager I envisioned to fill this position. He will make sure that the day-to-day operations of the governor's office are carried out expeditiously and in a fair manner.[40]

Clinton's reorganization shortly after Oliver's departure created a kind of triumvirate consisting of Pledger and Gloria Cabe, senior executive assistant for public relations and special projects, and Carol Rasco, senior executive assistant for policy and program areas. As Department of Finance and Administration chief, Pledger also was the secretary of Clinton's cabinet, and he would continue to work closely with the governor's office. Lest the news release be taken to suggest Clinton was sure he was running for president when he reorganized his staff on May 21, the governor elaborated during a political stop that night in Sioux City, Iowa, saying, "I wanted to make sure that if I do run [for president] that the office will run in a very efficient way, decisions will be made, initiatives will be followed up on, that problems will be resolved."[41] He did not say he wanted to keep the lieutenant governor in check, but some read this into his remarks.

I was scheduled to begin my duties Monday, September 9, but I was at the Capitol Friday, September 6, and, as the *Democrat* reported, I "already had [my] shirt sleeves rolled up as [I] smilingly greeted visitors to the governor's office." I told the reporters, "I'm honored and pleased to serve. Being a native son of Arkansas, I'm always pleased to try to do anything that will contribute to the well-being of the state."[42]

Just a few hours before—at 11 a.m..—I met with Tucker in what I would describe as a rancorous meeting. This was followed at 2:30 p.m. by a more amicable session at which a news release was authorized for distribution. The lieutenant governor had cooled off by then and we had a constructive visit. Reporters quoted Tucker as saying I was "the kind of person I would have hired as executive secretary if I were governor, whether I was running for something else or not. He's been a good personal friend and a supporter of mine."[43]

At least two veteran legislators saw my appointment as a signal Clinton was running for president. "Looks like he's running," Rep. Jodie Mahony (D-El Dorado) commented after reading the release from the governor's office. Mahony, who became a state senator two years later, added, "I don't know how the governor could have gotten a more qualified person [than I] in the state of Arkansas." State Senator Jerry Bookout (D-Jonesboro) called my appointment "an additional indicator" that Clinton had decided to make a bid for the White House. Meanwhile, I cautioned reporters about tying my appointment to a "go" decision by Clinton. I told them that we had had no discussion and my visit with him had no relation to that issue.

To political columnist Max Brantley, my hiring also was the "clearest sign yet," that Clinton had decided to run for president. Brantley knew friction was inevitable, though he erroneously attributed it to the clashing ambitions of Tucker and me to be governor.[44] Tucker's ambition was already known, but even if I had "flirted" in the past with the idea of seeking the post, it was not an option I considered. Although my health was good, I was sixty-eight at this point, and the family considerations that had stopped me before still existed. Brantley put the importance of my appointment this way:

> During his frequent absences, it is important to Clinton that he leave
> a firmly directed staff. It must project an image that Clinton, or at
> least his aides, are firmly in charge of the affairs of state.

My entrance as chief of staff, the columnist said, was "the clearest signal yet to Jim Guy Tucker that he better not go messing too much with gubernatorial prerogative." Tucker, he wrote:

> already has commandeered the gubernatorial limo on one occasion, has ordered a few staffers around, entered into negotiations over troubles in state departments and even, according to one source, riffled through confidential personnel files of a state agency. His ability to do such things is limited only by his reach; his brass; and now, Bill Bowen . . . Bowen is not shy. A fellow who stared down a bank takeover effort by the powerful Stephens family a few years back is a force to be reckoned with . . . Time will tell if these two strong-headed men can reach an accommodation, though both are smart enough to recognize the wisdom of such.[45]

Clinton formally announced he would seek the Democratic nomination for president from the Old Statehouse on October 3, 1991, and left immediately for the campaign trail.

A year before Clinton officially entered the presidential race, Central Arkansas Legal Services and the San Francisco–based National Center for Youth Services had notified the state that they were considering filing a class-action lawsuit on behalf of children served by Arkansas's foster care and protective services division. The center was considering separate litigation as well about overcrowding and understaffing problems in the Youth Services Centers at Alexander and Pine Bluff.[46] The warning was renewed before the Joint Budget Committee at a mid-March meeting during the 1991 General Assembly session.

"I don't think we will be able to defend the case adequately," Richard Dietz, director of the Division of Children and Family Services, told the legislators. His division, he said, needed eleven million to thirteen million dollars to hire more people and make improvements needed to stave off the litigation.[47] By letter, Clinton had asked the committee to add $2.2 million in state funds and a maximum of 250 staff positions to the division's $44 million budget with what Dietz said was the intention of trying to avert the lawsuit. "I'm not convinced it will," he confessed. Griffin "Griff" Stockley, an attorney with Central Arkansas Legal Services, confirmed this, saying Clinton's proposal was "just not acceptable to us."

Clinton held his ground, explaining in April that the system was "broke" and he would not defend it but that the National Center for Youth Law had failed to cite a state with a model system Arkansas could copy and had not convinced him that simply increasing the division's staff would "really reduce the number of kids getting abuse[d] and help more families stay together."[48] The governor said he had a plan to obtain more money for the agency, one that involved hiring expert consultants, using his emergency fund, and working on ways to secure more federal dollars for the division through matching programs, grants, and other sources.[49] He followed through by recruiting a panel of six national experts on June 14, and in August told the group he needed its recommendations for revamping the system by early November to assure their being included in an expected special legislative session.[50]

As promised, a ninety-three-page lawsuit accusing the state of failing to protect abused and neglected children was filed in federal district court on July 8, 1991.[51] In sometimes harrowing detail, the lawsuit cited specific cases in which abused children were moved repeatedly from one foster home to another, the state's failure to investigate serious reports of child abuse and the premature discontinuation of therapy required for troubled children.[52] Clinton told reporters he found the lawsuit "extremely disturbing" but he did not believe the situation was "purely a money problem" and that until the system could be revamped, he saw no reason to put more funds into it.[53]

In mid-August, William Grimm of the National Center for Youth Law told Clinton's panel of experts that his organization would rather reach a negotiated settlement than take the case to trial. The panel's recommendations "very well might form the basis for the plaintiff and the defendant sitting down . . . that means, over a period of time, we could move from one issue to another."[54] Two weeks later, DHS director Dr. Terry Yamauchi outlined an estimated $1.4 million in improvements that would be taken in Children and Family Services, including hiring forty-four additional family service workers to investigate child abuse cases and work with foster children.[55] Stockley commented that the steps were "an indication" the state was interested in trying to resolve the matters disputed in the lawsuit. Grimm was not so optimistic, noting that many of the recommendations had been made when the legislature was in session.

Now slightly on the defensive, Clinton asserted that children were his "top priority" and conceded he probably should have acted more quickly to put additional money into the beleaguered child welfare system. "If I had known for sure that we'd be able to run a modest surplus last year [the state ended the fiscal year on June 30, 1991, with a $15.9 million surplus], that we were not going to have the same financial problems that have bankrupted other states, I probably would have asked for the money to kick in a little earlier." He reiterated in the statement issued from the governor's office that he preferred to seek repair of the child welfare system itself before pumping more money into it, but he said his administration was "in high gear now and we're going to stay that way."[56]

Improvements were being implemented and negotiations were underway on the child welfare system when I became chief of staff. In meetings with Tucker before October 10, the lieutenant governor insisted the state had eight unresolved issues, including the lawsuit, that required a special legislative session to be called "forthwith." On October 10, Tucker and his staff met with Clinton's senior staff after I had prepared an eight-point memorandum on all of the issues the lieutenant governor had raised.[57] When Clinton came home briefly from the presidential campaign trail in mid-October, the governor used my paper to say he and top lawmakers agreed that the problems could be solved without a special legislative session, but he would not totally rule out the possibility of a special session.[58]

Before leaving for Washington, D.C., on Monday, October 21, Clinton's office issued a press advisory that the panel of national experts he had recruited would issue a twenty-page report the next day in which a sixteen million dollar plan was proposed to improve the state's child welfare system. He said the plan could serve as the basis for a settlement of the lawsuit and alleviate the need for a special legislative session. "I have a feeling that if we implement this plan, we will at least be ahead of the curve and will be doing as well as anybody else," Clinton said.[59] Six hours later, Tucker said:

> I disagree very strongly with those that advocate that rather than deal with the messy necessities of democracy—that is, the legislative process in the General Assembly—we simply work out an agreement among the experts and let a few selective people bless it and let a federal court order us to do it . . . I think it's a matter of policy that the state of Arkansas should not volunteer itself to federal court jurisdiction for the resolution of state problems. If you have a problem, you should take expeditious actions to solve the problems.[60]

Tucker and I were scheduled for a briefing session at 9:30 the next morning in the lieutenant governor's office. I arrived before Tucker and talked with staff member Howard Harper about "ways and means to improve communication" among Clinton, Tucker, our offices and staffs, and among department heads and commissions. Harper reiterated that Tucker was "distressed" Clinton had issued a press advisory Monday for a news conference on Tuesday and then left the state. After learning about the advisory on Monday, Tucker had demanded a copy of whatever it was Clinton was relying on to call a news conference. After some consultation, Carol Rasco supplied the copy at the end of the work day. Tucker let Clinton press aide Susie Whitacre know he was unhappy she was presuming to issue news releases for the governor when Clinton was out of state.

Harper also said Tucker was irked because during the legislative session, Clinton and his staff had met daily at 7 a.m. with House Speaker John Lipton and Senate President Pro Tempore Jerry Bookout to discuss upcoming business. Tucker infrequently attended these meetings, in part, Harper said, because Gloria Cabe presided when Clinton was absent. This seemed "irregular" to Tucker because he was the acting governor at those times. Harper went on to relate that Tucker was irritated as well when he or his chief aide, Neal Turner, asked Phyllis Anderson in Clinton's office for some information. Cabe responded by issuing a memorandum advising Clinton staff members not to deal with Tucker's aides except through the senior staff members to whom they reported.[61]

I assured Harper I recognized Tucker was acting governor when Clinton was out of state and made it a point to discuss ways to improve communications and specific assignments for the lieutenant governor, such as handling the aftermath of the Eaker Air Force Base closing in Mississippi County, water availability/sources issues, and the "stink" that hunters with camps on Big Island were raising about the U.S. Army Corps of Engineers plan to build a new lock and dam on the McClellan-Kerr Arkansas River Navigation System at Montgomery Point in southeastern Arkansas. In the midst of these statements, Attorney General Winston Bryant had issued an opinion in which he said Tucker had until October 31 to call a special session. The opinion contained the implication that Tucker could call a special session if Clinton did not.

The *Arkansas Democrat-Gazette* quoted Tucker as saying on the day he held his briefing with me that:

> We have two governors involved here. If, in fact, Gov. Clinton has a different view on it, then we're going to have to reconcile the different viewpoints. Obviously, if in fact the governor has a different opinion on this than I do, this is one of the awkward situations that's going to arise from having one governor on one day and another governor the next day.[62]

Clinton, campaigning in Washington, D.C., was quoted as saying that "No final decision has been made" about a special session. "The lawsuit hasn't been settled yet," he added. Whitacre said the governor's staff was trying to negotiate a settlement that "the plaintiffs will accept so we will be in a position of coming up with our own solution instead of one dictated by the court." This was a direct shot at Tucker, who was continuing to tell reporters a federal court order alone was not acceptable to him. Asked if he would call a special legislative session, Tucker replied, "that's not something we can address yet since the governor hasn't made a decision. That's premature."[63]

Meredith Oakley, a *Democrat-Gazette* editor/columnist, took Tucker's side, asking if the governor thought the child welfare system could be cleaned up administratively, "why hasn't he done so?" She also chided Clinton for not being "up to snuff" on the issue because he mixed up the funds that might serve as the source of financing changes in the child welfare system when he spoke at the news conference four days before.[64] Oakley also said of Clinton:

> He just wants to delay things into the new year so that it doesn't interfere with his long-awaited [presidential] campaign. He wants no controversy or undue attention to state problems to muddy the presidential waters.[65]

The day Oakley's column appeared, Tucker was being quoted in a news article as saying he might be able to compromise with Clinton over the handling of the child welfare system issue—but only if the compromise included a legislative session. Clinton, now campaigning in New York, was quoted as saying, "Well, how can we avoid having the federal courts rule on it? I mean, we've been sued in federal court. We've always been under the assumption that it would be the good thing that we could settle the suit and not go to trial. So if the suit is settled and doesn't go to trial, then I don't know that we need legislative" action.[66]

On the day these statements were made, I met with Jayme Dissly, Clinton's liaison with the Department of Human Services; Assistant Attorney General Angela Jegley; DHS chief counsel Deborah Nye; and Tucker to discuss how to achieve a negotiated settlement using recommendations made by the panel of experts.[67] The dispute between the "dueling governors" melted from the news pages thereafter. However, the situation intensified behind the scenes. On November 3, Clinton, Tucker, and I met at the governor's mansion. The next day, Tucker prepared a multipage memorandum giving his view of an "agreement" he felt had been achieved on the single issue of "mooting" the child welfare lawsuit. He asked for a detailed brief on the issues involved, desired strategy, and an assessment of liquidated dollar obligations to be delivered to him by November 25 so that he could call a special session immediately.[68] Tucker's memorandum led to a meeting among

Clinton, Pledger, Tucker, and me on November 5 in the governor's office where they agreed, among other points, to execute the memorandum but drop the November 25 target date for completion and choose instead a date in early December, at which time the memorandum would be taken to legislative leaders for their guidance. In an appearance on Pat Lynch's radio show that day, Tucker began backing away from his demand for a special legislative session, saying funding appeared to be available that would carry Children and Family Services through until the General Assembly convened in 1993 and said that if a "certain" administrative solution could be found, he could agree to it.[69] He noted legislators preferred not to be called into special session if it could be avoided.

Tucker and I met again from 2:45 to 4 p.m. on November 7, and during the meeting I made a point to ask the lieutenant governor what differences he saw with Clinton after the child welfare system issue was resolved. Tucker indicated the only difference would be one of style. I responded by citing the good reception Clinton was receiving from Democrats in New Hampshire, scene of the nation's first presidential primary, from Florida's leaders, and from Texas Gov. Ann Richards. I added that Clinton needed an elected ally in Arkansas "at this time" as Tucker would need Clinton when he ran for governor in 1994, and followed this up with a suggestion that Tucker go to Clinton and ask how he could help. I said I thought Tucker might encounter an invitation to resolve the child welfare matter without a session.[70] Tucker seemed to buy into the invitation and then we had a little historical discussion about the 1978 U.S. Senate race and the lieutenant governor's animosity about the help Clinton gave to Gov. David Pryor in the runoff primary in which Tucker was defeated, and the 1982 gubernatorial race in which Tucker finished third behind Clinton and Joe Purcell. He claimed all of that was behind him.

Eleven days later, I had a particularly confrontational meeting with Tucker from 2:30 to 4 p.m. The lieutenant governor's best friend, J. W. "Buddy" Benafield, was present as Tucker reiterated his grievances about Clinton maintaining control of the governor's office, which produced the sharpest exchange we had up to that point. It is fair to say he was angry: his face was flushed, his voice was raised, his eyes bulged, and he used, even for him, an uncommon number of epithets.[71]

Earlier in the day, Tucker had a confrontation with Dissly about his memorandum, to which he had not received responses. Dissly told him she had not seen the memorandum and was unaware or unsure of six items he said he had delineated. When I asked him to itemize the points, he demurred.[72] I went on to write:

> I responded that I knew she [Dissly] was aware generally of the main points at issue because I had had a meeting with her following his confrontation. I observed that his style was intimidating and that he was micro-managing the matter with 18 days remaining before the newest deadline for finalizing the memorandum. I observed that his style accommodated [accounted] in part for Mrs. Dissly's response to him and specifically for the fact that Carol Rasco was at home with a migraine headache. I observed that his style was not productive with the kind of environment needed for good work by this staff which was not used to this manner.[73]

Because of this and other matters we discussed, Tucker settled down a little. The meeting concluded with a little more productive discussion of the briefings that had taken place over the past ten days being illustrative of the staff's cooperation and concluded with my view that "good and timely execution of the November 4 memorandum coupled with a court order committing the appropriate Arkansas funds in the Children and Families legislation (candidly I am not clear on what is satisfactory to him here) which obviates the need for a session."[74] Tucker had the last shot, however, repeating his threshold demands: that he must have staff response, that it had to come by December 2 and preferably before, and legislative leadership must second any understanding reached during that week because Speaker Lipton and President Pro Tempore Bookout were scheduled to start a goodwill visit to Taiwan on December 7.

On December 30, Tucker told reporters, "The draft of a final [child welfare] plan, complete with precise funding figures, is still about two weeks away from completion."[75] The plan was seen as costing the state $17.3 million over eighteen months, with most of the money to come from the fund Clinton had cited earlier. Approving the appropriation probably would be the only direct legislative action required, Tucker added.

On January 24, 1992, Clinton sent a letter to legislators asking them to set aside February 19 to March 2 for a special session to deal with the child welfare system. "After several rounds of negotiation, it appears that we may be in a position to settle this case amicably," he said, adding that he wanted the General Assembly to approve the settlement before it was offered to Federal District Court Judge George Howard Jr. for his signature because it "may commit us to increased expenditures . . . in future years" for the Division of Children and Family Services.[76]

Clinton issued a call for the legislature to convene in special session Monday, February 24, to consider forty-two issues, chief among them being the child welfare settlement.[77] None was known to be controversial, and the session was expected to last only three days (under Arkansas's constitution, a minimum of three days is required to pass a bill). Even as the proclamation was being issued, Tucker was telling reporters it would be premature to say the child welfare system lawsuit was about to be settled. "There are still a lot of very serious issues outstanding. But I do think everyone—legislators, plaintiffs' counsels and the state's representatives—are all working in a good faith to try and put this matter to bed."[78]

Clinton arrived in Little Rock the morning the special session was to begin. He had been dogged by allegations he was a Vietnam War draft dodger, and a would-be singer named Gennifer Flowers had achieved notoriety by claiming she had had a twelve-year affair with the Arkansas governor. He had survived this to finish second in the New Hampshire primary and had told the nation on election night that he was the "Comeback Kid." Clinton went to the mansion in the early morning hours of February 24, where he had no more than three hours of sleep before he went to the Capitol for a briefing and to prepare for his address to the special session at 6 p.m. His address to the lawmakers, staff, and family gathered in the gallery lasted twenty-three minutes and was interrupted by applause eighteen times. I asked for a copy of his speech. It consisted of illegible longhand scribbles on the back of one page of a bill—a remarkable illustration of his communicating skills. Earlier in the day, Clinton spoke to his staff and senior aides in the Department of Finance and Administration conference room. After greeting each one present personally, he "slouched" to the table, reflected on the wear and unrelenting campaign pressures he was experiencing, and said, "I think I can win the nomination." His audience roundly applauded.[79]

On the second day of the session, the child welfare settlement was released between the state and the plaintiffs in the lawsuit, contingent on legislative approval. The trial scheduled in March on the lawsuit would be unnecessary if the settlement went through, but the federal court would have jurisdiction to enforce the agreement if the plaintiffs convinced the judge the state was failing to follow through. If the state complied with the plan through December 31, 1994, the case would be dismissed and the federal court would lose its jurisdiction. By the time the plan was revealed, the Senate already had adopted the appropriation bills for an oversight committee to determine whether the state was complying.[80] As expected, the legislators approved the plan and went home. Judge Howard subsequently signed the settlement and the issue was moot.

A serious situation developed November 29, 1991, when James Magee, a banker from Piggott/Blytheville, notified David Harrington, director of the Arkansas Industrial Development Department (now the Department of Economic Development) by telephone that he would be resigning as chairman of the Industrial Development Commission. Clinton's office received Magee's resignation letter dated December 2 on December 4. Within the day, Tucker asked me, on my return from the burial service for W. R. "Witt" Stephens Sr. in Prattsville, if there was a list of prospective appointees for the vacancy. Harrington told me he knew of no list, and I reported this to Tucker. On the afternoon of Thursday, December 5, I met with Tucker at his invitation, where I saw Magee's resignation letter for the first time and a list of five potential appointees.[81]

Cabe had been out of the office since noon Wednesday. When she returned on Friday, and I returned to the Capitol from the hanging of a portrait of retired Federal District Judge Elsijane Trimble Roy in the federal courthouse, I learned from her that Jim Lancaster of Sheridan had been selected to fill the vacancy.[82] I advised Tucker of this immediately. I was at a Pearl Harbor commemoration ceremony at Camp Robinson the morning of Saturday, December 6, and could not be reached. I learned soon that a member of Tucker's staff had picked up an appointment form but that the governor's office had processed Lancaster's appointment and it was a "done deal."[83] At the same time, Tucker called Wallace Fowler of Jonesboro to say he was appointing him to the AIDC position. Tucker then told press secretary Mike Gauldin to prepare a news release about Fowler's appointment even though Gauldin already had a release in his computer announcing Lancaster's appointment. With Gauldin's help, Tucker reached Clinton by telephone about 4 p.m. Clinton told Tucker he had signed a letter to Lancaster while in his office, but that he would support Fowler's appointment, given the circumstances.[84] Clinton returned to the state Sunday, December 8, but Tucker told John Troutt, editor and publisher of the *Jonesboro Sun,* about Fowler's appointment and the newspaper published the announcement Monday, December 9.

In a telephone conversation the morning of the *Sun's* article, Tucker told me he had come forward as he had because of inadequate information from Clinton's office and said flatly he thought I meant that Jim Lancaster's appointment was to occur in January to fill Edward Saig's seat to the First

District of AIDC when it became vacant.[85] I told Tucker that I would report under oath that I told him December 6 that Lancaster's appointment was to fill the Magee vacancy. He stuttered a little bit and hung up the phone to make another call.[86] Tucker now had demonstrated what he could and would do to reward his key supporters.

On Friday, December 27, Clinton's staff released a list of twenty-nine persons he had appointed to various boards and commissions. Of these, the terms of the incumbents in three of the posts would not expire until December 31, three on January 1, six on January 7, fourteen on January 14, and one on January 15.[87] Less than two weeks before, Attorney General Winston Bryant had released a pertinent opinion in response to a question from Clinton. Prepared by Assistant Attorney General Elisabeth Walker, it said a vacancy exists when an incumbent "dies, resigns, is removed or abandons the office." In 1967, the opinion noted, the state Supreme Court found that a vacancy exists when no incumbent is in place to discharge the duties of that office. "It thus seems clear that the Arkansas Supreme Court has taken the position that the office must in fact be vacant before an appointment may be made," Walker wrote.[88] Bryant followed up on January 2 with this public statement: "The law is that there has to be vacancy whenever an appointment is made; otherwise, the governor could make appointments now for everybody that fell due at any time . . . any appointment made prior to a vacancy occurring is not a valid appointment."[89]

In response to this, Clinton spokesperson Whitacre told reporters, "When the governor was here during the holidays, he spent a lot of time making appointments. He decided there was no reason not to go ahead and announce them. The appointments won't become effective until the terms expire, which is in agreement with the [attorney general's] opinion."

Bryant disagreed. "The point is the law is clear cut. The only appointment that could be made is an appointment to a position where a vacancy has occurred. For example, if someone indicates they are going to resign from the Arkansas Supreme Court effective February 1, there can be no appointment to that position until it is vacant."[90]

There was a "personality clash" between Tucker and Cabe, allegedly over the appointments, and the lieutenant governor fired her from the staff while Clinton was vacationing out of state.[91] Clinton and Tucker talked by telephone on Thursday, January 2, after which reporters learned Cabe was still on the job but had been reprimanded by the lieutenant governor. Tucker confirmed he had reprimanded Cabe and declared, "It is essential that I have complete trust and confidence in the judgment and the actions of all state employees who work in the office of the governor. The absence of such a relationship interferes with the performance of my constitutional duties and my relationship with Governor Clinton."[92]

The dispute was resolved when Clinton announced on returning to the state that Cabe would run his presidential campaign office in Washington, D.C. [the headquarters was and remained in Little Rock]. Clinton said he had wanted Cabe to be on his staff since October. Tucker insisted Cabe's joining the Clinton campaign was "never, never a part of the resolution" of his dispute with her.[93] The fifty-year-old Cabe, who had represented Little Rock's liberal Democratic Hillcrest/Heights neighborhood in the Arkansas House from 1979 to 1990, was known to be a thorough Clinton loyalist.

The Cabe blowup was not the only incident that made December a rough month. About 9 a.m. on Monday, December 30, eighteen activists—many in wheelchairs—associated with American Disabled for Attendant Programs Today (ADAPT) chained themselves to pipes, desks, and other furniture inside the governor's office to protest cuts in Medicaid, the state/federal medical care program for the poor and disabled, that were scheduled to take place on New Year's Day. The Arkansas demonstration was part of a national push to obtain federal funding for personal care services for the disabled, but the local protesters complained in particular that Clinton had ignored a December 18 letter outlining their arguments against the cuts.[94] Local ADAPT chapter president Dr. Terry Winkler said the group was prepared to remain in the governor's office indefinitely.

Cabe and other Clinton staff members called the sit-in a "publicity stunt" and blamed the cuts on the federal government even while expressing empathy for the group's plight. A line of state officials, including Tucker, paraded through the governor's office, trying to help negotiate an end to the occupation.[95] At about 7:30 p.m., Clinton spoke with the group on speaker phone and transformed the hostile community into supportive constituents in about ten minutes' time. The Democrat-Gazette reported on New Year's Day that Clinton had talked with the group, but attributed the end of the occupation to a settlement in which he had made the concessions they wanted.[96]

In May 1991, the board of trustees for the University of Central Arkansas in Conway voted to ask the General Assembly to repeal some invalid state segregation laws relative to the school. The talk of a possible special legislative session brought a movement on campus by some students to push for the inclusion of removal of the laws in the "call." The situation began coming to a head in November when two black UCA professors received threatening letters demanding that both leave. The letters prompted a third black professor to reveal publicly that he had resigned, effective at the end of the academic year, though he said he had not been threatened.[97]

The 1907 statutes under which UCA was created as Arkansas State Normal School stated that the institution was created "for the purpose of providing for the preparation and training of white persons, both male and female, citizens of the state desiring to teach in the state." Also, it said that "each county in the state shall be entitled to one scholarship for every 20 white teachers in the county."[98] The UCA students sent a letter to Clinton asking him to include removal of the laws in any special session call. On November 13, press secretary Mike Gauldin wrote a news release for his boss, who was campaigning in Michigan. It said:

> Although the racial references in the statutes establishing UCA are certainly void and UCA has been an integrated institution since 1955, I fully agree that such offensive relics of the past have no place in Arkansas today and without question should be eliminated as quickly as possible whenever they are discovered.[99]

The *Arkansas Democrat-Gazette* article on the statement from Clinton included a "Me, too" from Tucker, but the situation clearly made the lieutenant governor irate and set the stage for the rancorous meeting with me on November 15. Tucker complained bitterly that he knew nothing about the students' letter and that the news release had been issued while he was acting governor because Clinton was out of state. Tucker resented Clinton getting favorable headlines while he was "'relegated' to signing a flag lowering proclamation."[100]

The implication of the exchange was that Tucker wanted all letters addressed to the governor to be shared with him when he was acting governor. I asked him point-blank if he was asking us to treat Clinton as nonexistent when out of the state and if so, if he had forgotten his September 6 statement to me—raised with Clinton in mid-August—that there was the political office that did not transfer to him when Clinton was out of state. This settled Tucker down somewhat.

Tucker was prickly at best, and *Arkansas Business* no doubt contributed to this mood in mid-December 1991, when it featured an article titled "Governor Bowen," exploring whether I would oppose Tucker and seek to replace Clinton if he won the presidency. The news magazine said that I, "with [my] thousands of contacts in the banking and legal communities, would have no trouble raising the funds needed for a competitive statewide campaign."[101] The reporter even found a Republican who was enthusiastic about me. Former GOP state Senator Jim Keet, a Little Rock businessman, said he thought a Tucker-Bowen contest might be in the offing but now was not so sure. But if I ran, Keet added, "Bowen's administrative acumen and national connections in every segment of the economy, from manufacturing to the service industry, would provide Arkansas with needed contacts. He is well-respected, a hardball player with a heart."[102] Tucker could not have been comforted by this, but the article also demonstrated my determination to keep the peace. In response to a question about who was really filling the power vacuum in Clinton's absence, I replied: "I'm his [Tucker's] chief of staff, and my duty to him as acting governor is to see that the staff is responsive and the information flow open and accurate."

Floodwaters crushed southwestern and central Arkansas in mid-May 1990. No single place was hit harder than Hot Springs, where thirteen inches of rain within twenty-four hours sent a flash flood racing through downtown, causing an estimated five million dollars in damages.[103] A year later, the *Democrat-Gazette* reported downtown Hot Springs bore few physical scars from the six-foot wall of water that had rushed down Central Avenue. The business owners and city leaders had turned their thoughts to preventing future flooding. The city was considering participating in a $4.4 million study by the Army Corps of Engineers to find a feasible way to ease flooding— possibly by digging a tunnel through West Mountain Street to divert water around downtown. Hot Springs would have to come up with half the money for the study.[104]

In late 1991, veteran state Senator Eugene "Bud" Canada (D-Hot Springs), began an aggressive campaign for sixty thousand dollars in state funds to supplement a six hundred thousand dollar Department of the Interior grant U.S. Senator Dale Bumpers (D-AR) had obtained for the study. I had to tell Canada that all of the governor's emergency fund was committed and urged him to check with the state Soil and Water Conservation Commission. The commission could not help him. I next steered Canada to Maurice Smith, director of the Highway and Transportation Department. Smith committed one year of funding with conditions Hot Springs felt it could not accept. With no notice, Canada and the city's House members, Reps. James C. Allen and John Parkerson, called on Tucker. Without consulting Clinton's staff and with an incomplete understanding of emergency fund commitments, Tucker told Canada that Hot Springs could have sixty thousand dollars.[105]

Several state programs were shortchanged as a result, including one that was close to my heart—the match for federal funding designed to build Arkansas's academic scientific research capabilities. Tucker was unable to get Clinton to agree to issue a joint release announcing the funds, however. So the lieutenant governor "piggy-backed" a revelation of the commitment he had made for the sixty thousand dollars into a news release about what Bumpers had been able to achieve in obtaining six hundred thousand dollars from the Department of the Interior.

Still smarting from the governor's office news release about UCA, Tucker raised the issue at a December 13 staff meeting about mail to the governor's office and seemed to be implying that it should be routed to him. The volume of mail to Clinton as governor, some of it marked confidential and personal, was about 250 letters on Mondays when the legislature was not in session and another 150 during the remainder of the week—an average of eighty letters a day. Nothing was mentioned about the volume of telephone calls to the governor's office, which are numerous, and the drop-in visits, which are equally numerous (such as the one from Canada).[106] As he left for a meeting on the first floor of the Capitol, Tucker commented that with Clinton spending more and more time out of state campaigning and with his mind filled with presidential rather than state issues, Tucker expected to be involved more and more in running the state. Among other things, he announced that by February he wanted to have in hand plans for dealing with issues that could be expected to arise during the 1993 legislative session. Thereafter, according to legal counsel Field Wasson, the Clinton staff reached an "uneasy truce" with Tucker, and met with the lieutenant governor almost daily.[107]

No natural gas utility in the nation had had a more troubled existence, at least politically, since 1983 than Arkla, Incorporated, which had headquarters in Little Rock and Shreveport, Louisiana. The first real hint of impending financial disaster, however, came on November 21, 1991, when the firm's stock went "haywire" in trading on the New York Stock Exchange.[108] Trading of Arkla stock reached 3,499,500 shares. Its average during the previous thirty days was 330,720 shares, according to statistics from Standard and Poor's Corporation. The stock also hit its lowest level since 1962, dropping in price to $12 7/8 from $15 the day before. The company had sustained two troublesome quarters, losing $29.2 million in the second quarter followed by a $32.1 million loss in the third quarter of 1991. Investors were concerned about the natural gas industry as a whole, but also were speculating that

Arkla was going to cut its dividend and that the utility had cash-flow problems.[109] Two weeks later, Arkla put the Public Service Commission (PSC) on notice that it was completing a request for its first natural gas rate increase since 1987, of an unspecified amount, to be filed sometime between February 3 and March 2.[110]

On December 11, 1991, correspondent Dan Dorfman quoted energy analyst Alan Gaines on Financial News Network as saying Arkla had a "20 to 25 percent chance of going into Chapter 11 [bankruptcy] in six to nine months."[111] Trading in Arkla stock went into another tizzy, becoming the third-most-active issue on the NYSE, with slightly more than two million shares changing hands December 12. The stock closed at $11 7/8, down a point or 8.7 percent; it had been as low as $10 3/4 during the day. Thomas F. "Mack" McLarty, Arkla chairman, president and chief executive officer, responded in a written statement: "We are troubled by speculative statements made today about Arkla and the natural gas business . . . Questioning the solvency of Arkla is unwarranted and not supported by fact."[112]

In spite of McLarty's denial, the Clinton administration knew Arkla had real problems and more were on the way because an independent consultant had finished a study for the Public Service Commission in which a ninety-five million dollar rate decrease was recommended for the distribution portion of its business. Clinton, Tucker, I, and the rest of the staff met at the mansion from 7 to 11 p.m. on Wednesday, January 15, 1992. While the meeting was breaking up, I spoke privately with Clinton in the kitchen, telling the candidate I thought it was time for him to accept Secret Service protection. I also asked for Clinton's guidance on Arkla and was told it was "imperative that Arkla be negotiated to settlement immediately."[113]

In a telephone call on January 20, I told PSC chairman Sam Bratton what Clinton had said and bolstered the point with these observations: 1) Dick Bell of Riceland Cooperative, representing the industrial users, favored a settlement; 2) Attorney General Winston Bryant and Assistant Attorney General George Vena had expressed support, during the week ended January 17, of a settlement; 3) PSC general staff director Jerrell Clark observed in a meeting with Arkla's David Johnson that he thought settlement was appropriate, and 4) Tucker, in a meeting in my office on January 17, said he intended to visit with Clark about settlement/resolution of Arkla matters.[114] I added the litany of disasters that could/probably would happen to Arkla if left unattended (for example, at the worst, Chapter 11, or at the likely best, transfer of the headquarters/leadership to Houston), with the attendant black eye that Arkansas would be left with.

Bratton did not resist this compilation of downside projections. He agreed moving Arkla's headquarters would be a disaster to the state and to Clinton, and he invited me to meet with Clark. I met with Clark at 8 a.m. January 22 in the PSC director's office where I said I was there as the governor's agent, viewed the matters to be discussed as protected by attorney-client privilege, and that without equivocation, the governor viewed the possible loss of this corporate citizen as something that should be avoided if at all possible.

Among other points, I noted that 60 percent of Arkla's stock was held by institutional investors who had no loyalty to the company or its headquarters location and who had seen a substantial loss of value in their holdings in 1991 while the stock market otherwise was going up some 65 percent. Thus, Arkla's institutional investors were unhappy and could be expected to persuade non-Arkansas directors to look for a more favorable regulatory jurisdiction among the eleven states in which the company operated. I said I saw a move to Houston for Arkla as highly likely if the state could not help the firm work out its problems. I also observed to Clark that Arkla had something like $1.4 billion in debt and that a PSC public hearing on the issues surrounding the company probably would trigger a Standard and Poor's review of the utility's credit, possibly resulting in a loss of investment grade standing. I went on to recall that I had been on the board of Fairfield Communities in 1989, giving me the experience to point out what happens to a company when it drops to "junk bond" credit standing and then loses even that market. Fairfield was in bankruptcy by the end of 1989, I reminded Clark.[115]

At the time I thought Clark was receptive and cooperative, but this was before the discussion turned to many specific issues surrounding Arkla, when it became apparent the PSC director was not really as cooperative as I initially thought. For example, Clark questioned why Arkla should not be responsive to the agency's concerns for some control of natural gas costs and that the company's stockholder position, Standard and Poor's frailty on credit standing, and pressures on the board from out-of-state stockholders to move to a more favorable regulatory jurisdiction were subjective and outside the record at this time, making it difficult for him and the staff to give force and effect to them.

Even before Arkla filed its rate increase request, I prepared and sent a gloomy memorandum to Clinton in which I wrote, "the trend lines are worsening and the regulatory climate seems to be stalemated."[116] I told the future president that "at a time when Arkla gas rates are in the lowest quartile in the nation, its future is in the balance, its non-Arkansas directors are distressed about the regulatory climate in its home state as compared to the other states in which it operates; it is clear that Arkansas confronts not the possibility, but the probability, of a transfer of the headquarters to a more hospitable climate, e.g., Houston, and/or an acquisition/merger with one or more than viable gas distribution companies which would have the same effect as a headquarters change." I put Clinton on notice that he probably could not salvage Arkla on the home front.

Ten days after I wrote this memorandum, Arkla filed a $22.5 million rate increase (reduced later to $17.4 million) request for its distribution business with the PSC. The most unusual feature about this request was Arkla's proposal that residential rates (for "biscuit cookers" as founder W. R. "Witt" Stephens called them) go up 15.1 percent while heavy industrial customers were given cuts to 53.2 percent of what they then were paying.[117] Arkla chief operating officer Mike Means said that since natural gas deregulation in 1979, industries were free to "shop" for suppliers. If the company lost its heavy industrial users, who had long been subsidizing residential rates, the cost of gas for the "biscuit cookers" would shoot up even more.

Again, I talked with the PSC's Clark on March 4. Duff & Phelps had indicated it was preparing to downgrade Arkla's securities—a point I noted with concern. Clark responded he was aware of the credit report but that there were "differences in philosophy" at work in any Arkla settlement, including Arkansas Louisiana Gas Company's purchase of gas from AER (essentially itself) at a sixty million dollar markup. I replied that Arkla's gas costs to ratepayers were in the lowest quarter in the nation and substantially lower than those of a Fayetteville-based utility. Clark countered that "we don't set rates by comparison to others; moreover, the Fayetteville rates are too high and are being assailed."[118]

I observed that the settlement process involved representatives from the PSC staff, Arkla, the industrial users, and the attorney general's office and wondered aloud if it would be appropriate for me to be there in the future as an observer/mediator for the governor's office. Without rancor, Clark said there was no precedent for this and the appearances would be viewed as unusual. It was clear Clark would not welcome this but invited me to stay in touch through him.[119]

I next approached Attorney General Winston Bryant, but found him unwilling to intrude on or even to allow attorney W. M. "Mac" Norton and me on behalf of Arkla, to visit with his assistant, who was handling the Arkla case for Bryant's office.[120] By July, when Clinton had the Democratic nomination well in hand, I received notice from Arkla's David Johnson that a conference had been held at which all parties, except for Arkansas Gas Consumers (a coalition of industrial users) had agreed to reach a settlement of retroactive and prospective gas cost issues for Arkla, AER, and Arkansas Louisiana Gas Company. They also agreed to develop language committing Arkla to fulfill its obligation under the terms of the settlement as long as no signatory caused a breach of the agreement.[121]

A settlement was filed the day after Clinton's November 3, 1992, election. Arkla agreed to a $13.5 million rate increase on behalf of subsidiary Arkansas Louisiana Gas—an 11 percent increase for residential customers and about a 50 percent reduction for heavy industrial users. On November 17, Arkla announced a broad restructuring, saying it would chop seven hundred million dollars from its debt, sell its exploration and production company, Arkla Exploration, and rework its gas distribution system in the upper Midwest, among other changes. The plan was welcomed by Wall Street analysts, but ultimately came too late to satisfy the stockholders.[122] As expected and feared, Duff & Phelps in April 1993 lowered its rating of Arkla's senior debt securities, putting about two billion dollars of them in the below-investment grade or "junk bond" category. Moody's and Standard and Poor's had downgraded Arkla's debt to one level below investment grade a year before, but Duff & Phelps did not. Now, Duff & Phelps explained, "the financial improvement resulting from Arkla's strategic restructuring efforts to date has been slower than expected. Although Arkla has reduced the amount of debt outstanding, interest coverages remain thin."[123] The prediction eventually occurred: Arkla was sold, and its headquarters was moved to Houston.

In the spring of 1992, when Clinton still was only the "presumptive" nominee, I accepted an invitation from a teaching colleague at the American Bankers Association's Stonier Graduate School of Banking at Rutgers University to be an "executive-in-residence" at the University of Virginia's School of Business in mid-April. In Charlottesville, I regaled the classes to which I spoke with my insight into Bill Clinton. I told the students, for example, about the artifacts that filled Clinton's office in the Arkansas Capitol, such as busts of Abraham Lincoln, Winston Churchill, and Franklin D. Roosevelt. Statues of meercats, arm in arm, graced the fireplace mantel, and on the west wall was a photograph of a five-year-old Bill Clinton with grandfather and grandmother Cassidy of Hope on which the caption read: "It never hurt a good man to take a few lickins." On the north wall was an excerpt from an early unidentified Clinton speech that read: "The only way to save your soul is through public service." When Clinton was contemplating or arguing about an issue, it was his habit to meander around his office and touch these familiar artifacts. My report to the University of Virginia students related Clinton's background of a father who was killed in an automobile accident three months before Clinton's birth and of an abusive, alcoholic stepfather who made him feel he had to assume the duties of head of household when he was sixteen. I further described Clinton as a brilliant student at Georgetown University, where he served as president of both the junior and senior classes, two years as a Rhodes Scholar at Oxford, and a graduate of Yale's School of Law. Through all of this, Clinton knew his life's career would be public service because he had dedicated himself to this when he shook President John F. Kennedy's hand on a Boys Nation visit to the White House. A year later, I became one of two bankers to receive the ABA's distinguished alumni award from the Stonier Graduate School of Banking.[124] On my return to Little Rock from Virginia in April 1992, I found that Tucker was attempting to get Clinton to resign as governor.

Soon after my appointment as chief of staff, *Arkansas Gazette* cartoonist George Fisher produced a cartoon depicting me at a desk behind a nameplate reading "Acting Governor Wm. Bowen." Behind me was a caricature of Tucker, mopping the floor, and wearing a sweatshirt emblazoned with the words "Lt. Gov. and Capitol Valet de chambre." Tucker was scowling at Clinton, who was depicted on his way out the office door with suitcases in both hands saying, "Well, ta ta, Bill—I know you'll take good care of things in my absence." My relations with Tucker were tense for a few days after the cartoon appeared. About the time of the special session in February 1992 when Clinton's presidential campaign was gaining momentum, however, Tucker unexpectedly hung a framed copy of the cartoon behind his desk in the lieutenant governor's office, and we never thereafter had a strained word.

This is not to say Tucker didn't have his moments, some of which may have been caused by his chronic illness. For example, when I arrived to meet with Tucker about 11 a.m. March 2 in the lieutenant governor's office, Tucker was on edge and his hands were visibly shaking. Tucker explained that it was part of his illness. I brought Tucker five doughnuts, four of which he ate, and he was noticeably revived before our visit ended at noon.

Even before Clinton announced for president, Tucker had been insistent the Arkansas governor could and should resign, but this evolved into Tucker saying with good humor that, "I don't believe he will resign—even when he's elected president."[125] Tucker even said this publicly in a speech to the Hot

Springs National Park Rotary Club in April 1992, winning laughter and applause from his audience.[126] The next day, Tucker told reporters the state budget was in trouble because of spending practices under Clinton but denied he was criticizing the presidential candidate.[127] This came five days after a lengthy memorandum bearing Clinton's name had been sent to Tucker outlining "a clear role for you and your staff" in preparations for the 1993 General Assembly session. For example, Tucker was invited to be present with staff at all executive budget hearings and legislative package-building sessions.[128]

By this time, the media were referring to Clinton as the presumptive Democratic nominee for president. In August 1991, he had held out the possibility he might resign as governor if he won the nomination, but he shut

Cartoonist George Fisher's cartoon featuring Bill Bowen was published September 25, 1991. From *The Best of Fisher: 28 Years of Editorial Cartoons for Faubus to Clinton* (Fayetteville: University of Arkansas Press, 1993).

the door on this in April after speculation became rampant in Little Rock that he was about to leave the office to Tucker. Clinton said there was no need for him to resign because:

> Everybody involved has done such a great job, especially the fine leadership of Lt. Gov. Tucker, legislative leaders and the cabinet and staff. We've enjoyed a lot of cooperation and close communication. The challenges before the state are being managed in a proper way and I've been very proud of the way our state leaders have come together to make this work.[129]

The backdrop to this was that Tucker had met privately with Clinton at the mansion about 5:45 p.m. April 14 for the purpose of renewing his request that the governor resign. When Clinton emphatically declined, Tucker mounted a campaign to get key legislators to support his position but was told they did not agree.[130] Tucker met again with Clinton on April 21 and more heatedly than ever demanded that the governor resign, saying he was "frustrated to distraction and was even considering resignation himself." Shortly after this, Tucker ceased his demands that Clinton resign.

Clinton remained resolute in May that he would not resign as governor if he won his party's presidential nomination even though a poll by Mason-Dixon Political Media Research Incorporated, of Columbia, Maryland, commissioned by the *Arkansas Democrat-Gazette,* showed 75 percent of the 826 state voters surveyed thought he should.[131] After he had received the nomination, Clinton returned to Little Rock, where he told reporters he was not planning to resign. "I don't think I should be the first governor in American history to do this. I think it would set a precedent that I don't think would be good unless there is some real reason to do it."[132]

Even after being elected president November 3, Clinton told reporters he would not resign as governor until all the legal issues had been resolved in a lawsuit brought October 21 by Arthur English, political science professor at the University of Arkansas at Little Rock.[133] English, also chairman of Common Cause, said parts of the state constitution were in conflict about how the governor's office would be filled if Clinton resigned.[134] Pulaski County Circuit Court Judge John Plegge met his self-imposed deadline, ruling November 5 that it essentially was as I had been arguing—that Tucker as lieutenant governor would assume the duties and powers but not the office of governor when Clinton left it vacant.[135] State Republican Party chairman Asa Hutchinson insisted a special election had to be held to elect Clinton's successor as governor and grumped, "I don't think we need to have an acting governor for two years. He wouldn't have the mandate for leadership he needs."[136] Everyone but Tucker and the Democratic Party apparently wanted to appeal, but it was Attorney General Winston Bryant who won the foot race to the Arkansas Supreme Court.[137] Bryant said he would not be a candidate if there was a special election. The Supreme Court expedited the case and ruled December 4 that Tucker was the one who was right—he would occupy the office of governor for the remainder of Clinton's term, rising automatically via Amendment 6.[138] Tucker and Clinton spokesmen said the governor would resign before a special legislative session on a Medicaid funding crisis was held in mid-December so that Tucker could call the shots on it.

In early June 1992, I received a memorandum from David Watkins and David Buxbaum of Clinton's campaign in Little Rock setting forth a policy that had been adopted involving those who could attend and be reimbursed for the upcoming national Democratic convention in Chicago. Limited resources had to be allocated "carefully" with an eye toward remembering that the convention "must signal the beginning of the general election—not the end of the primary season. We do not want to repeat 1988's 'mistake of treating the convention as part celebration, part reward for an overworked staff. Everyone wanted to be there, and no one stayed back to organize and plan,'" Watkins and Bauxbaum said.[139] Attached was a list allocating 120 slots at the convention with a promise of five hundred dollars reimbursement for each with the decision about who would attend resting with each department head. The list included "GOVERNOR'S STAFF—Bill Bowen and 5 staff members." Jim Guy Tucker's name was not on the list, meaning he was being afforded no invitation or hotel accommodations at the convention. This reflected the continuing "strained relationship" between Clinton and Tucker. However, there had been nearly total cooperation between Tucker and the governor's office during the spring, and I acknowledged this by making my tickets to the convention, travel reservations, and hotel accommodations available to the lieutenant governor.[140] Tucker appropriately attended the convention.

The national transition team Clinton and his leadership initially put together contained no one from Arkansas or from business, consisting as it did of Mickey Kantor, Vernon Jordan, Vermont Gov. Madeleine Kunin, Warren Christopher and Henry Cisneros. I did not feel this was right and strongly recommended in a memorandum written well before the election that the president-elect's Hope friend since boyhood, Thomas F. "Mack" McLarty, be added to the team.[141] I also revealed in the memo that I had learned there was considerable concern in the leadership of the Clinton campaign about a takeover of the transition team by "Wilshire Boulevard" types who bill by the hour, to the exclusion of the campaign team that Clinton brought to the dance, including Eli Segal, David Wilhelm, George Stephanopoulous and Rahm Emmanuel.[142] I took steps to make sure the issue of McLarty's inclusion really was brought to the attention of both Clinton and his wife, after which the president-elect agreed, and McLarty joined the team.

The "changing of the guard" in Arkansas was scheduled for 11 a.m., Saturday, December 12, 1992. I met with Clinton in the governor's office at the Capitol about 3 p.m. December 11 to review our experiences. Among the many matters we discussed was a random reference to the Basel (Switzerland) Accord among European Community bank leaders to set minimum capital standards for the institutions. I thought to myself: how many U.S. bankers even know about the Basel Accord (an expression by international bankers of the need to strengthen commercial banks by increasing capital requirements), much less governors, even one just elected to the office of president?

During the meeting, Clinton said, "I want you to be in my administration." I responded: "You owe me no such consideration."[143] No particular office was discussed at the time. In fact, John Hart of the initial Clinton–Gore transition team had asked for my résumé when Hart assumed his duties two months before. I provided the résumé and sent a copy to McLarty with a memorandum in which I assured the administration I would have no conflicts of interest because I was retired and was willing to place my assets in a blind trust and resign from the board of First Commercial Bank. I told them, "my health is good and I would like to serve in any position found acceptable by the Transition Board—within reason."[144]

Tucker also met with Clinton's staff on December 11. I told the *Arkansas Democrat-Gazette*'s Jerry Dean that I was impressed with the way in which Tucker—on the eve of a super-charged General Assembly special session, his impending inauguration as governor and the looming regulator legislative session—had set staff members' minds at ease. "Jim Guy outlined completely and cordially what those who remain could expect during transition— that everyone [who wanted to] was expected to remain in place until he could interview staff members individually to learn where they would be comfortable in their jobs." I also told Dean I had enjoyed being a witness to Clinton's "relentless energy and his remarkable talent to read, absorb and understand in depth what's going on around him. It's been an experience I've deeply cherished."[145]

Bill Bowen with then president William Jefferson Clinton at the U.S. Capitol, September 29, 1994. Clinton was there to sign the Interstate Banking bill. *Official White House photograph.*

I had discussed the one negative I found in the job much earlier, telling Rachel O'Neal of the *Arkansas Democrat-Gazette* in an October 1991 interview that:

> people expect from their governor the impossible, sometimes. There's no counterpart of that in the private sector that I have seen. The request for jobs, attention, favors, et cetera, is unending.

From my years in the private sector, I knew the public had certain misgivings about government:

> It's sort of explained by what Neil Armstrong said as he sat on top of the missile that sent him to the moon. He was reminded that the missile was made of about a million parts, all manufactured by the lowest bidder and he was kind of dubious about whether or not it was going to work. Do you not feel that the private sector wonders how effectively the public sector is working? I think each looks on the other with some suspicion.[146]

What I was offered in August 1993 on the recommendation of Bruce Lindsey was the job of chief executive officer of the Farm Credit Administration.[147] I responded August 19 with a two-page letter to the president in which I summarized the history of the Farm Credit Administration and asked, "What would the role of a former commercial banker-lawyer be in this environment? First of all, I think a commercial banker would likely be suspect in the competitive environment that exists between the commercial banking system and the farm credit system . . . I believe it is fair to recommend to you that you not put a commercial banker in the job for fear that he or she would be severely handicapped without a farm background."[148]

Chapter Eight

William H. Bowen School of Law

Arkansas is unique in that it is the least populous state in the nation with two state-funded law schools. Formal legal education began in Little Rock in 1868 with the formation of the "Little Rock Law Class," a group of young men who studied law together at night in the capital city. Logic dictates that a law school should be located near the state's seat of government, so when the University of Arkansas established a law school in the 1890s, it did so not on the school's Fayetteville campus, but in the state's capital. Soon, however, disagreements over funding—or the lack thereof—arose between the law school and the university administration and after a few years, the law school broke away from the university and became an independent school. It was administered for decades by Dean John Carmichael and, although its name became the Arkansas Law School, many thought of it, and referred to it, as the Carmichael School of Law.

The Fayetteville campus continued to grow and in the 1920s established another law school. Fayetteville offered a day program, as opposed to the night school in Little Rock, and the school was accredited by the American Bar Association—a distinction that became even more important over time.

In Little Rock, many of my fellow members of the Bar and I became convinced that the capital city needed an accredited law school. In 1967, the Arkansas Law School graduated its last class and the University of Arkansas at Fayetteville opened an evening-only campus in Little Rock. The program grew quickly, as did the desire for a day program. In 1974, the Arkansas

General Assembly ended the Little Rock campus's affiliation with Fayetteville and instead, joined it to the new University of Arkansas at Little Rock. Like Fayetteville, the new UALR Law School enjoyed both American Bar Association accreditation and membership in the Association of American Law Schools. It fulfilled the pent-up demand particularly of nontraditional students who, for various reasons, could not relocate to Fayetteville for three years to attend law school. As a result of Bar influence, the new law school placed more of an emphasis on skills teaching than legal theory, which was the norm at the time.

By 1990, the UALR Law School was seeking a new dean to replace Lawrence H. Averill, Jr., who had resigned to take the position of administrative assistant to Chief Justice William Rehnquist of the United States Supreme Court. Long-time faculty member Fenton Adams served as acting dean for a year while the law school searched for a replacement.

The dean search process is one that often mystifies and confounds people who have never served on faculties. In almost all cases, a dean search committee is formed, chaired by a senior faculty member and comprised mainly of law faculty, with perhaps a university administrator, one or two alumni, and one or more law students as members. The search process is nationwide; announcements of the position are sent to all ABA-accredited American law schools and are advertised in various legal and academic publications, such as the *Chronicle of Higher Education* and the *American Bar Association Journal.* This process encourages outsiders to apply. Indeed, local applicants are often disadvantaged because they are known to the search committee and faculty and thus their weaknesses are evident, unlike outsiders who present only a positive face through their résumés and references.

As with most dean searches, different factions on the faculty wanted different strengths in the new dean. Some people thought that the next dean should be a scholar who by example would encourage and promote increased scholarship at the law school. Others argued that at this point in the school's history, a fund-raiser was needed to build endowment in order to strengthen the school's programs. During 1990–91, a nationwide search narrowed the field to one candidate, John Makdisi, a faculty member at Cleveland State University. After a lengthy negotiation with the UALR administration, however, he turned down the offer. Makdisi was the archetypal scholar-dean, with a strong academic background and a long list of publications. Once again, during 1991–92 the dean search committee conducted a nationwide search for a dean. This time the voices urging that a fundraiser with strong local ties be hired were more numerous, and I was interviewed for the job.

The search committee ultimately offered the position to professor Howard Eisenberg from Southern Illinois University. He was a good match for the UALR Law School because of his strong practice background (prior to his move to the academic world he had served first as the Wisconsin State Public Defender from 1972–78, and later as defender director and then executive director of the National Legal Aid and Defender Association from 1978–83) and his commitment to skills teaching.

Eisenberg enjoyed a successful four-year tenure as dean, but in 1995 he was offered the deanship at Marquette University, close to his and his wife's homes in Chicago and Madison. When he announced his resignation, several faculty members, led by professor Kenneth Gould, floated the idea of naming me dean for two years, with the idea that I could build on the fundraising effort that Eisenberg had begun while the school conducted a thorough nationwide search for the next dean. Chancellor Charles E. Hathaway was agreeable to the plan, as was I. In July 1995, at age 72, I became dean of the law school.

The three most pressing needs during my tenure were to conduct a significant fundraising effort for the school, to ensure a successful sabbatical inspection for reaccreditation by the American Bar Association and the Association of American Law Schools, and to facilitate the selection of a successor dean. Assisted by two capable administrators, associate dean Charles Goldner Jr. and law library director Lynn Foster, I planned to be an "external" dean—one who actively participated in activities and organizations outside of the law school and the academe.

My first task, however, was to attend a "dean school" for new administrators at Wake Forest University in June. There I was warned by speakers to beware of tenured faculty, a myopic central administration, a nonsupporting alumni body, and a shortfall in financial support. In my first letter to alumni, however, I stated that these cautions might be appropriate for the normal school, but they had little application here. I assumed the deanship just three years after the law school had moved to new and spacious facilities next to MacArthur Park. Just one year before, in 1994, *National Jurist* magazine had ranked law schools by student satisfaction and UALR School of Law ranked thirteenth out of 165.

My fundraising approach included several aspects. First, I used my extensive contacts to generate gifts to the law school. The Altheimer Foundation, established from the estate of attorney Benjamin J. Altheimer, had long been a supporter of the law school, funding salary enhancement for a faculty position and an annual lectureship. I served as a trustee of the foundation and enthusiastically supported the foundation's decision to donate $450,000 from the dissolution of the trust to an endowment to underwrite the Altheimer Distinguished Professorship and the Altheimer Lectures. I was also responsible for a gift of ten thousand dollars from the Bernice Jones Trust to fund a joint study of a health law program by the law school and the University of Arkansas for Medical Sciences.

I also sought to galvanize alumni support of the law school. During my first year as dean, more than one hundred alumni attended a reception at the Governor's Mansion. In February 1996, 150 alumni attended a dinner and ceremony at the Excelsior Hotel celebrating the law school's twentieth anniversary as part of UALR. At the dinner, various law school supporters were honored, including Federal District Judge Henry Woods, Judge William R. Wilson, former state Senator Max Howell, Rep. Ray Thornton, James B. Sharp, and Byron Eiseman. The year marked a coming of age of the alumni association of the law school.

During the same year, the law school prepared for its accreditation visit, which happened once every seven years. The visit required a huge amount of preparation. A self-study, along with many appendices, was prepared, reflecting the law faculty's view of the school's strengths and weaknesses and its success or failure at meeting the American Bar Association standards. The law school's long range planning committee, chaired by Professor Foster, carried out the self-study process and drafted the report, which was then edited and approved by the faculty. At the end of February the inspection team arrived, comprised of law faculty members from different schools around the United States, one practicing attorney, and one university counsel. The team visited for three days, meeting with students, faculty, university administrators, alumni, and members of the legal community. They were impressed by the facility and the good relations between students and faculty. At the exit interview for the accreditation review team, Chancellor Hathaway described the law school as "a jewel in the University's crown." The team's report was favorable. It was reviewed by the ABA's accreditation committee, which ultimately required the law school to report back on three main areas—addressing the adequacy of financial resources to operate the school's programs, resolving acoustic problems in two large classrooms, and creating a provision for security similar to tenure for our writing instructors and clinic supervising attorneys. This was the first accreditation report that was not highly critical of the law school facilities, and the committee recognized that we were already working to resolve all three issues.[1]

The new law school building should have been an inspiration for fundraising, but it proved not to be the case from 1992–96. In fact, in that first year, with a new dean on board in a new building, and with a lot of attention focused on the school, the school received only $255,000 in donations. I realized we needed a development office. Julie Baldridge Speed emerged as the top choice for development director. She immediately went about formalizing our outreach effort, our solicitation records system, and organized a team of student and alumni supporters. Her legislative experience, both with Associate Justice Ray Thornton when he was in Congress, and Bill Clinton when he was in the governor's office, added needed insight into state and federal funding sources.

One concern for me, as for any dean, was what former Dean Eisenberg called the "brooding omnipresence of the two law schools issue."[2] Beginning at least in the 1990s, there was a biennial question in the legislature whether Arkansas needed two state-supported law schools. Even lawyers seemed to be of the opinion that there were too many lawyers. While Fayetteville's school has a larger enrollment and faculty, only UALR held night classes and it enrolled more part-time students. Bar passage rates continued to be high at UALR (in February 1996, 92.2 percent passed the bar examination) and the two schools cooperated productively. By the end of the decade, the legislature was no longer questioning the need—still, outside fundraising remained an important part of the dean's job.

During my two years as dean, professor Glenn Pasvogel chaired the dean search committee and conducted a nationwide search for a dean who would continue the fundraising effort and also raise the school's reputation among its peers. Rodney K. Smith, a faculty member at the Capital School of Law in Columbus, Ohio, made a favorable impression on both the faculty and the university administration. Smith had been dean at both Capital and the University of Montana law schools. In June 1997, I stepped down and Smith assumed the deanship July 1. My support for the law school, however, continued.

In December 1998, Chancellor Hathaway and Dean Goldner approached me about making a gift to the law school. Within the month, I agreed to donate $2.5 million in Regions Bank stock and cash between December 1998 and January 2000. The endowment from this gift was used to establish the

Bowen Scholars Program. Bowen Scholars are chosen on the basis of merit, need, and what they can offer to the student body. The gift was, and remains, the largest in the law school's history—although I will readily cede that record to anyone who would like to contribute more.

In 1999, the law school faculty honored me by naming the law school after me. The naming ceremony was held outside on Thursday, April 27. Students, faculty, and several hundred local attorneys attended. President William Jefferson Clinton gave the keynote address in a lineup that included such speakers as Chancellor Hathaway, UA board of trustees chairman Tommy May, former White House chief of staff Mack McLarty, then law school dean Rod Smith, and student bar president Derrick Smith. It was a proud moment for me as Clinton described my recall from retirement by saying, "I wasn't surprised when you agreed not to grow old, but to help the young."[3]

During the ceremony, I referenced a 1996 speech by Alan Greenspan, chairman of the Federal Reserve System, who added a new yardstick to measuring market performance. He asked if "irrational exuberance had unduly escalated asset value." Borrowing from that language, I told the audi-

Bill Bowen shares a laugh with then president William Jefferson Clinton in Little Rock during the ceremony to rename the UALR School of Law after Bowen, April 27, 2000.

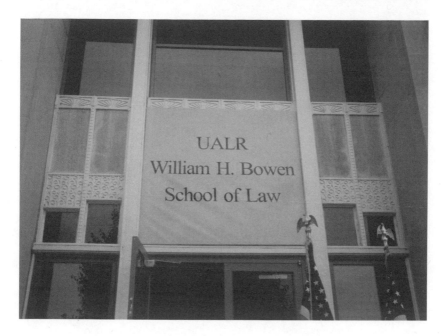

The renamed UALR William H. Bowen School of Law in Little Rock.

ence about my "rational exuberance" for the direction that the law school was heading. I told them how proud I was of the excellent faculty, the fact that ten percent of the student body was African American, and that women made up nearly fifty percent of the enrollment. I pointed out the distinctiveness of the night division, which allows students who are employed full-time or who care for families during the day to attend classes. I believe that this serves both our students and our community well, and our graduates serve in the public and private sectors with distinction. I firmly believe that supporters of the school should be exuberant and I know that the William H. Bowen School of Law is a, indeed if not the, "jewel" in UALR's crown.

Epilogue

The book is finally done! It focuses too much attention on me, but it seems that an autobiography requires it. Not enough attention is given to former UALR Chancellor Chuck Hathaway for commissioning the book, nor to Laura Miller, for compiling these remembrances—nor to President Clinton, who is especially generous in his gracious forward. To them and the guidance of others listed in the introduction, I close with my heartfelt appreciation.

William H. Bowen

Appendix

National Advisory Board Members, 1972–1998

1972—FOUNDING MEMBERS

James E. Davis	Board chairman, Winn-Dixie Stores, Inc.—Jacksonville, FL
Dr. Neil E. Harlan	McKinsey & Company, Inc.—Washington, D.C.
Henry Henley, Jr.	President, Cluett, Peabody & Co.—New York, NY
Marvin Hurley	Executive vice president, Houston (Texas) Chamber of Commerce
J. S. McDonnell	McDonnell-Douglas, Inc.—Portland, OR
Sidney A. McKnight	Executive vice president, Montgomery Ward and Co.—Chicago, IL
Frank Pace, Jr.	Corporation for Public Broadcasting—New York, NY
John G. Phillips	President of Louisiana Land and Exploration Co.— New Orleans, LA
George Stinson	President of National Steel Corp.—Pittsburgh, PA
Thomas R. Vaughan	Chairman, Freeport Mining Co.— New York, NY
Kemmons Wilson	Founder and Board Chairman, Holiday Inns, Inc.—Memphis, TN
Charles H. Murphy, Jr.	President, Murphy Oil Corp.—El Dorado, AR
Fred Pickens	Attorney and chairman of the board of UA trustees—Newport, AR
Robert E. L. Wilson, III	Lee Wilson & Co. and chairman of the Bank of Wilson, AR

1972—NEW MEMBERS

William Seawell	President, Pan American World Airways, Inc.—New York, NY
H. L. Hembree	President, Arkansas Best Corp.—Fort Smith, AR

1975—NEW MEMBERS

The Right Reverend John Maury Allin	Bishop of the Episcopal Church—New York, NY
W. Carroll Bumpers	President, Greyhound Leasing & Financial Corp.—Phoenix, AZ
Charles M. Kittrell	Executive vice president, Phillips Petroleum Co.—Bartlesville, OK
Raymond H. Rebsamen	CPA, owned and operated a conglomerate of companies engaged in printing, insurance, auto sales, finance, and banking—Little Rock, AR

1977—NEW MEMBERS

W. Donham Crawford	President, Edison Electric Institute—New York, NY
Frederick D. Watkins	President, Aetna Insurance Co.—Hartford, CT

1978—NEW MEMBERS

E. H. Boullioun	President, Boeing Commercial Airplane Co.— Seattle, WA
J. Lynn Helms	Chairman, President, and CEO of Piper Aircraft Corp.—Lock Haven, PA

1980—NEW MEMBER

Sam F. Segnar	President and CEO, InterNorth, Inc.—Omaha, NE

1981–82 NEW MEMBERS

Ray C. Adam	President and CEO, NL Industries, Inc.—New York, NY
William P. Stiritz	Chairman and CEO, Ralston Purina Co.—St. Louis, MO
Jackson T. Stephens	Chairman and CEO, Stephens, Inc.—Little Rock, AR

1983—NEW MEMBERS

R. R. Baxter	President and CEO, CF Industries, Inc.—Long Grove, IL
M. D. Matthews	Chairman, President, and CEO of Houston Natural Gas Corp.—Houston, TX

1984—NEW MEMBER

William Dillard, Sr.	Chairman and CEO, Dillard Department Stores—Little Rock, AR

1985—NEW MEMBERS

Robert H. Dedman	Chairman, Club Corporation of America—Dallas, TX
John H. Johnson	Founder, publisher, and chairman, Johnson Publishing Co.—Chicago, IL
William N. Small	Admiral, U.S. Navy—born in Little Rock, AR
Donald J. Tyson	President and CEO, Tyson Foods, Inc.—Springdale, AR

1988—NEW MEMBERS

Dr. Mary L. Good	President, Signal Research Center, Inc.—Des Plaines, IL
Joe M. Henson	President and CEO (Ret.), Prime Computer, Inc.—Natick, MA
Fred W. Smith	President and COO, Donrey Media Group—Las Vegas, NV
Jerry L. Maulden	Chairman, Entergy Arkansas—Little Rock, AR
Mack McLarty	Chairman and CEO, Arkla Gas Co., Inc.—Little Rock, AR

1989–1990—NEW MEMBERS

J. Virgil Waggoner	President and CEO, Sterling Chemicals, Inc.—Houston, TX
Frank D. Hickingbotham	Chairman and CEO, TCBY Enterprises—Little Rock, AR
J. B. Hunt	Chairman, J. B. Hunt Transport Services—Lowell, AR
Charles D. Morgan	Chairman and CEO, Acxiom Corp.—Conway, AR
W. Thomas Stephens	President and CEO, Manville Corp.—Denver, CO

1991—NEW MEMBERS

Dale P. Jones	President, Halliburton Co.—Dallas, TX
Charles T. Meyer	Chairman, Meyer's Bakeries—Little Rock, AR
General William Y. Smith	President (Ret.), Institute for Defense Analysis—Alexandria, VA
William R. Toller	Chairman and CEO, Witco Corp.—Greenwich, CT

1992—NEW MEMBERS

Maya Angelou	Poet, author, and Reynolds Professor of American Studies at Wake Forest University—Winston-Salem, NC
George W. Edwards, Jr.	President and CEO, Kansas City Southern Railway Co.—Kansas City, MO
Harry C. Gambill	President, Trans Union Corporation—Fullerton, CA

F. S. Garrison	President and CEO, American Freightways, Inc.—Harrison, AR
Jerry Jones	Owner Dallas Cowboys—Dallas, TX
Patricia P. "Patti" Upton	President and CEO, Aromatique, Inc.—Heber Springs, AR
Helen Robson Walton	Civic leader, Sam Walton's widow—Bentonville, AR

1993–94 NEW MEMBERS

Col. Lloyd L. Burke	U.S. Army (Ret.)—Hot Springs, AR
Ernest G. Green	Managing Director, Lehman Brothers and one of the Little Rock Nine—the nine African American students who integrated Little Rock's Central High School in 1957—Washington, D.C.
Harry Thomason	Television producer—Los Angeles, CA
Elizabeth Peck Williams	Broadway producer, winner of the 1992 Tony Award and 1993 Olivier Award for Best Musical —New York, NY
Dr. Farris W. Womack	Executive VP and CFO, University of Michigan—Ann Arbor, MI

Notes

Chapter One: The Boy From Altheimer

1. Tom Brokaw, *The Greatest Generation* (New York: Random House, 1998), xix.

2. Willard B. Gatewood, "The Arkansas Delta: The Deepest of the Deep South," in *The Arkansas Delta: Land of Paradox* ed. Jeannie Whayne and Willard B. Gatewood (Fayetteville: University of Arkansas Press, 1993), 5.

3. Gatewood, 19–20.

4. William Oats Ragsdale, *They Sought a Land: A Settlement in the Arkansas River Valley, 1840–1870* (Fayetteville: University of Arkansas Press, 1997), 1–14.

5. Ragsdale, 91–92.

6. Bill Bowen, "Lois Ruth Falls Bowen," *Pope County Historical Quarterly*, 22, no.1 (March 1988): 3–10.

7. *Arkansas Gazette*, November 12, 1907.

8. *Arkansas Gazette*, November 14, 1886.

9. Ibid.

10. *Agricultural Yearbook*, United States Department of Agriculture, 1920.

11. Kim Allen Scott, "Plague on the Homefront: Arkansas and the Great Influenza Epidemic of 1918," *Arkansas Historical Quarterly*, 47, no. 4 (1988): 311–43.

12. Scott, 340.

13. *Agricultural Yearbook*, United States Department of Agriculture, 1935.

14. Russell Bearden, "Jefferson County's Worst Disaster," *Arkansas Historical Quarterly*, 43, no. 4 (1984): 332.

15. *Arkansas Gazette*, April 16, 1927.

16. *Arkansas Gazette*, April 19, 1927.

17. *Arkansas Gazette*, April 20, 1927.

18. Bearden, 325–28.

19. Pete Daniel, *Deep'n as it Come: The 1927 Mississippi Flood* (New York: Oxford University Press, 1977), 11.

20. Daniel, 10.

21. Mary Rathbone, *Castle on the Rock 1881–1985: History of the Little Rock District Army Corps of Engineers* (Little Rock: U.S. Army Engineers District, 1990), 47.

22. *Agricultural Yearbook*, 1935.

23. T. J. Woofer Jr., *Landlord and Tenant on the Cotton Plantation* (New York: Negro University Press, 1969), xxiii.

24. Nan E. Woodruff, *As Rare as Rain: Federal Relief in the Great Southern Drought of 1930–31* (Urbana: University of Illinois Press, 1985), 5–6.

25. *Agricultural Yearbook*, United States Department of Agriculture, 1931.

26. T. H. Watkins, *The Great Depression: America in the 1930s* (Boston: Little, Brown and Co., 1993), 61.

27. Roger Lambert, "Hoover and the Red Cross in the Arkansas Drought of 1930," *Arkansas Historical Quarterly*, 29, no. 1 (Spring, 1970): 9.

28. Woodruff, 30–31.

29. Lambert, 18.

30. Watkins, 114.

31. Paul E. Mertz, *The New Deal Policy and Southern Rural Poverty* (Baton Rouge: Louisiana State University Press, 1978), 20.

32. David Eugene Conrad, *The Forgotten Farmers: The Story of Sharecroppers in the New Deal* (Urbana: University of Illinois Press, 1965), 44.

33. Conrad, 61.

34. Mertz, 28.

35. Angie Haymon, in interview with Laura Miller, April 8, 1997, Altheimer, Arkansas. Tape and transcripts housed at the University of Arkansas at Little Rock Archives and Special Collections.

Chapter Two: Becoming a Navy Fighter Pilot

1. Arkansas National Guard Museum exhibit.

2. Robert James Maddox, *The United States and World War II* (Boulder, CO: Westview Press, 1992), 113.

3. Gordon W. Prange, with Donald M. Goldstein and Katherine V. Dillon, *Miracle at Midway* (New York: McGraw-Hill Book Co., 1982), xi.

4. Donald M. Goldstein and Katherine V. Dillon, *The Williwaw War: The Arkansas National Guard in the Aleutians in World War II* (Fayetteville: The University of Arkansas Press, 1992), vii.

5. Goldstein and Dillon, 243.

6. Goldstein and Dillon, 242.

7. S. Charles Bolton, "World War II and Economic Development," *Arkansas Historical Quarterly*, 61, no. 2, (Summer 2002):141–43.

8. Samuel Hynes, *Flights of Passage: Reflections of a World War II Aviator*, (Annapolis: Naval Institute Press, 1988), 45.

9. Wesley Price, "Fear," *The Saturday Evening Post*, August 12, 1944.

10. The combat team consisted of myself, Aycock, Beall, and Rosen—all Arkansans—as well as H. E. "Dit" Mongovan of Maine and Bill Ducharme of New York.

11. Hynes, 95.

12. The peacetime draft of 1940, with updating amendments through World War II, Korea, Vietnam, and numerous military engagements through the summer of 1972, ended in the summer of 1973. Unless mobilized and placed on active duty, reservists and guardsmen were viewed as "weekend" warriors because of drill one weekend a month and two weeks of summer training.

Chapter Three: Learning to be a Tax Lawyer

1. Michael J. Bennett, *When Dreams Came True: The GI Bill and the Making of Modern America,* (Washington: Brassey's Inc., 1996), 22.

2. John A. Kirk, *Redefining the Color Line: Black Activism in Little Rock, Arkansas, 1940–1970* (Gainesville: University Press of Florida, 2002), 32.

3. Kirk, 60–72.

4. Kirk, 61.

5. *Anderson v. Robinson,* 115 F. Supp. 776 (D. Mont. 1953).

6. *Kuhn v. Thompson,* 48 AFTR 1373 (E.D. Ark. 1953).

7. *KOMA, Inc. v. Commissioner, Tulsa Broadcasting Co. v. Commissioner,* 189 F.2d 390 (10th Cir. 1951).

8. *Collector of Revenues v. KOMA, Inc.,* 218 F.2d 530 (10th Cir. 1955).

9. *Chandler v. Judicial Council of the 10th Cir.,* 398 U.S. 74, 90 S. Ct. 1648 (1970).

Chapter Four: Building a Tax Law Practice

1. *Cheney v. Stephens, Inc.,* 231 Ark. 541, 330 S.W.2d 949 (1960).

2. *W. S. Bushmiaer v. United States,* 230 F.2d 146 (8th Cir. 1956).

3. *W. S. Bushmiaer v. United States,* 146 F. Supp. 329 (W. D. Ark. 1956).

4. *Dortch v. N.Y. Life Ins. Co.,* 268 F.2d. 149 (8th Cir. 1959).

5. *Estate of Minnie V. Parkin v. United States,* 1971 WL 369 (E. D. Ark.).

6. *Barrineau v. Brown,* 240 Ark. 599, 401 S.W.2d 30 (1965).

7. Ron Wolfe, "Gangster Gained Respectability in Hot Springs, the Story Goes," *Arkansas Democrat-Gazette,* March 13, 2003.

8. Ibid.

9. *Stephens v. United States,* 216 F. Supp. 854 (E. D. Ark. 1963).

10. *Ark. Bank and Trust Co. v. United States,* 224 F. Supp. 171 (W. D. Ark. 1963).

11. *Izard v. Ark. Savings and Loan Assn. Board,* 239 Ark. 670, 393 S.W.2d 245 (Ark. 1965).

12. *Bell v. Commissioner,* Tax Ct. Memo 1957–201.

13. *Beaver v. Commissioner,* 55 T. C. 85 (1970).

Chapter Five: Commercial Banking

1. Carol Griffee, "Laws Permitting Multi-bank Firms Seen by Bearden," *Arkansas Gazette,* August 19, 1974.

2. Ernest Dumas, "Banking Future at Stake, Foes and FABCO Say," *Arkansas Gazette,* June 27, 1970.

3. Ibid.

4. "FABCO Bill Passed, Sent to Governor," *Arkansas Gazette,* January 30, 1971.

5. Doug Smith, "House Passes Bill on Bank Expansion of Branch Services," *Arkansas Gazette,* February 2, 1973.

6. Statement of Condition. Commercial National Bank. Little Rock, Arkansas. June 30, 1971.

7. Carol Griffee, "Attempt to Remove State's Usury Law to Begin Next Year," *Arkansas Gazette,* December 21, 1973.

8. Leland DuVall, "Laws on Usury Help Machinery of the Fed Work," *Arkansas Gazette,* October 21, 1973.

9. Ibid.

10. "Usury Bill Amended to Give the States Power to Override," *Arkansas Gazette,* August 14, 1974.

11. Ibid.

12. "Bid to Raise Interest Limit Called Moot," *Arkansas Gazette,* October 18, 1974.

13. Ernest Dumas, "'57' Defeated by Large Margin; 2 Amendments Apparently Win," *Arkansas Gazette,* November 6, 1974.

14. "Bid to Raise Interest Limit Called Moot."

15. Ibid.

16. "Arkansas Bankers Oppose More Holding Companies," *Arkansas Gazette,* August 29, 1974.

17. Ibid.

18. John Brummett, "Extra Session of Assembly Ruled Illegal," *Arkansas Gazette,* June 3, 1980.

19. "Proposal for Legislature to Set Ceiling on Usury Goes Down to Defeat," *Arkansas Gazette,* November 5, 1980.

20. Leroy Donald, "Proponents on Both Sides Unsure of Defeats' Effects," *Arkansas Gazette,* November 16, 1980.

21. David Palmer and Leroy Donald, "Bill Further Pre-empts Arkansas Usury Law," *Arkansas Gazette,* October 18, 1980.

22. Steele Hays, "Challenge of Bank Act Upheld; Interest Ruling Stuns State's Lenders," *Arkansas Gazette,* December 23, 1980.

23. Dave Edmark, "U.S. Law Upheld In Usury Reversal," *Arkansas Gazette,* February 24, 1981.

24. Ibid.

25. David R. Palmer, "Credit Council to Fight Usury Battle at County Level," *Arkansas Gazette,* July 11, 1982.

26. *1982 Arkansas Elections. A Compilation of Primary, Run-Off and General Election Results for State and District Offices* (Little Rock: Secretary of State's Office, Elections Division, 1982), 82.

27. Doug Smith, "Vote Solidly Supports Proposal Increasing Interest Rate Ceiling," *Arkansas Gazette,* November 3, 1982.

28. Ibid.

29. "Expanded Services Prepared LR Bank for New Decade," *Arkansas Democrat,* April 13, 1980.

30. Ibid.

31. Randy Tardy, "CNB Thrives," *Arkansas Democrat*, March 22, l981.

32. Ibid.

33. Randy Tardy, "CNB Officers Term 1980 a Good Year in Report," *Arkansas Democrat*, March 11, 1981.

34. "CNB Thrives."

35. "Bank Acquisition Gains Approval," *Arkansas Gazette*, October 28, 1981.

36. Leroy Donald, "2 LR Banks May Merge, Begin Study," *Arkansas Gazette*, May 27, 1982.

37. Ibid.

38. Ibid.

39. Ibid.

40. David R. Palmer, "It's 'Business as Usual' While LR Banks Study Merger Possibility," *Arkansas Gazette*, May 28, 1982.

41. Ibid.

42. "First National, Commercial Plan To Finish Merger by End of Year," *Arkansas Gazette*, June 4, 1982.

43. David R. Palmer, "Question of Bank Merger Boils Down to Amount of Competition for Loans," *Arkansas Gazette*, December 19, 1982.

44. Ibid.

45. "Federal Comptroller's Office Approves Planned Merger of CNB, First National," *Arkansas Gazette*, May 28, 1983.

46. Ibid.

47. "Deadline Passes for Agency to Oppose LR Bank Merger," *Arkansas Gazette*, June 28, 1983.

48. Max Brantley, "Merging Banks Hire Consultant," *Arkansas Gazette*, July 2, 1983.

49. Carol Griffee and John Brummett, "Stephens Drops Bid to Take Over Bank," *Arkansas Gazette*, July 13, 1983.

50. "Bank Directors Study Response to Stock Offer," *Arkansas Gazette*, July 12, 1983.

51. Carol Griffee and John Brummett, "Stephens Drops Bid to Take Over Bank." *Arkansas Gazette*, July 13, 1983; p. 1A.

52. Ibid.

53. Ibid.

54. "Official Time of Birth to be 4:20 p.m.," *Arkansas Democrat*, July 31, 1983.

55. Ibid.

56. Ibid.

57. "Edwin C. Kane Retires; Banker in LR 30 Years," *Arkansas Gazette*, August 6, 1983.

58. "Vinson to Fill Chairmanship Held by Kane," *Arkansas Gazette*, August 18, 1983.

59. "Stephenses, Investors Arrange to Buy Control Of FABCO for $60 Million," *Arkansas Gazette,* October 22, 1983.

60. "Cravens Leaves Post At First Commercial; Bowen Has New Title," *Arkansas Gazette,* January 27, 1984.

61. Ibid.

62. "Holding Firm Seeks to Obtain Second Bank," *Arkansas Gazette,* September 10, 1983.

63. "Morrilton Bank to Be Acquired," *Arkansas Gazette,* January 29, 1984.

64. "Bank Board Urges Accepting Offer," *Arkansas Gazette,* May 5, 1985.

65. "Bank Firms Sign Pact to Merge," *Arkansas Gazette,* July 23, 1985.

66. "S. Arkansans Named to Posts In Bank Firm," *Arkansas Gazette,* July 19, 1984; "CEO of Bank Goes to Grace," *Arkansas Gazette,* July 23, 1987.

67. "Grace Elected President of First Commercial Corporation," *Arkansas Gazette,* December 24, 1988.

68. "Bowen to Advise Fed for 1984," *Arkansas Gazette,* November 16, 1983.

69. "Oklahoma Bank Shut; State Firms Buy It," *Arkansas Gazette,* January 9, 1987.

70. "First Commercial Reports 19 Percent Earnings Drop," *Arkansas Democrat,* January 21, 1987.

71. "LR Company Offers to Buy Harrison Bank," *Arkansas Gazette,* September 2, 1987.

72. "First Commercial Earnings Up 37 Percent," *Arkansas Gazette,* April 20, 1988.

73. Dave Wannemacher, "Benton Bank in Deal," *Arkansas Democrat,* July 23, 1988.

74. James M. Hopkins, "Price of Benton Bank $16.75 Million," *Arkansas Gazette,* October 1, 1988.

75. James M. Hopkins, "Firm Plans to Buy Bank in England," *Arkansas Gazette,* August 17, 1988.

76. James M. Hopkins, "Bank Going to Cabot Via England," *Arkansas Gazette,* August 18, 1988.

77. Howard Coan, "Bank May Be Boring, But It's Successful," *Arkansas Democrat,* March 19, 1989.

78. Ibid.

79. William H. Bowen and Barnett Grace to First Commercial Corporation shareholders, April 21, 1989. In the author's possession.

80. C. S. Heinbockel. "First Commercial Cuts Deal," *Arkansas Gazette,* July 18, 1989.

81. Dave Wannemacher, "Firm Logs Record Earnings," *Arkansas Gazette,* January 17, 1990.

82. Dave Wannemacher, "First Commercial Seeks to Form Trust Company," *Arkansas Gazette,* March 1, 1990.

83. James Scudder, "Lottery Opponents, Supporter Square Off," *Arkansas Gazette,* May 12, 1990.

84. Dave Wannemacher, "LR Bank Buys Memphis S&L," *Arkansas Gazette*, June 16, 1990.

85. Ibid.

86. Ibid.

87. Steve Barnes, "Get Ready, Arkansas—Bowen Retiring," *Log Cabin Democrat* (Conway, AR), April 22, 1990.

Chapter Six: Private Sector—Public Service

1. "59 Ex-Arkansans Accept Invitation to Visit, See How Things Are Going," *Arkansas Gazette*, October 13, 1963.

2. Ibid.

3. "Ex-Arkansans Say State's Progress is Fantastic," *Arkansas Gazette*, October 20, 1963.

4. "History—Interstate 630 Route, Little Rock, Arkansas," unpublished history, Arkansas Highway and Transportation Department, n.d.

5. *Arkansas Gazette*, January 7, 1969, and January 23, 1969.

6. Commercial National Bank of Little Rock, *National Advisory Board*, annual report, 1971, 2-3.

7. Ibid.

8. Commercial National Bank of Little Rock, *The 1972 Report of the National Advisory Board*, 10.

9. Ibid.

10. Commercial National Bank of Little Rock, *The Buffalo Hunter Versus the Environmentalist*, 1973 Report of the National Advisory Board, 6.

11. Ibid.

12. Commercial National Bank of Little Rock, *The People's University—Viewpoints on Continuing Education*, 1974 report of the National Advisory Board.

13. First Commercial Bank, *History of the National Advisory Board (1971-1998)*, (as outlined in excerpts from each year's annual report), 4.

14. Commercial National Bank of Little Rock, *The Power Shift—Arkansas' Opportunity*, 1976 Report of the National Advisory Board.

15. Commercial National Bank of Little Rock, *Arkansas' Water: A Fragile Wealth*, 1977 Report of the National Advisory Board.

16. Ibid.

17. Commercial National Bank of Little Rock, *Energy for Arkansas: A Challenge to Survival*, 1978 Report of the National Advisory Board. "Hard" and "soft" paths refer to the way physicist Amory B. Lovins divided the energy debate. "Hard" was his terminology for the past and existing use of massive coal, gas, and nuclear-fired electric generating stations; "soft" was conservation and the use of renewable resources.

18. Commercial National Bank of Little Rock, *The Road Ahead: Economic*

Development For Arkansas In The Decade Of The Eighties,1979 Report of the National Advisory Board, 15.

19. *The Road Ahead.*

20. "LR Bank Creates Scholarship Fund; $300,000 Pledged," *Arkansas Gazette,* April 15, 1980.

21. Commercial National Bank of Little Rock, *Arkansas Agriculture: The Renewing Miracle,* 1980 Report of the National Advisory Board, 18.

22. Marilyn Hodoway (executive assistant, Regions Bank), in interview with Carol Griffee, June 28, 2001.

23. Commercial National Bank of Little Rock, *Aging in Arkansas,* 1981 Report of the National Advisory Board, 23–24.

24. Commercial National Bank of Little Rock, *Images And Realities of Arkansas,* 1982 Report Of The National Advisory Board. This document was accorded first place honors for 1982 annual reports in the National Federation of Press Women's annual communications contest.

25. Ibid.

26, Ibid.

27. Carol Griffee, "Science, Technology Authority Holds Organizational Meeting, Elects Officers," *Arkansas Gazette,* July 7, 1983.

28. Ibid.

29. First Commercial Bank of Little Rock, *Toxicology: Today's Target For Tomorrow In Central Arkansas,* 1983 Report of the National Advisory Board, 8.

30. First Commercial Bank of Little Rock, *Capital: The Missing Link,* 1984 Report of the National Advisory Board, 18–20.

31. First Commercial Bank of Little Rock, *Leadership Formula For Arkansas,* 1985–86 Report of the National Advisory Board, 7.

32. *Leadership Formula for Arkansas.*

33. John Brummett, "Shroud Lifts; Grand Idea for States Gives Rise to Mysterious Gathering," *Arkansas Gazette,* August 7, 1986.

34. Scott Morris, "Business Council to Take Spotlight," *Arkansas Gazette,* September 11, 1988.

35. *Leadership Formula For Arkansas,* 10.

36. "Business Council to Take Spotlight."

37. Robert Reich, the major presenter at the National Advisory Board's 1987 meeting, later became secretary of labor in President Bill Clinton's cabinet.

38. First Commercial Bank of Little Rock, *Toward a New Arkansas Economy,* 1987 Report of The National Advisory Board, 6–16.

39. *Toward a New Arkansas Economy.*

40. Arkansas Business Council Foundation, *In Pursuit of Excellence— Recommendations for Reform of Education in Arkansas,* Little Rock, September 1988.

41. First Commercial Bank of Little Rock, *A Partnership For Arkansas,* 1988 Report of the National Advisory Board, 3.

42. "Bank Board Backs Report on Education," *Arkansas Gazette,* October 23, 1988.

43. "Arkansas Business Council Changed But Alive and Well," *Arkansas Gazette,* January 13, 1991.

44. "Bank Board Backs Report on Education."

45. Ibid.

46. Act 250 of 1997. Bureau of Legislative Research.

47. First Commercial Bank of Little Rock, *The Arkansas Research Center,* 1990 Report of the National Advisory Board, 4.

48. *The Arkansas Research Center,* 5.

49. Ibid.

50. *The Arkansas Research Center,* 12.

51. First Commercial Bank of Little Rock, *Progress Report: The Arkansas Institute—A Center for Public Policy Research,* 1991 Report of the National Advisory Board, 2.

52. David Smith, "Think Tank Ready with Funds, Leader," *Arkansas Gazette,* September 26, 1991.

53. "Arkansas Institute Hires Californian as Top Executive," *Arkansas Democrat-Gazette,* December 30, 1992.

54. Ibid.

55. Jake Sandlin, "Arkansas Institute Communication Tool, its President Says," *Arkansas Democrat-Gazette,* June 7, 1993.

56. John Ahlen, Ph.D. (president, Arkansas Science and Technology Authority), in interview with Carole Griffee, July 2, 2001.

57. First Commercial Bank of Little Rock, *The 90s—Arkansas' Decade,* 1992 Report of the National Advisory Board, 18–19.

58. *Maximizing the Potential,* 1993–94 Report of the National Advisory Board, 14–15.

59. Ibid.

60. Ibid.

61. *Maximizing the Potential.*

62. First Commercial Bank of Little Rock, *Arkansas: Looking Ahead,* 1995 Report of the National Advisory Board.

63. Ibid.

64. Ibid.

65. First Commercial Bank of Little Rock, *High Technology in Arkansas: 'You Don't Have a Choice,'* 1996 Report of the National Advisory, 3.

66. After leaving the Commerce Department, Dr. Good retired to Little Rock, where she became a managing principal in a venture capital firm. In 1999, she was a driving force in the legislative establishment and funding of the Donaghey College of Information Science and Systems Engineering at the University of Arkansas at Little Rock, where she is now the dean.

67. *High Technology in Arkansas*.

68. Bob Lancaster, "An Assortment of Lesser Bests," *Arkansas Times,* June 15, 2001.

69. Mike Huckabee, a Republican, was lieutenant governor when Jim Guy Tucker resigned the office on July 15, 1996, after his conviction on fraud charges in federal court.

70. First Commercial Bank of Little Rock, *Arkansas Tourism: The Giant Awakens*, 1997 Report of the National Advisory Board, 31.

71. The group acquired this name because it was headed by Madison Murphy, a son of National Advisory Board founding member Charles H. Murphy Jr. of Murphy Oil.

72. First Commercial Bank of Little Rock (now Regions Bank), *Streamlining Arkansas State Government,* 1998 Report of the National Advisory Board, i.

73. James "Skip" Rutherford, in conversation with author, June 9, 2001.

74. Cynthia Howell, "LR Board," *Arkansas Democrat-Gazette,* January 26, 1996.

Chapter Seven: Governor Clinton's Chief of Staff

1. John Brummett, "Will Clinton Run Again?," *Arkansas Gazette,* January 14, 1990.

2. Michael Arbanas, "Tucker to Run for Governor; Clinton Mum," *Arkansas Gazette,* February 20, 1990.

3. Ibid.

4. John Reinan, "Carving a Cable Business," *Arkansas Gazette,* March 27, 1990.

5. John Brummett, "Tucker Ends a Free Ride for Clinton," *Arkansas Gazette,* February 20, 1990.

6. James Merriweather, "Clinton to Run Again," *Arkansas Gazette,* March 2, 1990.

7. Ibid.

8. James Merriweather, "Clinton Names Cabe to Head Campaign," *Arkansas Gazette,* March 15, 1990.

9. Valerie Smith, "Cabe Runs up $17,000 Tab," *Arkansas Gazette,* February 9, 1990.

10. "Grocery Tax Necessary, Tucker says," *Arkansas Gazette,* March 4, 1990.

11. John Reed, "Tucker Claims His Health Plan 'Meat, Potatoes,'" *Arkansas Gazette,* March 17, 1990.

12. James Merriweather, "Tucker Says State Lacks Leadership," *Arkansas Gazette,* March 22, 1990.

13. John Reed, "Clinton Trumpets Triumph," *Arkansas Gazette,* March 24, 1990.

14. John Reed, "Tucker Pulls Out of Race," *Arkansas Gazette,* March 27, 1990.

15. Ibid.

16. Marilyn Porter, in interview with Carol Griffee, September 2, 2001.

17. James Merriweather, "Tucker Files; Roy Now Reconsidering," *Arkansas Gazette,* March 29, 1990.

18. Anne Farris, "Tucker Ahead, Roy Gaining, Poll Shows," *Arkansas Gazette,* May 16, 1990.

19. James Merriweather, "Tucker Tosses His Money After Roy's," *Arkansas Gazette,* May 25, 1990.

20. Scott Morris, "Tucker May Squeak by Without a Runoff," *Arkansas Gazette,* May 30, 1990.

21. "Arkansas Election Results 1990." Elections Division, Arkansas Secretary of State, 9.

22. "Tucker Spent $473,788," *Arkansas Gazette,* June 30, 1990.

23. "Arkansas Election Results 1990," 9.

24. Ibid.

25. Noel Oman, "Fund-raiser to Cut Tucker's $399,000 Debt," *Arkansas Democrat-Gazette,* November 7, 1991.

26. Paul Barton, "Clinton Back in National Picture," *Arkansas Gazette,* November 8, 1990.

27. Max Brantley, "For Tucker, a Second Beginning," *Arkansas Gazette,* November 23, 1990.

28. Scott Morris, "Clinton Turning Toward the Mainstream," *Arkansas Gazette,* April 11, 1991.

29. Ibid.

30. Jeffrey Stinson, "Clinton, DLC Move to Take Center Stage," *Arkansas Gazette,* May 5, 1991.

31. Jeffrey Stinson, "Clinton's Speech Brings Delegates to Their Feet," *Arkansas Gazette,* May 7, 1991.

32. Ibid.

33. Ibid. and Bowen Memorandum to Carol Griffee, June 24, 2001.

34. Max Parker, "He Forms Exploratory Committee, Resigns as Chairman of DLC," *Arkansas Gazette,* August 16, 1991.

35. *Walls et al. v. Hall, Secretary of State. Arkansas Reports.* Volume 202; 999. Opinion delivered October 13, 1941.

36. William H. Bowen. Memorandum, "Creation of alliance among BC, his staff cabinet, and JGT," December 18, 1991, 1.

37. Scott Morris, "Tucker Ready to Take Reins if Clinton Decides to Run for President," *Arkansas Gazette,* August 20, 1991.

38. William H. Bowen. Memorandum to Carol Griffee. June 24, 2001.

39. Ibid.

40. Scott Morris, "Bowen Named Governor's Chief of Staff," *Arkansas Gazette,* September 7, 1991.

41. Ibid.

42. Larry Rhodes and Rachel O'Neal, "Ex-bank CEO Named Clinton Chief of Staff," *Arkansas Democrat,* September 7, 1991.

43. Scott Morris, "Bowen Named Governor's Chief of Staff," *Arkansas Gazette,* September 7, 1991.

44. Max Brantley, "Clinton's Top Guns at Odds," *Arkansas Gazette,* September 19, 1991.

45. Ibid.

46. Mark Oswald, "State May Face Lawsuit Over Child Welfare System," *Arkansas Gazette,* March 14, 1991.

47. Ibid.

48. Mark Oswald, "Clinton Rejects Jump in Child Welfare Fund," *Arkansas Gazette,* April 11, 1991.

49. Ibid.

50. Max Parker, "Clinton Calls for Child Welfare Proposal," *Arkansas Gazette,* August 14, 1991.

51. Scott Morris, "State Failing Abused Kids, Lawsuit Says," *Arkansas Gazette,* July 9, 1991.

52. Mark Oswald and Scott Morris, "Clinton Calls Neglect Suit Disturbing," *Arkansas Gazette,* July 10, 1991.

53. Ibid.

54. Cory S. Anderson, "Plaintiffs Are Willing to Settle Suit," *Arkansas Gazette,* August 15, 1991.

55. Mark Oswald, "DHS Steps Forward with Changes," *Arkansas Gazette,* August 28, 1991.

56. Scott Morris. "Child Welfare Funds Lagged, Clinton Concedes." *Arkansas Gazette.* August 31, 1991.

57. Bowen memorandum, December 18, 1991.

58. Scott Morris, "Session Not Needed, Clinton, Legislators Agree," *Arkansas Gazette,* October 16, 1991.

59. Rachel O'Neal, "$16 Million Child Welfare Plan May Settle Lawsuit, Clinton Says," *Arkansas Democrat-Gazette,* October 23, 1991.

60. Ibid.

61. Ibid.

62. Rachel O'Neal, "Struggle Over Session Looms," *Arkansas Democrat-Gazette,* October 24, 1991.

63. Ibid.

64. Meredith Oakley, "'Dualing' Governors at Odds on Special Session," *Arkansas Democrat-Gazette,* October 25, 1991.

65. Ibid.

66. Rachel O'Neal, "Tucker Insists Session Necessary," *Arkansas Democrat-Gazette,* October 25, 1991.

67. William H. Bowen. Memorandum to file. November 15, 1991.

68. Bowen memorandum, December 18, 1991, 3.

69. Larry Rhodes, "Tucker Hints at Race for Governor," *Arkansas Democrat-Gazette,* November 6, 1991.

70. William H. Bowen. Memorandum, "Meeting with J.G.T." November 7, 1991, 1–2.

71. Bowen memorandum, November 15, 1991.

72. Ibid.

73. Ibid.

74. Ibid.

75. Larry Rhodes, "Tucker Sees Accord Soon in Child Suit," *Arkansas Democrat-Gazette,* December 31, 1991.

76. The Associated Press, "Clinton Letter Announces Dates for Special Session," *Arkansas Democrat-Gazette,* January 27, 1992.

77. Larry Rhodes, "Proclamation Calls Legislature into Special Session Monday," *Arkansas Democrat-Gazette,* February 20, 1992.

78. Rachel O'Neal, "Could Settle Suit, Tucker Says," *Arkansas Democrat Gazette,* February 20, 1992.

79. Ibid. and Bowen Memorandum to Carol Griffee, June 24, 2001.

80. Rachel O'Neal, "Accord Comes in Welfare Suit Against State," *Arkansas Democrat-Gazette,* February 26, 1992.

81. William H. Bowen. Memorandum, "Wallace Fowler Appointment to AIDC." December 12, 1991, 1.

82. *Arkansas Democrat-Gazette,* February 26, 1992; Bowen memorandum, December 18, 1991; and Bowen memorandum December 12, 1991. Lancaster, brother of Senate chief of staff Bill Lancaster and novelist Bob Lancaster, later was elected for three terms to the Arkansas House of Representatives. He was defeated for the state Senate in 2000.

83. Bowen memorandum, December 12, 1991.

84. Ibid.

85. The reference apparently was to Edward Saig of West Memphis. However, the official book of boards and commissions in the secretary of state's office at the Arkansas State Capitol shows (on page 179) that Saig's term on the commission expired January 14, 1991, making it unlikely I would have been referring prospectively to him as Tucker claimed.

86. Bowen memorandum, December 12, 1991.

87. Noel Oman and Rachel O'Neal, "Cabe Forced from Staff, Sources Say," *Arkansas Democrat-Gazette,* January 1, 1992.

88. Ibid.

89. Rachel O'Neal, "Cabe Gets Reprimand, Stays on Job," *Arkansas Democrat-Gazette,* January 3, 1992.

90. Ibid.

91. Bowen memorandum, June 4, 2001, 2.

92. "Cabe Gets Reprimand, Stays on Job."

93. Rachel O'Neal, "Cabe to Manage Clinton HQ in Washington," *Arkansas Democrat-Gazette,* January 10, 1992.

94. Marvon Johansen Browning, "Governor's Office Siege Part of National Effort," *Arkansas Democrat-Gazette,* December 31, 1991.

95. Ibid.

96. Noel Oman, "Clinton Call, Concessions End Protest by Disabled," *Arkansas Democrat-Gazette,* January 1, 1992.

97. Jay Meisel, "Black Professor Resigns at UCA as Students Push Removal of Racist Laws," *Arkansas Democrat-Gazette,* November 13, 1991.

98. Rachel O'Neal and Jay Meisel, "Clinton Says State Should Erase Race from UCA Charter," *Arkansas Democrat-Gazette,* November 14, 1991.

99. Ibid.

100. Marking the death of former Speaker of the House Means Wilkinson of Greenwood.

101. Kane Webb, "Governor Bowen," *Arkansas Business,* December 16–22, 1991.

102. Ibid.

103. Elizabeth Lowry, "Downtown Damage Set at $5 Million," *Arkansas Democrat-Gazette,* May 22, 1990.

104. Elizabeth Lowry, "'90 Flood Damage Still Lingers." *Arkansas Democrat-Gazette,* May 19, 1991.

105. Bowen memorandum, December 18, 1991.

106. Ibid.

107. Field Wasson, in telephone interview by Carol Griffee, October 1, 2001.

108. Andrew Moreau, "Arkla Stock Declines in Frenzied Trading," *Arkansas Democrat-Gazette,* November 22, 1991.

109. Ibid.

110. Terry Lemons, "Arkla Rate Increase on PSC Agenda," *Arkansas Democrat-Gazette,* December 4, 1991.

111. Randy Tardy, "Arkla Denies Impending Bankruptcy Reported on TV," *Arkansas Democrat-Gazette,* December 4, 1991.

112. Ibid.

113. William H. Bowen. Memorandum to Carol Griffee, January 20, 1992.

114. Ibid.

115. Ibid.

116. William H. Bowen. Memorandum to Bill Clinton, "Arkla Situation," February 7, 1992, 1.

117. Andrew Moreau, "Opponents Want Another $6 Million Cut in Arkla Request," *Arkansas Democrat-Gazette,* October 27, 1992.

118. William H. Bowen. Memorandum on Telephone Visit with Jerol [Jerrell] Clark, March 4, 1992.

119. Ibid.

120. William H. Bowen. Memorandum re: "Conference with Winston Bryant and His First Assistant," March 10, 1992, 2.

121. David Johnson to William H. Bowen, "Memorandum Reflecting Meeting with Parties to APSC Docket No. 91-093-U on July 2, 1992."

122. Hal Brown, "Arkla to Streamline, Jettison $700 Million in Debt," *Arkansas Democrat-Gazette,* November 18, 1992.

123. Randy Tardy, "Arkla Slips to 'Junk Bond' Rating," *Arkansas Democrat-Gazette,* April 27, 1993.

124. *Arkansas Democrat-Gazette,* June 22, 1993.

125. Bowen memorandum, June 24, 2001.

126. Mark Gregory, "As Clinton Chases Dream, Tucker Faces Reality," *Arkansas Democrat-Gazette,* April 23, 1992.

127. Ron Fournier (Associated Press), "Clinton's Spending Created Budget Crisis, Tucker Says," *Arkansas Democrat-Gazette,* April 12, 1992.

128. Bill Clinton to Jim Guy Tucker "Planning for the 1993 General Assembly," April 7, 1992.

129. Noel Oman, "Clinton Says He Won't Resign if Nominated," *Arkansas Democrat-Gazette,* April 11, 1992.

130. Ibid.

131. Noel Oman, "Clinton Won't Quit as Governor," *Arkansas Democrat-Gazette,* May 23, 1992.

132. "Clinton Rules Out Idea of Resigning," *Arkansas Democrat-Gazette,* July 24, 1992.

133. "Clinton to Reserve Governorship Plans Until Suit Resolved," *Arkansas Democrat-Gazette,* October 24, 1992.

134. Elizabeth Caldwell, "Judge Aims for Nov. 5 Ruling in Governor Successor Suit," *Arkansas Democrat-Gazette,* October 24, 1992.

135. Elizabeth Caldwell, "Tucker is Heir, Judge Rules," *Arkansas Democrat-Gazette,* November 6, 1992; p. 1A.

136. Ibid.

137. Elizabeth Caldwell, "Bryant Appeals Succession Ruling," *Arkansas Democrat-Gazette,* November 10, 1992.

138. Rachel O'Neal, "It'll be Governor Tucker, Court Rules," *Arkansas Democrat-Gazette,* December 5, 1992.

139. David Watkins/David Buxbaum, Clinton for President Inter-Office Memorandum to Department Heads, "National Convention Travel and Housing Policy," June 3, 1992.

140. Ibid.

141. William H. Bowen. Memorandum "Clinton-Gore Transition Corporation," October 26, 1992.

142. Ibid.

143. Ibid.

144. William H. Bowen to Mack McLarty, "Consideration for an Appointment in the Clinton-Gore Administration," November 9, 1992.

145. Jerry Dean, "As Clinton Exits Governor's Office, Most Staff to Stay," *Arkansas Democrat-Gazette,* December 12, 1992.

146. Rachel O'Neal, "Bowen Defines 1 Negative of Job," *Arkansas Democrat-Gazette,* October 28, 1991.

147. Bowen memorandum, June 24, 2001, 7.

148. William H. Bowen letter to President William J. Clinton, "August 4, 1993 Memorandum to the President from Bruce Lindsey Recommending Appointment of William H. Bowen for Chairman, Farm Credit Administration," August 19, 1993.

Chapter Eight: William H. Bowen School of Law

1. "Annual Report, Academic Year 1996–1997," School of Law and Law Library, University of Arkansas at Little Rock, June 30, 1997.

2. *Arkansas Business,* April 17–23, 1995.

3. UALR Campus Update, May 1, 2000.

Index